JAZZ BASS

COMPENDIUM

JAZZ BASS
COMPENDIUM

SIGI BUSCH

Music typesetting and layout: Hans-Jörg Rüdiger

English Translation: Dale Jayne

Cover art by Buzz

Printed by Kohlhammer und Wallishauser GmbH, Hechingen, Germany

Notensatz und Layout: Hans-Jörg Rüdiger

Englische Übersetzung: Dale Jayne

Cover-Grafik: Buzz

Druck: Kohlhammer und Wallishauser GmbH, Hechingen, Germany

Order No. 15000

CONTENTS

INHALT

The real purpose of books is to trap the mind into doing its own thinking. (Christopher Morley)

Der eigentliche Sinn von Büchern ist der, den Verstand in eine Falle zu locken, damit er anfängt, selbständig zu denken. (Christopher Morley)

PREFACE TO THE NEW EDITION

More than ten years have passed since the first edition of the "Jazz Bass Compendium" was published. Since jazz bass playing has in that time continued to evolve, I think it would be worthwhile to examine and verify the many new techniques, concepts, and refinements.

In addition to my own 20 years experience as a musician and teacher, the advice and criticisms of friends, students and fellow musicians have helped me considerably in compiling this new edition.

By working through the book, you will undoubtedly gain a great deal of motivation and ideas for your own playing and practicing. This book is not designed by the common concept "Beginner to Advanced". Instead it treats individual subjects such as "Left Hand", "Right Hand", "Coordination", etc. in depth. The decisive reason for this is that in my many years of experience, I never met the "typical" bass student, who learns by a single method that fits all. Abilities, talents and motivation are different for each individual. Therefore it is up to the user to find his very personal way through the Jazz Bass Compendium.

This book has not been designed for the absolute beginner. It is assumed that the reader has not only a basic knowledge of music theory, but also possesses basic skills in instrumental technique.

Bassists who teach themselves from the beginning run the risk of learning to many mistakes from the start. You can avoid these pitfalls by studying under the guidance of a good teacher. The teaching and performing experience of our classically trained colleagues can be very helpful, especially in regard to good intonation and in order to develop a solid left hand technique. The focus of this book will therefore be confined mainly to the aspects of jazz bass playing.

Hopefully the Jazz Bass Compendium offers a voyage of discovery, experimentation, encourages selfawareness, inventiveness, and enables each an experience in jazz that is extremely personal.

Special thanks to Hans-Jörg Rüdiger, Buzz, Paul Hellmer, Randall Nordstroem, and Hans and Veronika Gruber for their great support. I also wish to thank the many jazz bass students with whom I have worked. Their enthusiasm made the book possible.

Best wishes

VORWORT ZUR NEUAUSGABE

Die vorliegende Überarbeitung des "Jazz Bass Compendiums" basiert auf dem, was sich bei der ersten Ausgabe bewährt hat. Darüber hinaus hat es natürlich in den letzten Jahren eine Reihe von Entwicklungen und Erkenntnissen gegeben, bei denen es sich lohnt, sie ausführlich zu betrachten, sie zu bewerten und sie gegebenenfalls zu berücksichtigen.

Dabei habe ich mich bemüht, über meine persönlichen, mehr als zwanzigjährigen Erfahrungen als Musiker und Pädagoge hinaus, Anregungen und Kritik von Freunden, Studenten und Mitmusikern einzubeziehen.

Sie werden durch die Beschäftigung mit diesem Buch sicherlich eine Menge von Anregungen und Ideen für Ihr eigenes Spielen und Üben erhalten. Zudem sehen Sie, daß es nicht nach dem herkömmlichen Konzept "Anfänger bis Fortgeschrittene" aufgebaut ist. Vielmehr werden einzelne Lernfelder wie "Linke Hand", "Rechte Hand", "Koordination" etc. jeweils gesondert behandelt.

Ausschlaggebend für diese Vorgehensweise ist meine über lange Zeit gewachsene Erfahrung, daß es *den* typischen Baßschüler, der nach einem allgemein gültigen Lernschema vorgehen könnte, nicht gibt. Die jeweiligen Fähigkeiten, Talente und Bedürfnisse sind äußerst unterschiedlich ausgeprägt. Einen Weg durch das Jazz Bass Compendium zu finden, liegt demzufolge in der Verantwortung des Benutzers.

Ausgangspunkt für das Studium dieses Kompendiums sollten schon vorhandene instrumentale und musiktheoretische Grundkenntnisse sein.

Die Chance für einen völligen Anfänger, als Autodidakt Fehler vor allem im instrumentaltechnischen Bereich zu machen, sind doch ziemlich groß. Ein guter Instrumentallehrer hilft, diese Klippe zu umschiffen. Gerade hierbei kann die enorme Erfahrung unserer klassischen Baßkollegen auch für die nur an Jazz interessierten Kontrabassisten sehr nützlich sein. Das gilt besonders für eine gute Intonation und bei der Entwicklung der Technik für die linke Hand. Aus diesem Grunde habe ich mich in diesem Buch vor allem auf jazzbezogene Aspekte konzentriert.

Ich hoffe, daß mit Hilfe des Buches musikalische Entdeckungsreisen in den verschiedenen "Lernfeldern" möglich werden. Üben wird dabei zum Probehandeln, fördert das Experimentieren und Erfinden. Die sich so ergebenden, sehr persönlichen Erfahrungen ermöglichen es, mit viel Freude Jazz zu erleben und zu spielen.

Besonderen Dank an Hans-Jörg Rüdiger, Buzz, Paul Hellmer, Randall Nordstroem, sowie Veronika und Hans Gruber für ihre tolle Unterstützung. Auch bei meinen Baßschülern möchte ich mich an dieser Stelle noch einmal bedanken. Ihr Tatendrang machte dieses Buch erst möglich.

Alles Gute

GLOSSARY

arco	to be played with the bow
pizz, pizzicato	to be plucked with the finger
ϕ	denotes the position of the thumb
MM 80 (♩ = 80)	metronome marking (80 beats per minute)
i	right index finger
m	middle finger
a	ring finger
/ or \	glissando (glide), ascending or descending
E-S	"E" string
A-S	"A" string
D-S	"D" string
G-S	"G" string
┌──┐	keep the same left hand position
8va	to be played one octave higher than written
loco	to be played as notated

Chord symbols*

C	C major triad (root, major third, perfect fifth)
CΔ, Cmaj7	C major seventh chord (root, major third, perfect fifth, major seventh)
$C\Delta^{\sharp 11}$	C major seventh chord with the raised eleventh added. (Lydian chord)
$C6^{9}$	C major chord with the added major sixth and major ninth
C7	C major triad with a minor seventh. (Dominant seventh chord)
$C7^{9}$	C dominant seventh with the added ninth
$C7^{\flat 9}$	C dominant seventh with the lowered (minor) ninth
$C7^{\sharp 9}$	C dominant seventh with the raised (augmented) ninth)
$C7^{13}$	C dominant seventh chord with the added thirteenth
C–, Cm, Cmin	C minor triad
C–7	C minor triad with the minor seventh
$C\text{–}^{\Delta}$, Cm(maj7)	C minor triad with the major seventh
Cø, $C\text{–}7^{\flat 5}$	C minor seven flat five, or C half-diminished (root, minor third, diminished fifth, minor seventh)
C^{o}	C diminished triad (root, minor third and diminished fifth)
$C^{o}7$	C diminished seventh chord. (root, minor third, diminished fifth, diminished seventh, C,E♭,G♭,B♭♭)
C7sus4	C dominant seventh with the fourth replacing the third
$\frac{A}{F}$	Polychord: An A major triad over an F major triad (superimposed major triads)
CΔ/B	Major seventh chord with the note B in the bass
II V progression	A chord progression using the chords built on the II and V degree of a given scale
Turnaround	A standard chord progression, mostly at the end of a phrase, e.g. I VI II V I

* Although there are other ways of notating the chord symbols, I have used those which I have most frequently encountered.

GLOSSAR

arco	mit dem Bogen gestrichen
pizz, pizzicato	mit den Fingern gezupft
ȸ	Daumenaufsatz (D.A.S.)
MM 80 (♩ = 80)	80 Schläge in der Minute (Metronomeinstellung)
i	Zeigefinger der rechten Hand
m	Mittelfinger der rechten Hand
a	Ringfinger der rechten Hand
⁄ oder ⁀	Glissando (der Finger der linken Hand rutscht bis zum nächsten Ton auf- oder abwärts)
E-S	E Saite
A-S	A Saite
D-S	D Saite
G-S	G Saite
┌──┐	Die Klammer zeigt an, daß die gewählte Lage der linken Hand beibehalten wird
8va	beginnend von diesem Zeichen wird, der Übersichtlichkeit halber, eine Oktave tiefer notiert
loco	ab hier gilt wieder die ursprüngliche Notation

Akkordsymbole*

C	C Durdreiklang
CΔ, Cmaj7	C Durvierklang mit großer Septime, Durseptakkord
$C\Delta^{\sharp 11}$	C Durvierklang mit großer Septime und übermäßiger Undezime (lydischer Akkord)
$C6^{9}$	C Dur mit großer Sexte und großer None
C7	C Durvierklang mit kleiner Septime, meist in der Funktion eines Dominantseptakkordes
$C7^{9}$	C Durvierklang mit großer None
$C7^{\flat 9}$	C Durvierklang mit kleiner None
$C7^{\sharp 9}$	C Durvierklang mit übermäßiger None (kleiner Dezime)
$C7^{13}$	Dominantseptakkord mit zugefügter 13 (Tredezime)
C–, Cm, Cmin	C Molldreiklang
C–7	C Molldreiklang mit kleiner Septime
$C\text{–}^{\Delta}$, Cm(maj7)	C Molldreiklang mit großer Septime
Cø, $C\text{–}7^{\flat 5}$	halbverminderter Akkord mit kleiner Terz, kleiner Septime und verminderter Quinte
C^{o}	verminderter Dreiklang mit kleiner Terz und verminderter Quinte
$C^{o}7$	verminderter Septakkord, bestehend aus drei kleinen Terzen (C, E♭, G♭, B♭♭)
C7sus4	Vierstimmiger Septakkord auf C, bei dem die Terz durch die Quarte ersetzt wird
$\frac{A}{F}$	polytonaler Akkord, bei dem über einem F Durakkord ein A Durdreiklang liegt
CΔ /B	Durseptakkord mit dem Ton B (deutsch: H) im Bass**
II V Verbindung	Begriff aus der (Jazz-) Harmonielehre: Kadenzfolge mit Akkorden auf der II. und V. Stufe einer (temporären) Tonika
Turnaround	Akkordfolge, die zu einem Ausgangsakkord zurückführt, z.B. I VI II V I

* Für die Akkordsymbole habe ich die Schreibweise gewählt, die ich am häufigsten angetroffen habe. Daneben gibt es noch zahlreiche andere Schreibweisen.
** In diesem Buch wird – wie üblich im Jazz – die angloamerikanische Schreibweise beibehalten, d.h. der (deutsche) Ton "H" wird mit "B" beziffert.

I THE RIGHT HAND

1. General

In bass playing, the right hand fulfills different functions:

- causes the strings to vibrate by plucking them *(pizzicato)*
- control dynamics
- responsible for maintaining good time
- control sound

1.1 The Position Of The Right Hand

The best results will be achieved when...

- the right hand is positioned at the end of the fingerboard
- the thumb is placed at the right edge and held stationary in order to provide leverage for the fingers
- the fingers are held almost parallel to the strings
- the hand and forearm are in a straight line
- the shoulders are not lifted

See if you can properly pluck the G string. Use the full length of the index finger of your right hand to build tension in the string by pulling it toward you. Release the string by sliding the finger off in such a way that it comes to rest against the neighboring string and the fingerboard. If there was enough the string will vibrate.

Observe this movement carefully and exactly. Take your time.

1.2 How Different Attacks Effect The Sound

Listen to the effects that the different attacks have on the sound. Use the full range of dynamics from extreme loud to extreme soft. Decide which dynamic is best suited for walking bass and which would be best suited for solos. Pluck the string repeatedly while slowly moving the right hand up from the end of the fingerboard. The sound becomes lighter and softer as the hand moves up the fingerboard. You can observe changes of color. The sound becomes lighter and softer as the hand moves up the fingerboard, and harder and louder as it is moved toward the bridge. The change of position also effects the overtone spectrum.

Next change the angle at which the finger plucks the string. If you pluck the string with your fingertip at a right angle to the fingerboard the tone will be more distinct and pointed. If you pluck using the finger in a more parallel manner to the string the sound will become more supple, rounder, and fuller. At this point small factors such as the condition of your skin and the length of your finger play a role.

Because the finger after the release of the string hits not only the adjacent string but also the fingerboard we also get a more percussive color.

Study the way other bass players position their right hand (e.g. by watching video tapes) and imitate them. Experiment with these movements.

I DIE RECHTE HAND

1. Allgemeines

Die rechte Hand erfüllt mehrere Aufgaben:

- durch sie werden die Saiten in Schwingungen versetzt *(Pizzicato)*
- durch sie wird die Dynamik gesteuert
- sie ist zum überwiegenden Teil verantwortlich für die rhythmische Gliederung (Timing)
- sie hat großen Einfluß auf den Klang

1.1 Die Haltung der rechten Hand

Gute Ergebnisse erzielen Sie mit der folgenden Haltung:

- die Hand befindet sich am Ende des Griffbretts
- der Daumen liegt am rechten Rand des Griffbretts
- alle Finger liegen fast parallel zu den Saiten
- Hand und Unterarm bilden eine gerade Linie (nicht abknicken)
- die Schulter wird nicht hochgezogen

Zupfen Sie zuerst einmal die G-Saite mit möglichst viel Fläche des Zeigefingers (seitlich). An einem bestimmten Spannungspunkt läßt der Finger die Saite los und diese fängt an zu schwingen. Anschließend schlägt der Finger auf die danebenliegende Saite und das Griffbrett auf.

Beobachten Sie diesen Bewegungsablauf mehrmals, in aller Ruhe und sehr genau.

1.2 Der Einfluß auf den Sound

Hören Sie, welchen Einfluß verschiedene Anschlagsvarianten auf Ihren Sound haben. Spielen Sie dazu das gesamte Spektrum von extrem laut bis fast nicht mehr hörbar und entscheiden Sie, welcher Bereich optimal für *walking bass* und welcher Bereich gut für das Solospiel geeignet ist. Zupfen Sie nun die Saite mehrmals hintereinander und schieben Ihre rechte Hand vom Ende des Griffbretts allmählich nach oben. Hören und erfahren Sie, wie der Klang sich dabei verändert. In der Mitte des Griffbretts gezupft wird der Sound leiser und weicher, am Ende dagegen härter und lauter. Auch die Obertöne verändern sich.

Variieren Sie nun den Anschlagswinkel und beobachten Sie dabei, wie sich die Klangfarben ändern. Wenn Sie mit der Fingerkuppe zupfen, im rechten Winkel zum Griffbrett, wird der Ton schärfer und spitzer. Wenn Sie mit der Längsseite des Zeigefingers und im spitzen Winkel zum Griffbrett zupfen, wird der Klang weicher, runder und kräftiger. Dabei spielen auch scheinbar so geringe Faktoren wie die Beschaffenheit Ihrer Haut und die Länge Ihrer Finger eine Rolle.

Dadurch, daß der Finger nicht nur auf die daneben liegende Saite, sondern auch auf das Griffbrett aufschlägt, erhält der Klang eine weitere, perkussive Farbe.

Beobachten Sie die Haltung der rechten Hand bei anderen Bassisten (Videos eignen sich dafür hervorragend).

Applying these techniques you will have a large palette of colors at your disposal to create your own personal sound.

Imitieren Sie verschiedene Handstellungen und prüfen Sie die klanglichen Auswirkungen.

Mit diesen Erfahrungen steht Ihnen sicherlich eine reiche Palette von Klangfarben für Ihren ganz persönlichen Sound zur Verfügung.

1.3 Effect On The Timing

Check out now, how a smooth and steady movement of your right hand has an impact on your timing. To start with play the following exercise at a slow tempo (♩ = 60) only with your index finger. Concentrate on a constant tempo, one dynamic, and a consistent rhythmic placement of the individual notes. Record the exercise and listen carefully to what you played. Can you discover any irregularities? Analyze any deviation you might have made. When did it occur and why? How can you avoid these mistakes?

1.3 Der Einfluß auf das Timing

Untersuchen Sie nun, welchen Einfluß ein runder, gleichmäßiger Bewegungsablauf auf Ihr Timing hat. Spielen Sie die folgende Übung in einem ruhigen Tempo (♩ = 60), zu Beginn nur mit dem Zeigefinger "i". Konzentrieren Sie sich auf ein gleichbleibendes Tempo, auf eine gleichmäßige Dynamik und auf die gleichbleibende rhythmische Plazierung der Noten. Nehmen Sie die Übung auf (Kassettenrecorder o.ä.) und prüfen Sie, was und wie Sie gespielt haben. Analysieren Sie eventuelle Fehler. Wann und warum sind sie entstanden? Wodurch lassen sie sich abstellen?

2. Exercises For The Right Hand

2.1 Basic Exercises

The indications of the fingers are the same as those used for the guitar.

"i" – index finger
"m" – middle finger
"a" – ring finger

Practice exercises 1 and 2 on both the D and A string as well.

2. Übungen für die rechte Hand

2.1 Grundlegende Übungen

Die Bezeichnungen für die verschiedenen Finger der rechten Hand stammen aus der Gitarrentechnik:

"i" für den Zeigefinger
"m" für den Mittelfinger
"a" für den Ringfinger

Spielen Sie die Übungen 1 und 2 auch auf der D- und auf der A-Saite.

1

2

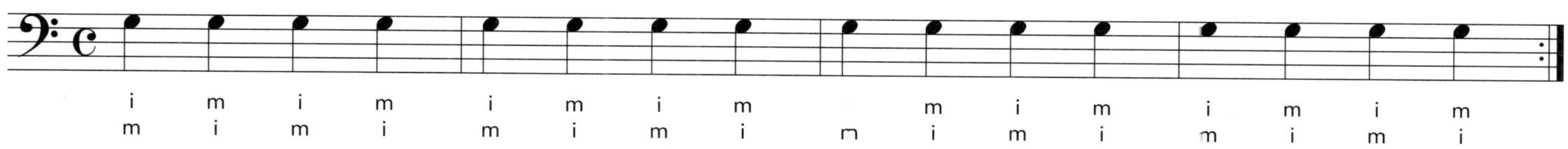

3

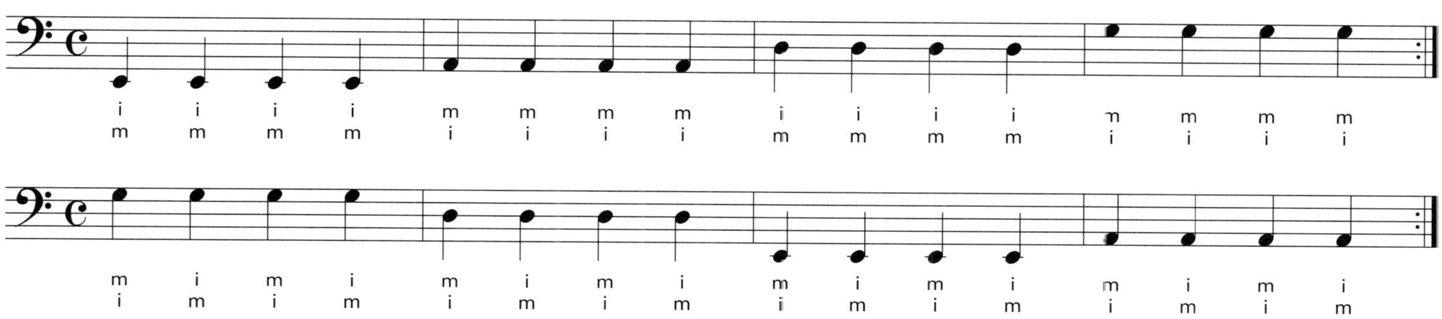

Special consideration must be given for achieving a *pizzicato* on the lowest string (E on most basses). Immediately after plucking the string, the finger turns to the inside and comes to rest against the thumb. This movement differs from that used with the other strings. You must give extra attention to this, above all in the context of string crossing.

Ein Sonderfall ergibt sich beim *Pizziccto* auf der tiefsten Saite (bei den meisten Bässen die E-Saite). Nachdem der Finger die Saite angezupft hat, dreht er sich nach innen und schlägt auf den Daumen. Dieser Bewegungsablauf ist etwas anders als der auf den anderen Saiten und verlangt daher besondere Aufmerksamkeit, vor allem im Zusammenhang mit einem Saitenwechsel.

4

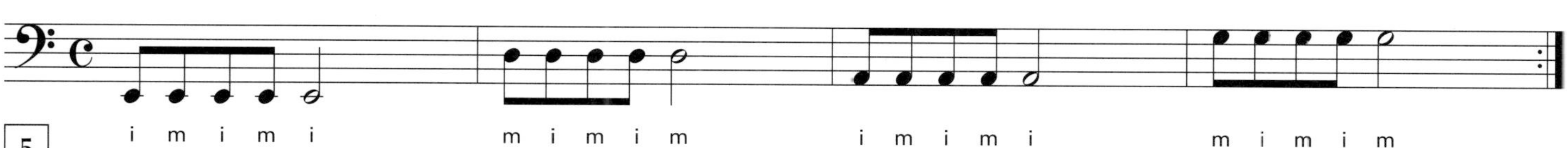

5

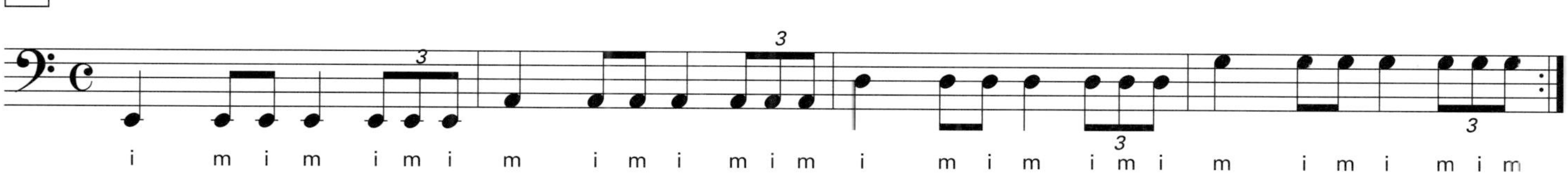

Find the tempo for the exercises at which you feel most comfortable. Set the metronome for that tempo and practice the exercise with the metronome. Gradually increase and decrease the tempo in small steps. For a start, a metronome click on beats 2 and 4 of the measure will help you keep the tempo constant.

Testen Sie, bei welchem Tempo Ihnen die Übungen besonders gut gelingen. Stellen Sie die Metronomzahl dieses Tempos fest und üben Sie von da aus schrittweise nach oben (schnelleres Tempo) und nach unten (langsameres Tempo). Ein Metronomklick auf 2 und 4 hilft Ihnen zu Beginn, das Tempo konstant zu halten.

2.2 Crossing Strings

Play the following exercises using:

- the index finger
- the middle finger
- using combinations of both fingers:
  i m i m or m i m i

2.2 Verbindung mit Saitenwechseln

Spielen Sie folgende Übungen in allen möglichen Varianten:

- mit dem Zeigefinger
- mit dem Mittelfinger
- mit Kombinationen beider Finger:
  i m i m oder m i m i

6 7

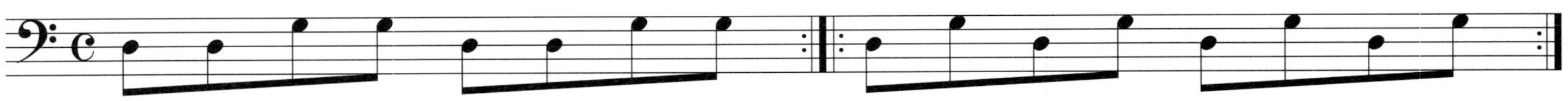

8 9

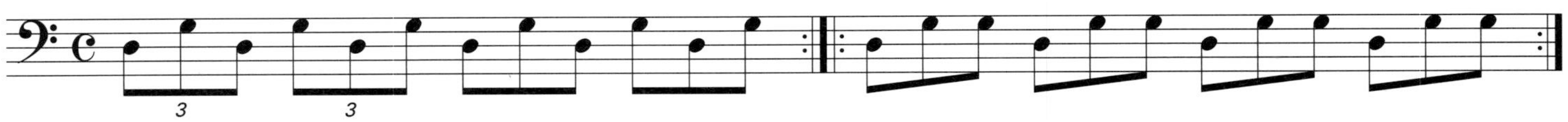

10 11

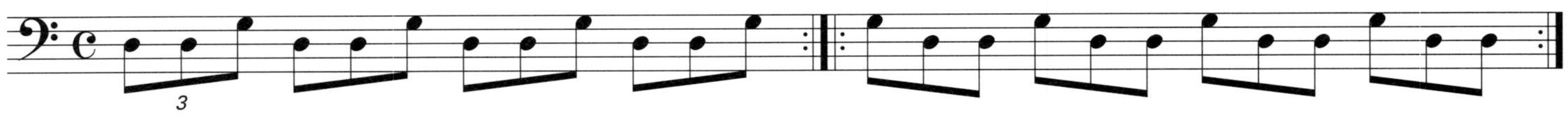

12 13

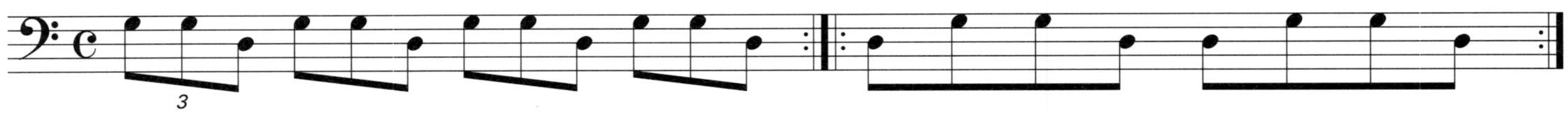

14 15

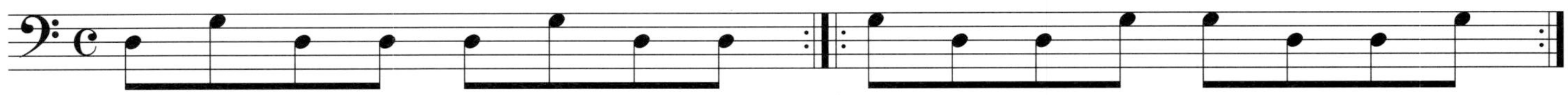

16 17

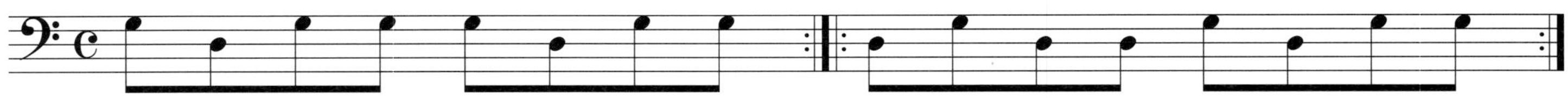

18 19

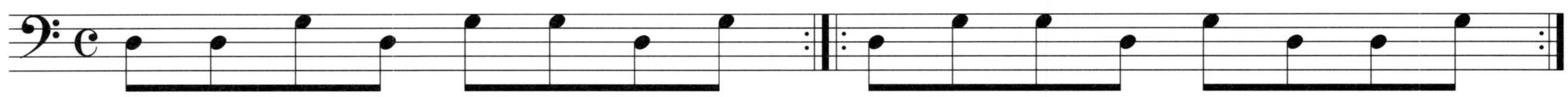

20 21

22

Practice the proceeding exercises using different combinations of strings:

- the D and A strings
- the A and E strings
- the E and D strings
- the E and G strings (difficult)
- the A and G strings

Spielen Sie die vorigen Übungen auch mit verschiedenen Kombinationen von Saitenwechseln:

- auf der D- und A-Saite
- auf der A- und E-Saite
- auf der E- und D-Saite
- auf der E- und G-Saite (schwierig)
- auf der A- und G-Saite

Examples:

Beispiele:

If you need to increase the endurance of your left hand, instead of playing the open strings try using thirds, fourths, fifths on two strings; sixths, sevenths and octaves across three strings; tenths across four strings.
Here are some examples:

Falls Sie etwas für die Kondition Ihrer linken Hand tun wollen, spielen Sie statt der Leersaiten Terzen, Quarten, Quinten (über zwei Saiten), Sexten, Septimen und Oktaven über drei Saiten oder Dezimen über vier Saiten. Dazu einige Beispiele:

2.3 Various Groupings

In this exercise triplets are grouped in sets of four notes, while eighth notes are grouped in sets of three. In the beginning be sure to give the first note of each group an accent.

2.3 Verschiedene Gruppierungen

Hierbei sind Triolen in Vierergruppen und Achtelnoten in Dreiergruppen eingeteilt. Betonen Sie zu Beginn jeweils die erste Note einer Gruppe.

Alternating: "i m i m" oder "m i m i"

Immer abwechselnd: "i m i m" oder "m i m i"

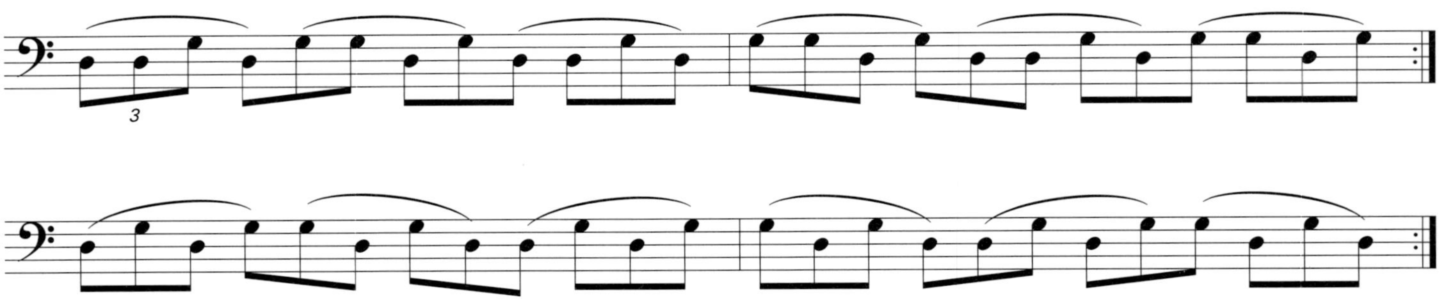

SUGGESTION FOR PRACTICING:
Use the exercises above to improve your timing! Add alternating accents to different notes in the groups; the second, third and fourth note in a group of four notes, or the second and third note in a three note group.

ÜBEHINWEIS:
Die oben stehenden Übungen lassen sich auch sehr gut als Timing-Übungen nutzen! Spielen Sie Akzente auf verschiedenen Noten der Gruppen, bei Vierergruppen wechselnd auf der 2., 3. und 4. Note, bei Dreiergruppen mal auf der 2. und anschließend auf der 3. Note.

3.The Right Hand Three-Finger Technique

3. Die Dreifingertechnik der rechten Hand

3.1 Application

Adding the use of the ring finger adds interesting possibilities and is recommended in the following cases.

- By difficult crossing of strings.

3.1 Anwendungsmöglichkeiten

Der Einsatz des Ringfingers bietet interessante Möglichkeiten und empfiehlt sich z.B. in folgenden Fällen:

- Bei schwierigen Saitenwechseln.

Example: *Freedom Jazzdance*

Beispiel: *Freedom Jazzdance*

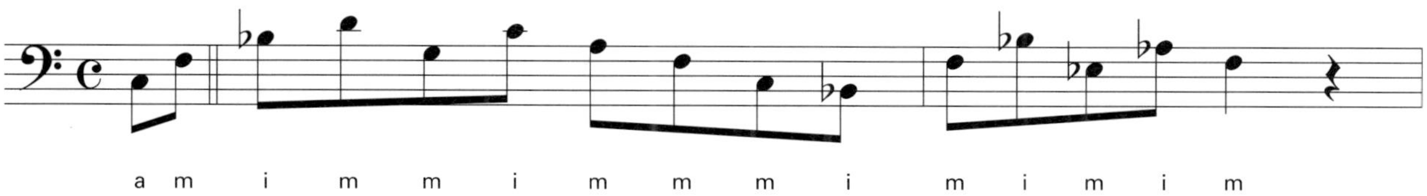

Example: *Anthropology*

Beispiel: *Anthropology*

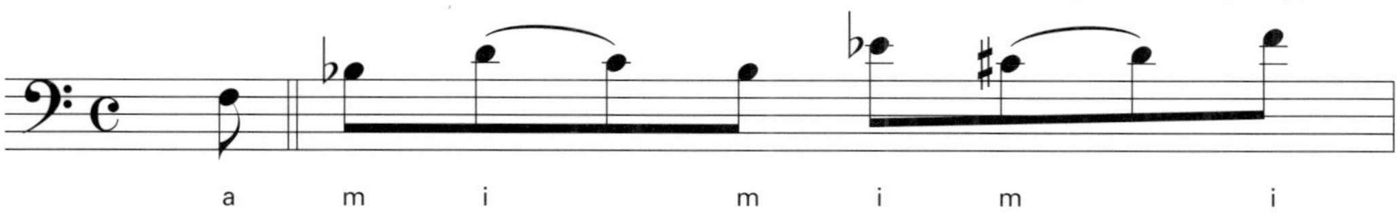

- Playing a melody or a solo in parallel octaves.

- Oktavparallelen beim Spielen einer Melodie oder eines Solos.

Example: *All The Things You Are* – use "i" for the upper octave, "a" for the lower.

Beispiel: *All The Things You Are* – "i" für die obere, "a" für die untere Oktave.

- A walking bass line in octaves at a slow tempo.

- Oktaven bei einer langsamen Walking Bass Linie.

Example: Blues in B♭, bars 1-8

Beispiel: Blues in B♭, Takt 1-8

- Playing strings of triplets in a theme at a fast tempo.

- Das Spielen von schnellen Triolen und Triolenketten innerhalb eines Themas.

Example: *Toys* by Herbie Hancock, bars 13-15

Beispiel: *Toys* von Herbie Hancock, Takt 13-15

Example: ***Donna Lee*** **by Charlie Parker**

Beispiel: ***Donna Lee*** **von Charlie Parker**

- Playing strings of triplets in a solo.

- Das Spielen von Triolenketten innerhalb eines Solos.

Examples:

Beispiele:

1

2
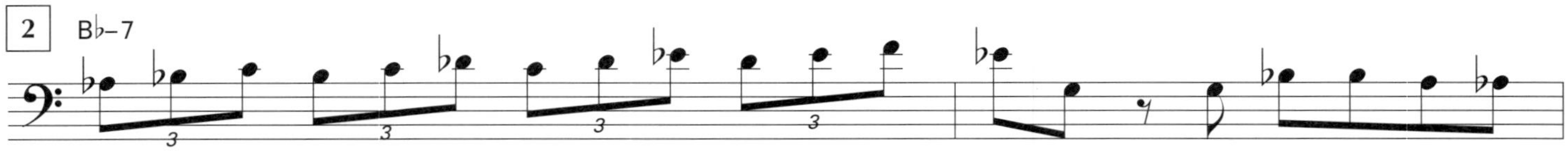

3

4
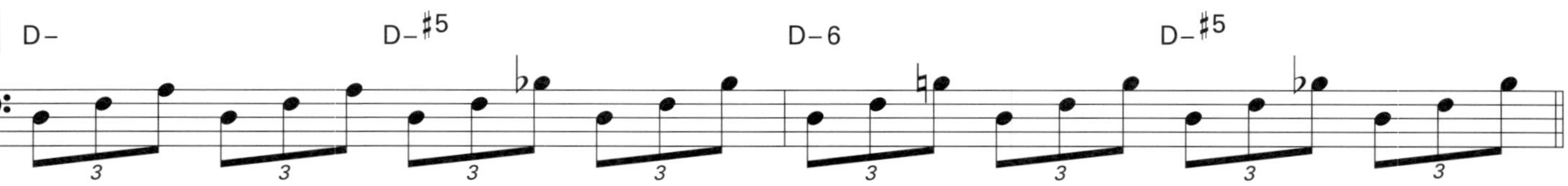

5
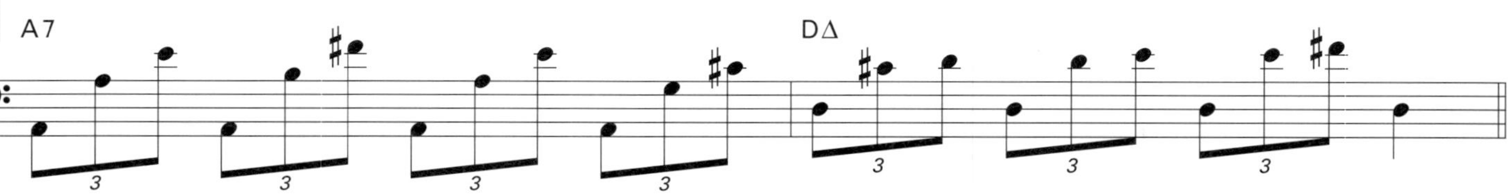

6

Niels Henning Œrsted Pedersen is a bass player who is renowned for his very efficient three-finger technique.

Sehr effizient und musikalisch sinnvoll wird die Dreifingertechnik z.B. von Niels Henning Œrsted Pedersen eingesetzt.

3.2 Exercises For The Three-Finger Technique

To strengthen the ring finger

- you could invent and play your own simple straight and even quarter note exercises;
- use only the ring finger while practicing exercises 2.1 and 2.2. Start very softly at first to avoid blisters;
- practice the following exercises.

3.2 Übungen für die Dreifingertechnik

Um den Ringfinger zu kräftigen, können Sie

- eigene, einfache Übungen entwickeln und spielen, (z.B. gleichmäßig durchlaufende Viertel);
- alle unter 2.1 und 2.2 aufgeführten Übungen nur mit dem Ringfinger zupfen, zu Beginn am besten sehr leise um eine evtl. Blasenbildung am Finger zu vermeiden;
- die folgenden Übungen spielen.

1

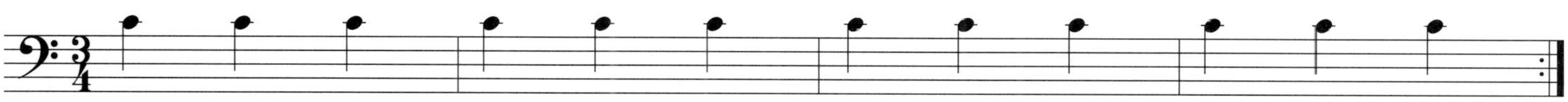

a m i a m i etc.
m i a m i a etc.
i a m i a m etc.

2

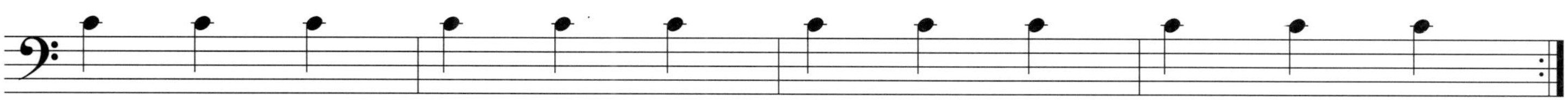

i m a i m a etc.
m a i m a i etc.
a i m a i m etc.

3 **4** **5** **6**

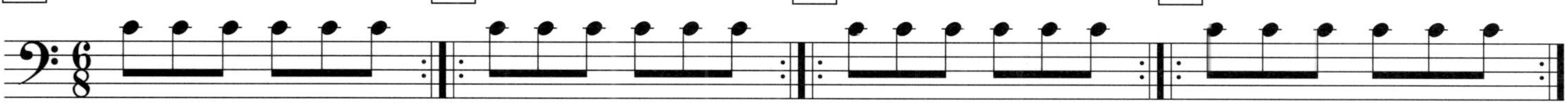

3: a m i m i m / m i m a m a
4: a m a i m i / a m a m a m
5: i a i m i m
6: a m i m a m

7 **8** **9**

7: a m a m a m a m
8: a m i m a m i m
9: a m a m a m a m

10 **11** **12**

10: m a m a m a m a
11: a m a m a m a m
12: m a m a m a m a

13 **14** **15**

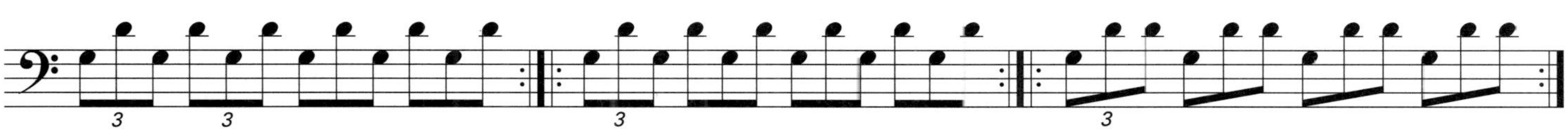

13: a m a m a m a m a m a m
14: a i a i a i a i a i a i
15: a m a m a m etc. / m a m a m a etc.

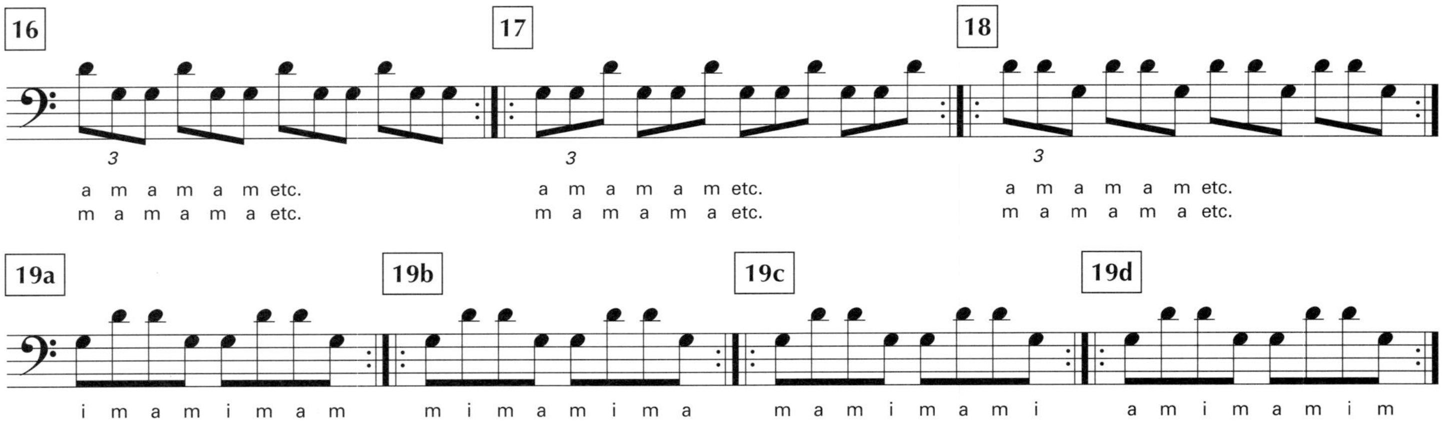

Use the fingerings given for exercise 19a-d also with exercises 20-25.

Die folgenden Übungen 20-25 werden jeweils mit den Fingersätzen der Übung 19a-d gespielt.

Analyze exercise 36. The accents superimpose six groups of four notes over the triplet rhythm. Compare this to the exercises in paragraph 2.3.

Invent your own exercises. Practice scales in parallel octaves.

Analysieren Sie die Übung 36. Über dem Triolenrhythmus im 4/4 Takt liegen sechs Vierergruppen. Der Fingersatz rechts ist ebenfalls in Vierergruppen eingeteilt. Vergleichen Sie dazu die Übungen unter 2.3.

Entwickeln Sie selbst eigene Übungen! Üben Sie Tonleitern in Oktavparallelen.

3.3 Rhythmic Exercises For The Right Hand Three-Finger Technique

3.3 Rhythmische Übungen für die Dreifingertechnik der rechten Hand

3.4 Preliminary Exercises: "Drops"

3.4 Vorbereitende Übungen für "Drops"

II THE LEFT HAND

1. The Left Hand Position

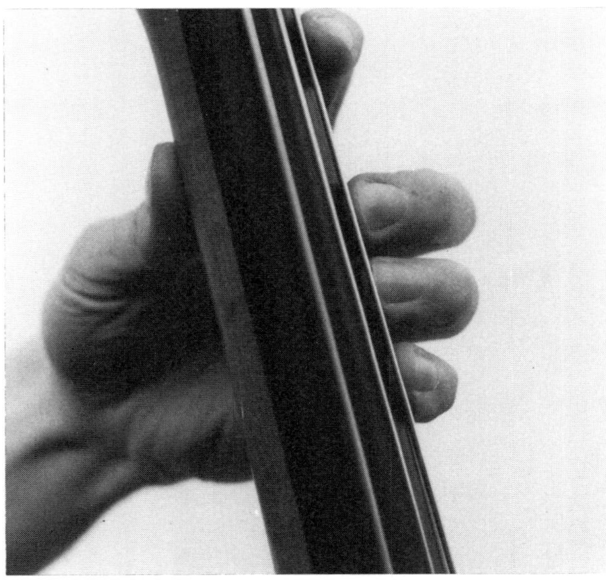

II DIE LINKE HAND

1. Die Stellung der linken Hand

2. Exercises For The Left Hand

2.1 Intonation

Good intonation is the sign of a good bassist. Use the bow and practice very slowly in order to gain control.

2. Übungen für die linke Hand

2.1 Intonationsübungen

Sicherheit in der Intonation kennzeichnet einen guten Bassisten. Spielen Sie die folgenden Übungen ganz langsam mit dem Bogen, damit Sie sich gut kontrollieren können.

When changing positions use your hand as a unit without extreme movements. The hand may slide up and down the fingerboard, yet it should keep the same balanced position. Always keep the first finger on the string.

Pluck only the first note in each measure. Slide from one tone to the other while keeping contact with the string.

A noticeable improvement in intonation will be gained when one is first able to "hear" each note in his head before he plays it. To practice, sing the second note of each measure (on beat three) before you play it.

Beim Lagenwechsel auf- oder abwärts bleibt der erste Finger immer auf der Saite liegen und drückt diese gegen das Griffbrett. Die Stellung der linken Hand verändert sich nicht, nur der Unterarm bewegt sich nach oben oder unten.

Gleiten Sie mit den angegebenen Fingern von einem Ton zum anderen. Zupfen Sie nur den ersten Ton in jedem Takt und behalten Sie immer Kontakt mit der Saite.

Bemerkenswerte Verbesserungen bei der Intonation ergeben sich, wenn man die zu spielenden Töne innerlich klar hört, bevor sie gespielt werden. Singen Sie deshalb die Töne auf der Zählzeit 3 in den folgenden Takten bevor Sie sie spielen.

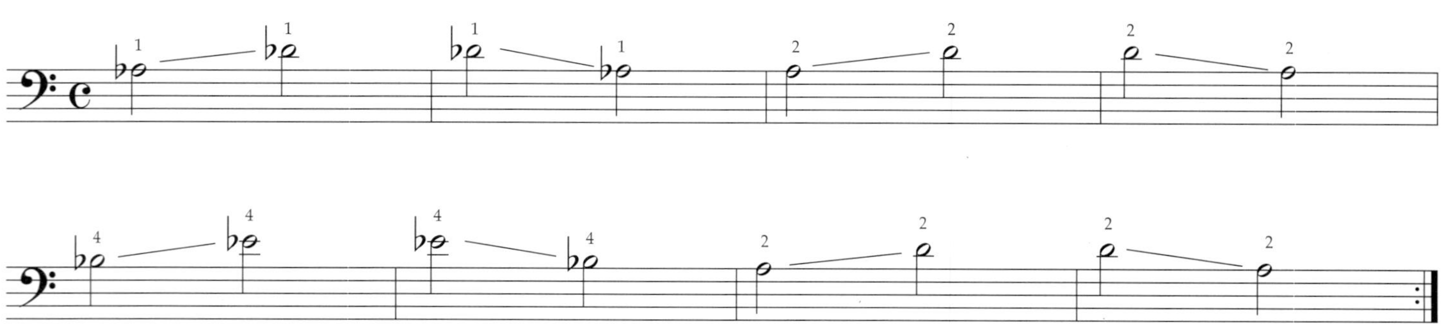

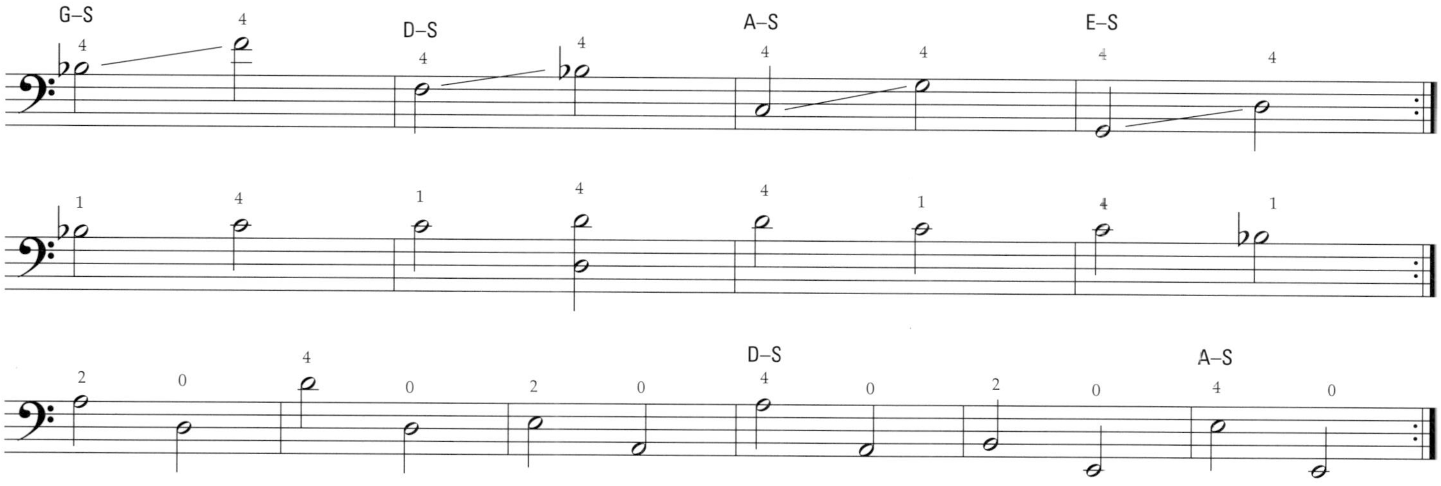

Begin these exercises at a very slow tempo (♩ = 44). Practice both *arco* and *pizzicato*.

Beginnen Sie diese Übungen mit dem Tempo ♩ = 44, sowohl gestrichen als auch gezupft.

Good intonation can also be developed through the use of "Drones". Drones are long, unchanging, low-piched tones similar to the ones produced by the bagpipe or hurdy gurdy. Jerry Coker used this as an improvisation device in his "Drones For Improvisation". A drone can be easily produced on an electronic keyboard by using a low-piched wind or string sound. Over the drone one then plays intervals, scales, chords, etc., on the bass. Playing against the constant reference tone provided by the drone makes it much easier to make pitch corrections.

Hal Crook calls this device "pitch axis" in his "Creative Comping For Improvisation", Vol. 1, Rottenburg, 1992.

Für die Entwicklung einer guten Intonation sind die sog. "Drones" sehr gut geeignet. Darunter versteht man allgemein einen tiefen, permanent klingenden Ton, ähnlich einem Bordun bei einer Drehleier oder einem Dudelsack. Jerry Coker hat diese Idee aufgegriffen als Grundlage für verschiedene Improvisationen (s. "Drones for Improvisation", Hialeah, Fl. U.S.A. 1985). Zu einem Drone, den man übrigens auf einem Keyboard mit einem tiefen bläser- oder streicherähnlichen Klang auf einem Ton schnell selbst erstellen kann, werden Intervalle, Skalen, Akkorde etc. gespielt. Durch den andauernd zu hörenden "Referenzton" ist eine evtl erforderliche Korrektur des gespielten Tons viel einfacher vorzunehmen.

Hal Crook benutzt dafür den Begriff "Pitch Axis" (Creative Comping For Improvisation Vol. 1, Rottenburg 1992).

2.2 Exercises To Strengthen The Left Hand

For Beginners:

Practice the following exercises very slowly. On the G string finger the note D. Compare the pitch with that of the open D string. Practice for short periods in the beginning. Stop immediately if the hand or arm becomes overtired or begins to hurt. Relax the left arm, hand and fingers. Massaging the arm will help. Lengthen the practice time by a few seconds each day.

After five or six days of practice, put the exercise a half step down. e.g. from D to D♭, then to C, etc. Also practice it on the D, A, and E strings. This will increase the overall strength of the left hand and counteract the danger of "Tendonitis" (inflammation of the tendons).

These exercises are also very good for warmups, especially before a performance.

2.2 Übungen zur Kräftigung der linken Hand

Für Anfänger: Greifen Sie mit der linken Hand den Ton "D" auf der G-Saite (mit der leeren D-Saite vergleichen!) und spielen Sie die folgenden Übungen sehr langsam. Üben Sie anfangs nicht zu lange. Wenn die Hand oder der Arm sich verhärten oder gar schmerzen – sofort aufhören. Lockern und entspannen Sie den linken Arm, die Hand und die Finger. Massieren des Arms hilft dabei. Verlängern Sie die Übezeit jeden Tag um ein paar Sekunden.

Verlagern Sie die Übungen nach ca. 5-6 Tagen um einen Halbton nach unten, d.h. in Richtung Griffbrettsattel. Übertragen Sie sie dann auf die D-, A- und E-Saite. Nach dieser Methode wird die linke Hand ganz allmählich gekräftigt. Die immer latente Gefahr einer Sehnenscheidenentzündung wird so fast ausgeschaltet.

Darüber hinaus eignen sich die Übungen auch sehr gut zum Aufwärmen und Einspielen, z.B. vor einem Job.

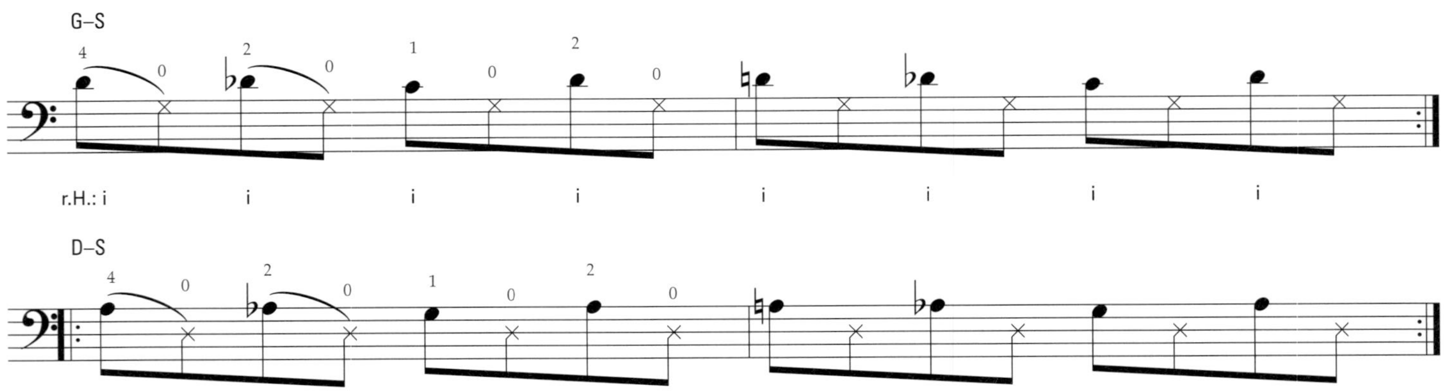

The notes marked with "x" are to be pulled off with the left hand.

Die mit "x" gekennzeichneten Noten werden mit den Fingern der linken Hand abgezogen.

In the following "conditioning exercise" you are to strike the string with an ascending movement of the finger on your left-hand hard enough so that the note can be heard loud and clear. The descending notes are plucked in a manner very similar to the left hand *pizzicato* used in the preceding exercise.

Play all notes with equal strength and dynamics. Listen critically.

Bei der nächsten Konditionsübung schlagen die Finger der linken Hand bei der Aufwärtsbewegung so stark auf die Saiten, daß die Töne gut zu hören sind. Abwärts werden die Töne mit links gezupft, ähnlich wie bei der vorigen Übung.

Achten Sie auf eine gleichmäßige Lautstärke aller Töne.

Studies using the Circle of Fifths

Studien im Quintenzirkel

Every bassist knows the feeling where the left hand is almost ready to fall off while playing a ballad or an up-tempo tune (♩ = 360). You should integrate such pieces into your daily practice routine.

Jeder Bassist kennt das Gefühl, wenn einem bei einer Ballade oder einer Up-Tempo-Nummer (♩ = 360) die linke Hand fast "abfällt". Integrieren Sie deshalb entsprechende Stücke in Ihr Übungsprogramm!

2.3 Left Hand *Pizzicato*

Pluck the notes that occur on beats 2 and 4 with your right hand, and hit the fingerboard with your left finger very hard to sound the notes on beats 1 and 3 (hammer-on technique).

2.3 *Pizzicato* mit der linken Hand

Nur die auf 2 und 4 fallenden Töne werden gezupft, die auf 1 und 3 werden durch hartes Aufschlagen des Fingers auf Saite und Griffbrett zum Klingen gebracht.

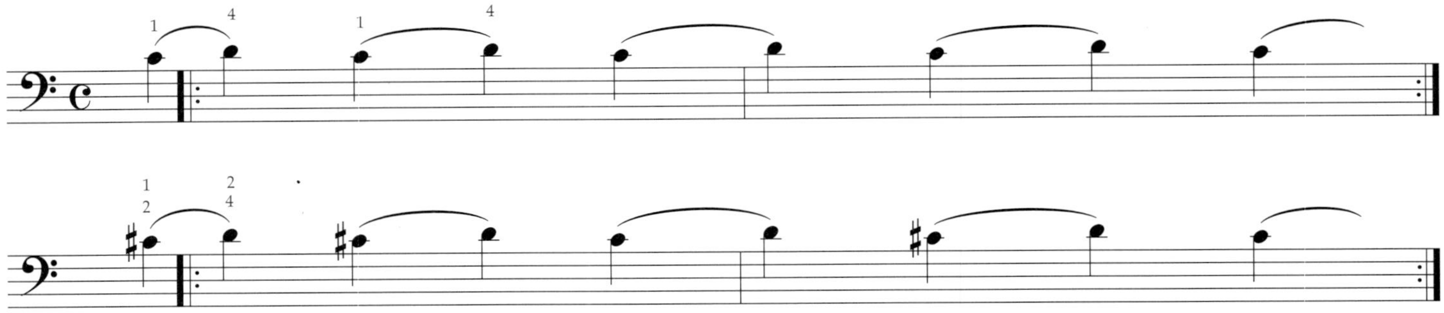

For these exercises pluck the offbeats and make the downbeats sound by pulling off the string with the fourth (or second) finger of the left hand (pull-off technique).

Nur die auf 2 und 4 fallenden Noten werden gezupft, die auf 1 und 3 werden durch "Abziehen" der Saite mit der linken Hand zum Klingen gebracht.

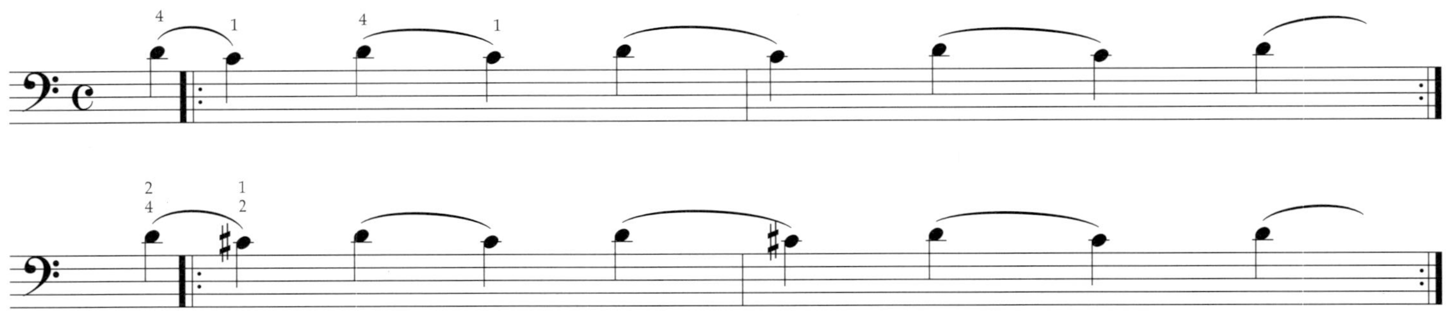

Transpose the above exercises to different pitches.

When you think that the exercise sounds good on the G string, practice it again on the D, and A strings. One needs much more strenght in order to play it on the E string.

Bewegen Sie sich auch hier langsam nach unten (bzgl. der Tonhöhe).

Wenn Sie der Meinung sind, daß die Übungen auf der G-Saite gut klingen, übertragen Sie sie auch auf die D- und die A-Saite. Auf der E-Saite kosten sie sehr viel Kraft.

2.4 Preperation: Articulation

Eighth notes are executed in a similar way. The notes that land on the downbeat will be "hammered" or "pulled off", and the notes on the offbeats (the "and") are plucked. The following exercises will help develop the typical swing phrasing and articulation.

2.4 Vorübung Artikulation

Achtelnoten werden ganz ähnlich ausgeführt. Die auf "und" fallenden Achtel werden gezupft, die auf das Metrum fallenden werden "gehämmert" oder "abgezogen". Diese Abfolge erleichtert eine typisch swingende Phrasierung und Artikulation.

Hammer-on / **Hämmern**

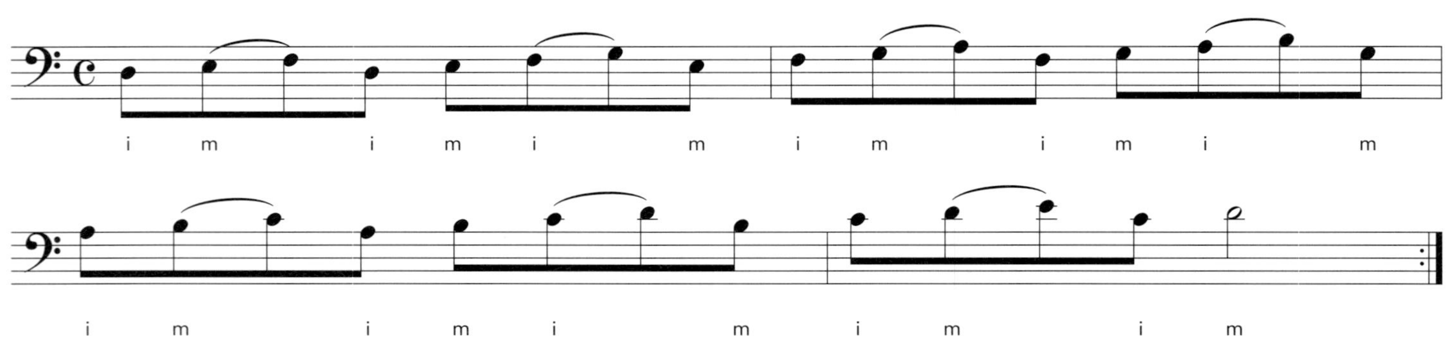

Pull-off

Abziehen

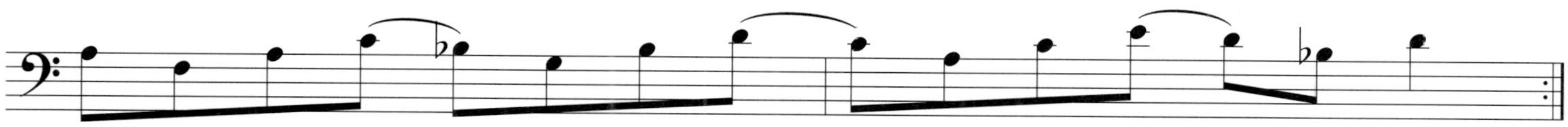

To receive maximum benefit from these exercises, practice them using scales. (See Chapter VIII, p. 150ff)

Diese Übungen sind besonders effektiv in Verbindung mit dem Üben von Skalen (siehe Kapitel VIII, S. 150ff).

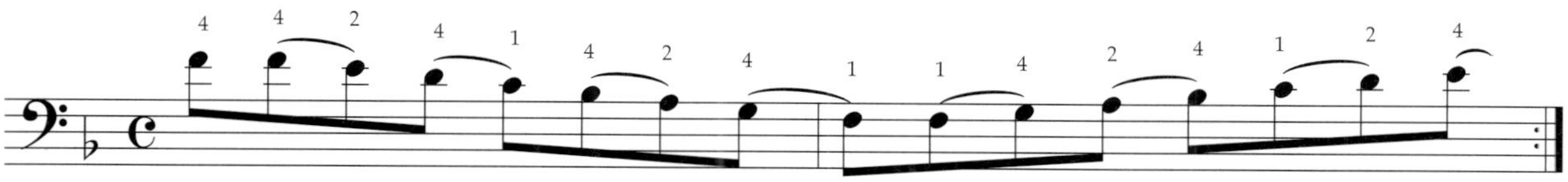

Pull-off

Abziehen

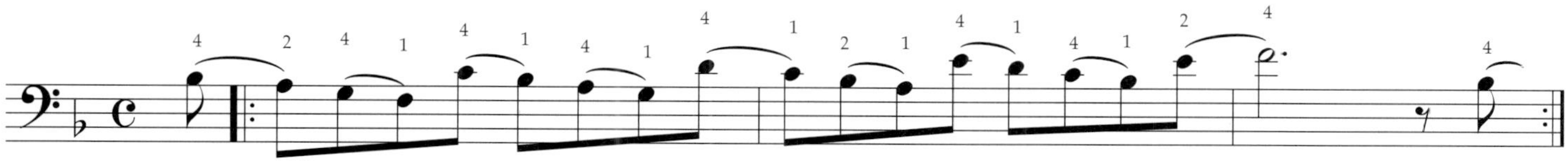

Hammer-on and Pull-off

Hämmern und Abziehen

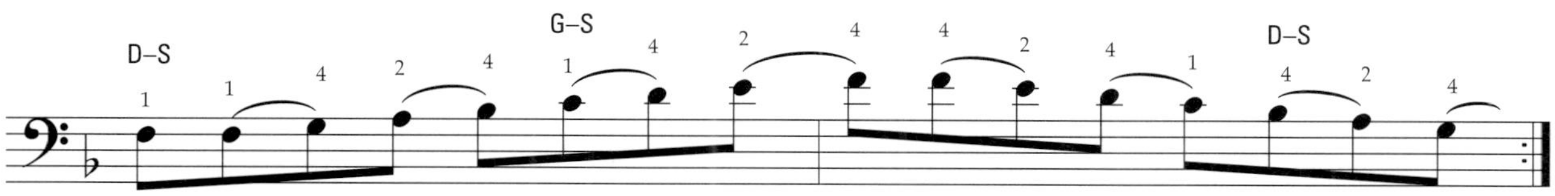

2.5 Intonation Exercises Combined With Shifting Positions

At first glance it might be difficult to see the value in these exercises, but after practicing them for a time, you will come to realize just how effective they really are. They will bring a great improvement in your intonation and ability to shift positions.

Half position

2.5 Intonationsübungen in Verbindung mit Lagenwechseln

Diese Übungen erscheinen Ihnen zunächst vielleicht sehr trocken. Wie effektiv sie tatsächlich sind, macht sich erst nach einiger Zeit bemerkbar. Sie bringen rasch enorme Verbesserungen bei der Intonation und beim Lagenwechsel.

Lagenwechsel 1/2 Lage

The following exercises continue the same principles as before. Begin with the half position from G♯ and move in half steps ascending (up to the note A, third finger) and then descending as you did in the first exercises. Do them on all strings. Develop exercises of your own.

Üben Sie die folgenden Lagenwechsel nach dem gleichen Prinzip wie die vorhergehenden Übungen. Beginnen Sie in der halben Lage mit dem Ton G♯ und bewegen Sie sich wie bei den ersten Übungen in Halbtonschritten bis zum Ton A (3. Finger) zuerst nach oben und dann wieder nach unten. Übertragen Sie alle Übungen auf alle Saiten und erfinden Sie eigene Übungen.

Be sure that the first finger stays in contact with the string. (See page 24)

Achten Sie darauf, daß der 1. Finger immer den Kontakt mit der Saite behält. (Siehe Seite 24)

Repeat the following exercises a number of times using different fingerings in different positions. Use the bow. (You may also use a "drone" as a reference. See page 25.)

Üben Sie alle nachstehenden Übungen mit den verschiedenen Fingersätzen in allen Lagen, x mal wiederholt, am besten mit dem Bogen. (Vielleicht zu einem Drone? Siehe Seite 25).

Position shift exercise using one position

Lagenwechselübungen 1 Lage

Position shift exercise using 1 1/2 positions

Lagenwechsel über 1 1/2 Lagen

Position shift exercise using 2 positions

Lagenwechsel über 2 Lagen

2.6 Shifting Positions Combined With Crossing Strings

2.6 Lagenwechsel kombiniert mit Saitenwechsel

Exercise:

Übung:

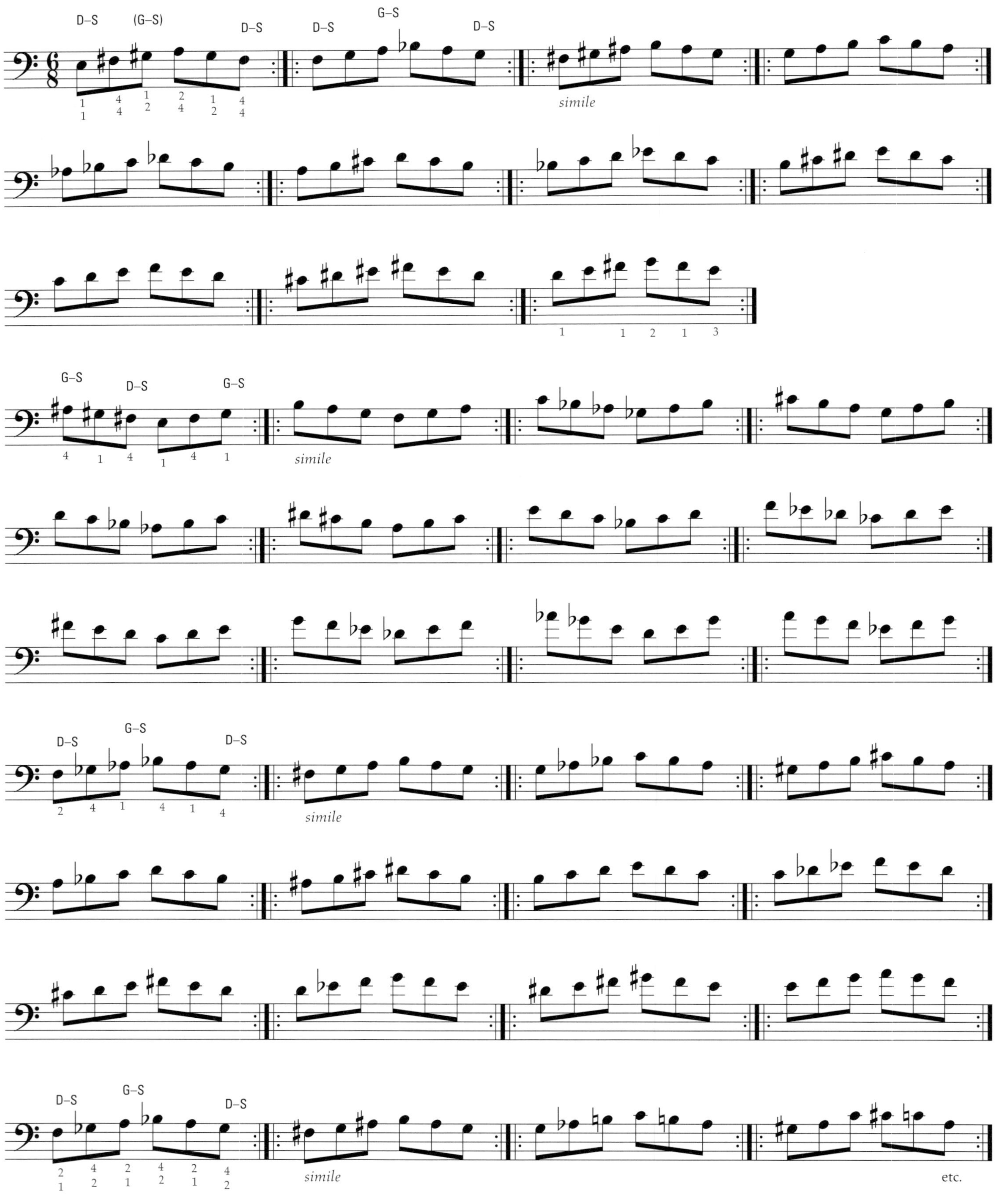

2.7 Studies In Shifting Positions

2.7 Lagenwechselstudien

1

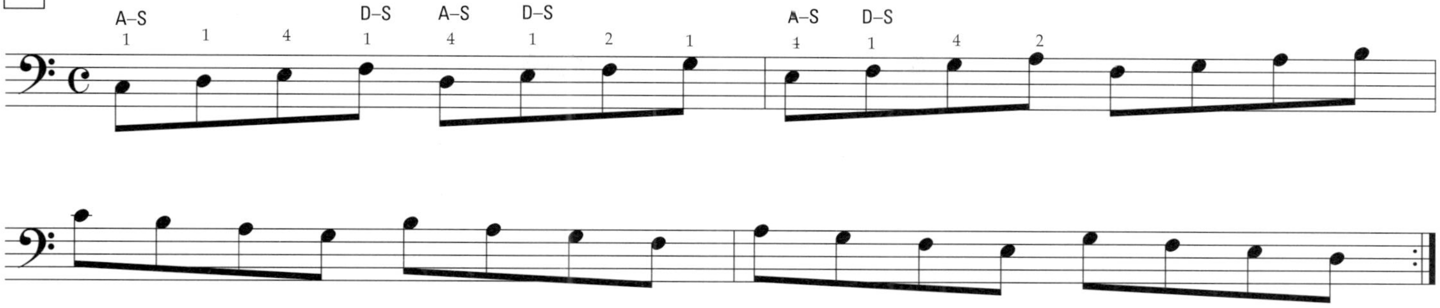

Exercise 2 is constructed of so called "Digital Patterns". The notes of the scale, C major used here consisting of the steps from 1 to 7. (step 8 is the same as step 1)

The pattern for this exercise is 1 2 3 5, 2 3 4 6, 3 4 5 7, etc. Exercise 3 consists of 1 2 4 5, 2 4 5 6 etc.

With these patterns one can develop different studies for all the modes and scales. Practice these patterns with compositions which use half-time chord progressions like *Confirmation, Joy Spring,* and *Giant Steps*. Use patterns like 1 3 4 5 for minor chords and 3 5 6 7 for major chords. These patterns are often used by musicians who can't think of something more original. The value of these lie more in gaining instrumental technique than as a melodic device.

Übung 2 basiert auf sog. "Digital-Patterns". Die Töne einer Skala, hier C Dur, erhalten Zahlen von 1 bis 7 (8 ist wie 1).

Das Pattern bei dieser Übung ist 1 2 3 5, 2 3 4 6, 3 4 5 7, usw. Übung 3 besteht aus 1 3 4 5, 2 4 5 6 usw.

Mit diesen Patterns kann man zu allen Dur- und Mollskalen inklusive ihrer verschiedenen Modi technische Studien entwickeln. Üben Sie diese Patterns auch über Kompositionen mit halbtaktigen Akkordverbindungen wie z.B. *Confirmation, Joy Spring, Giant Steps* o.ä. mit Patterns wie 1 3 4 5 für Mollakkorde und 3 5 6 7 für Durakkorde. Häufig hört man solche Patterns auch in Improvisationen von Musikern, denen sonst wenig einfällt. Ihr Wert liegt jedoch meines Erachtens mehr im instrumentaltechnischen, weniger im melodischen Bereich.

2

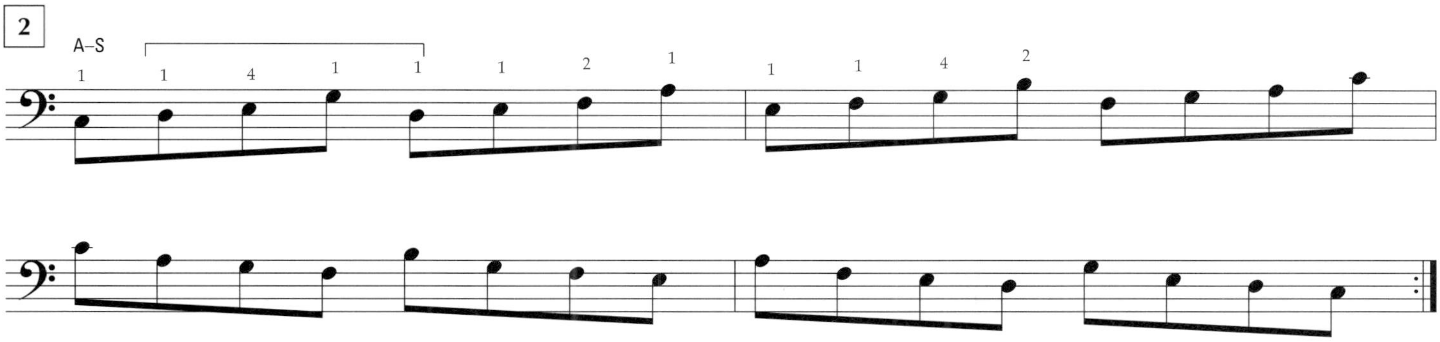

3

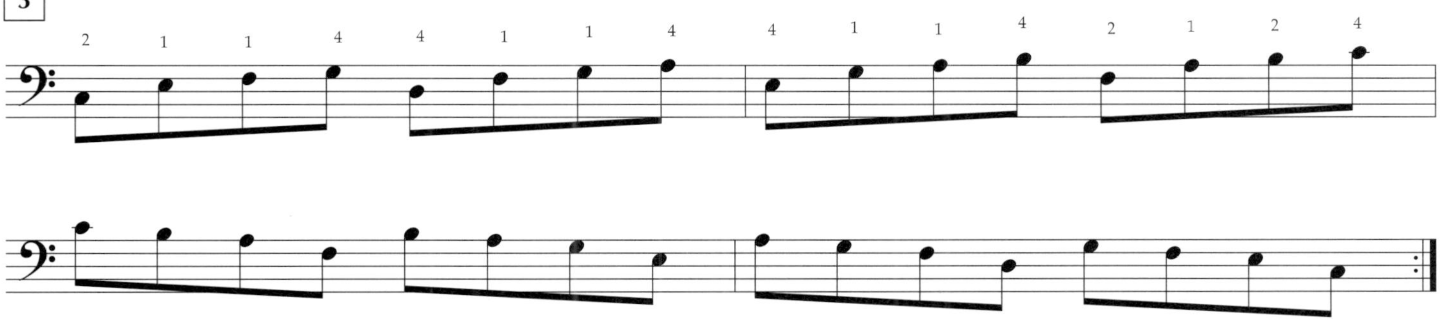

4

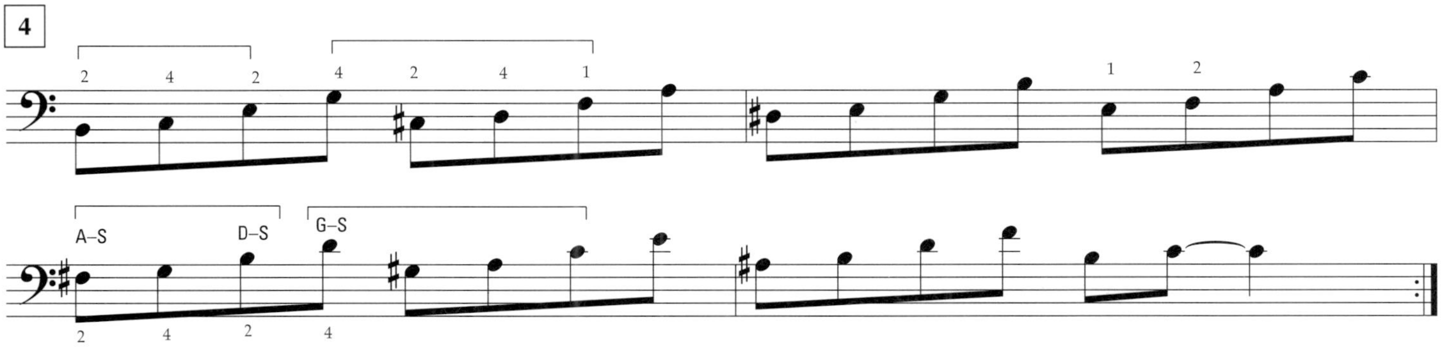

Work out your own fingerings for the left hand.

Finden und notieren Sie selbst den Fingersatz für die linke Hand.

5

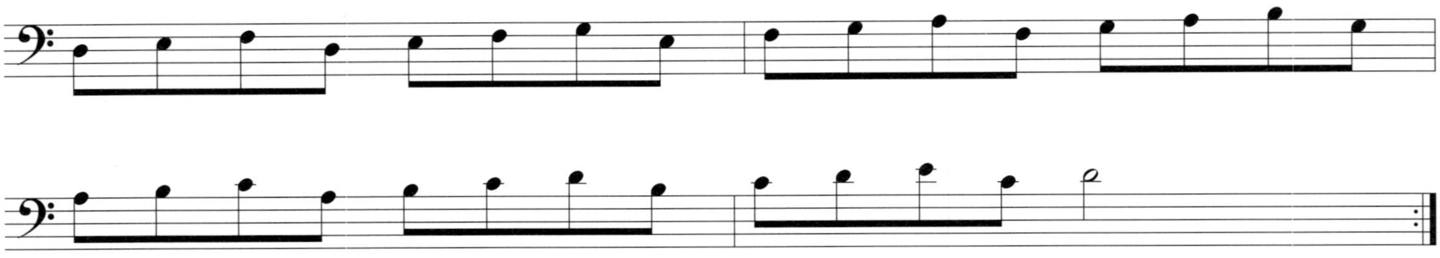

6

7

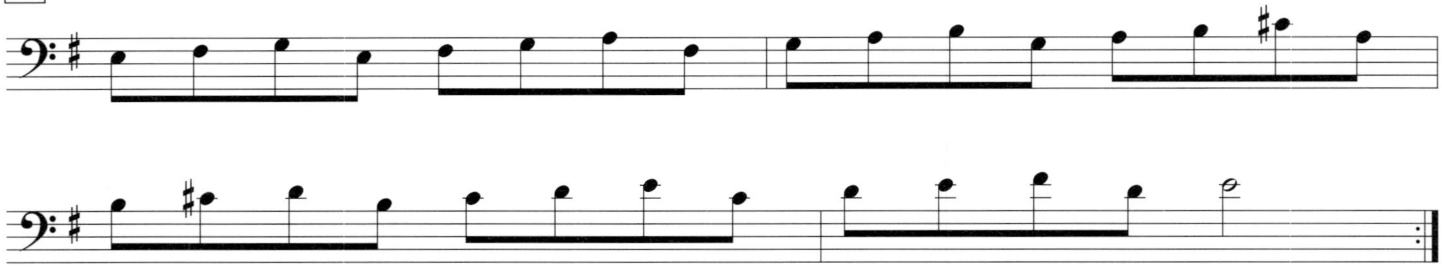

8

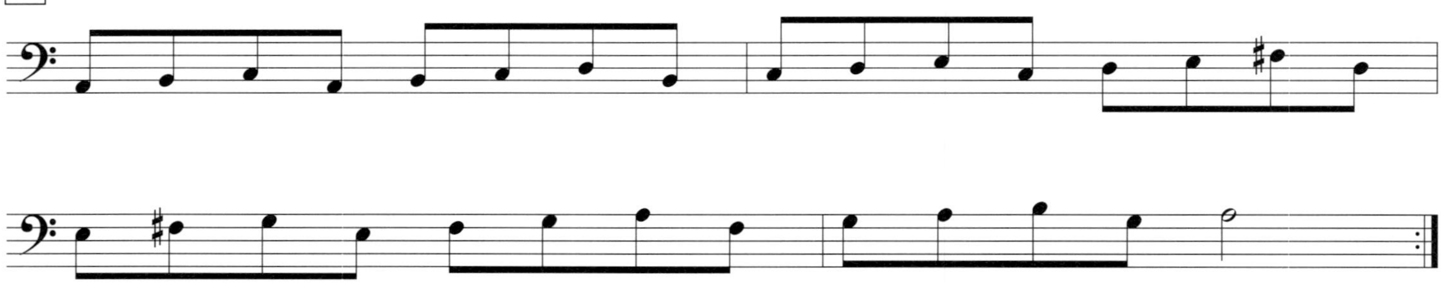

9

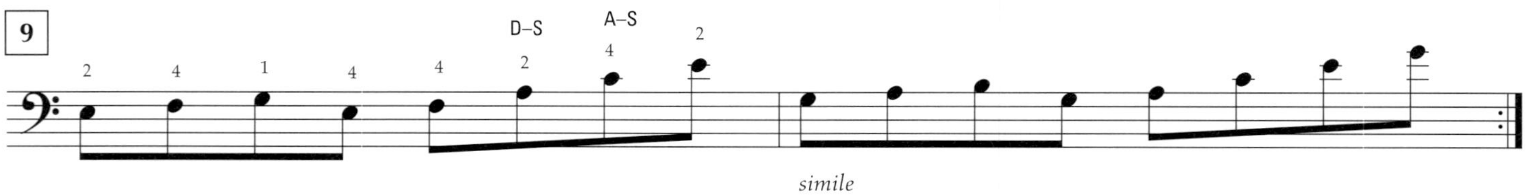

10

NOTE:
This study is based on the chord changes of Herbie Hancock's *Maiden Voyage*.

ANMERKUNG:
Diese Etüde basiert auf den Akkorden von *Maiden Voyage* von Herbie Hancock.

2.8 Vibrato

Through the following exercises one will gain a well controlled vibrato and a livelier tone. When playing jazz you should try and match the vibrato with a rhythmical subdivision of the note, e.g. a single triplet for the length of a quarter note. This applies mostly at slow tempos.

Preliminary exercises:

In order to raise the tone by a half-step, roll the left hand using the fingertip as a pivot. In the first exercise: Finger an A♭ on the G string. Change the pitch by using wrist action to roll the finger up and to raise the tone and down to lower it. The notation of the pitches are approximate in the following example!

2.8 Das Vibrato

Durch die folgenden Übungen bekommen Sie ein gut kontrolliertes Vibrato – Ihr Ton wird lebendiger. Beim Jazzspielen sollten Sie versuchen, das Vibrato innerhalb der "Time", also des Zeitmaßes, anzuwenden, z.B. in Achteltriolen bei einem langsamen Tempo.

Vorübung:

Rollen Sie die linke Hand über die Fingerkuppen so ab, daß der Tonhöhenunterschied fast einen Halbton beträgt. Bei der ersten Übung greifen Sie mit der linken Hand ein A♭ auf der G-Saite, dann rollen Sie den Finger durch eine Drehung des Handgelenkes und verändern so die Tonhöhe nach oben und dann wieder entgegengesetzt nach unten. Die untenstehende Notation ist demnach nur eine Annäherung!

1

2

Practice this using the second finger: **Üben Sie nun das Ganze mit dem 2. Finger:**

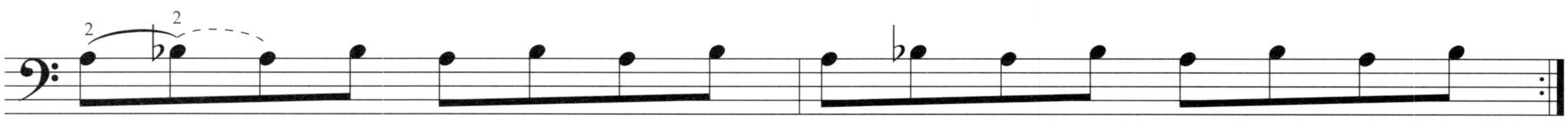

Using the fourth finger: **Nun mit dem 4. Finger:**

3

Using triplets (same tempo): **Im gleichen Tempo Triolen:**

4

5

6

2.9 The Trill

Even though trills on the bass are seldom used in jazz, they are important devices to use for strengthening the left hand. Play the following exercises using the bow. Play them on all strings and in all positions. (The lower strings demand more strength). Practice slowly, evenly, and pay attention to your rhythm.

2.9 Der Triller

Triller werden im Jazz auf dem Baß ziemlich selten gespielt. Trotzdem sind sie wichtig zur Kräftigung der linken Hand. Die unten stehenden Übungen werden mit dem Bogen gestrichen. Spielen Sie auch diese wieder auf allen Saiten (auf den unteren kosten Sie sehr viel Kraft) und in allen Lagen. Üben Sie langsam und gleichmäßig und achten Sie auf den Rhythmus.

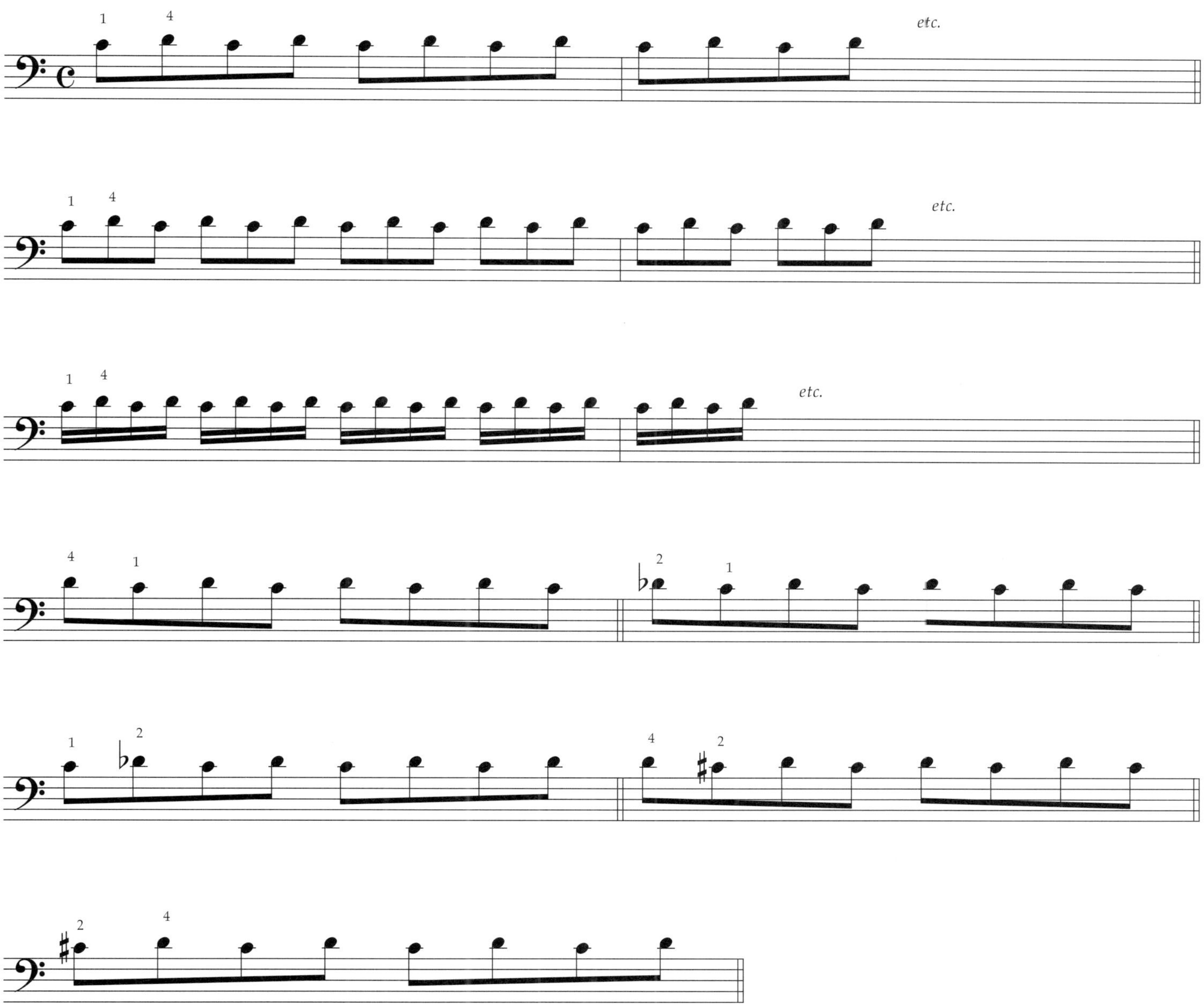

Study:

Studie:

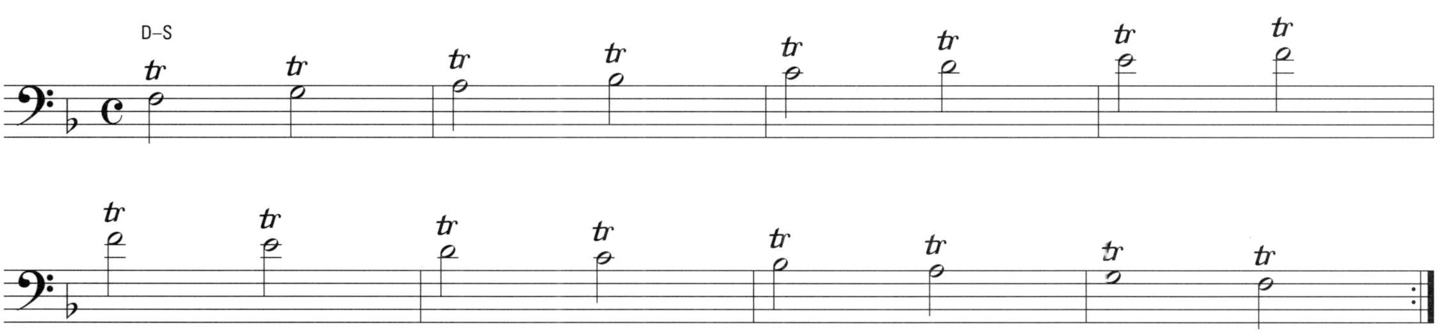

III COORDINATING BOTH HANDS

1. Various Exercises

The coordination of the hands has a great influence on timing and sound. Parallel movements of the hands are much simpler than movements in opposite directions. Determine which of the exercises are the easiest for you and which are the most difficult. If you have a problem with timing or sound, see if it maybe due to bad coordination between the hands.

III KOORDINATION DER HÄNDE

1. Verschiedene Übungen

Die Koordination beider Hände hat einen sehr starken Einfluß auf Timing und Sound. Meistens sind parallele Bewegungen der Hände einfacher auszuführen als gegenläufige. Beobachten Sie, welche der nachstehenden Übungen für Sie einfach und welche nicht so einfach zu spielen sind. Prüfen Sie, ob Defizite im Timing oder ein nicht zufriedenstellender Sound vielleicht ihre Ursache in der fehlerhaften Koordination beider Hände haben könnten.

1

parallel: i m i m etc.
gegenläufig: m i m i etc. **(contrary motion)**
a m a m etc.
m a m a etc.

2

i m i m etc
m i m i etc.
a m a m etc.
m a m a etc.

3

1. as above 1. wie oben
2. a m i m etc.
m i m a etc.
i m a m etc.

4

m a m i m a m i

5

as 3 wie 3

6

as 4 wie 4

7

as 1 wie 1

8

as 1 wie 1

9

as 3 wie 3

10

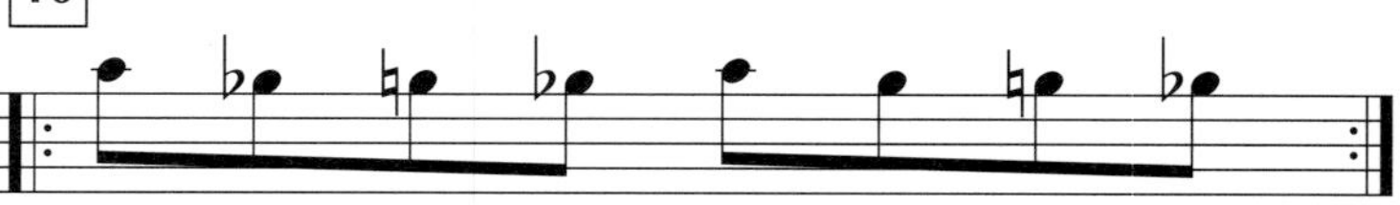

as 3 wie 3

11

a m i a m i
m i a m i a
i a m i a m

12

as 11 wie 11

13

as 11 wie 11

14

as 11 wie 11

15

a m i m a m i m a m i m
m i m a m i m a m i m a
m a m i m a m i m a m i

16

as 15 wie 15

Alternate using the following fingering patterns:
1. imim, 2. mimi, 3. amam, 4. mama

Üben Sie abwechselnd:
1. imim, 2. mimi, 3. amam, 4. mama

Be careful to keep a precise rhythmic flow and an even dynamic. The critical points will occur with position shifts and/or string crossings.

Achten Sie auf eine gleichbleibende Dynamik und auf präzisen rhythmischen Fluß. Kritische Punkte sind Lagen- und/ oder Saitenwechsel!

Use these fingerings with the right hand:
imim, mimi, amim, mima, imam, amam, mama

Üben Sie rechts mit den Fingersätzen:
imim, mimi, amim, mima, imam, amam, mama

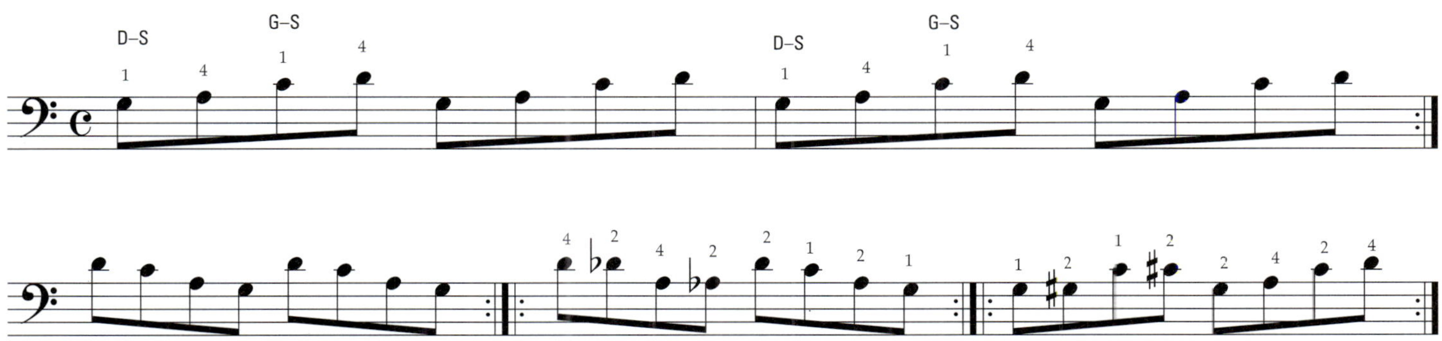

PRACTICE TIP:
These coordination exercises can be used with all the scale exercises in Chapter VIII. Practice using differnt scales in combination with different right hand fingerings.

ÜBEHINWEIS:
Auch diese Koordinationsübungen können Sie mit allen Skalenübungen (Kapitel VIII) verbinden. Üben Sie verschiedene Skalen mit jeweils verschiedenen Fingersätzen der rechten Hand.

Transpose these exercises to all strings and all positions.

Transponieren Sie diese und die folgenden Übungen in alle Lagen und auf alle Saiten.

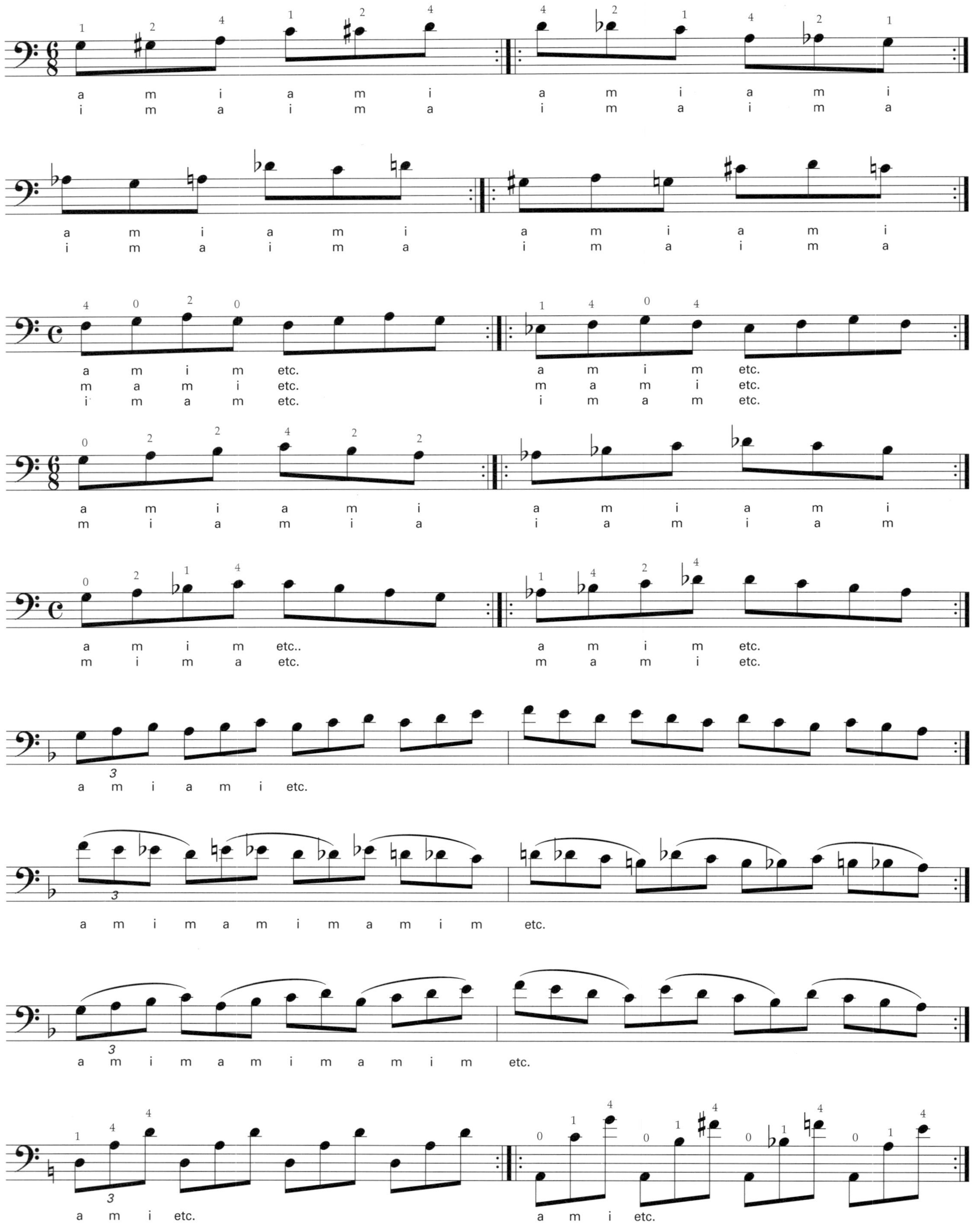

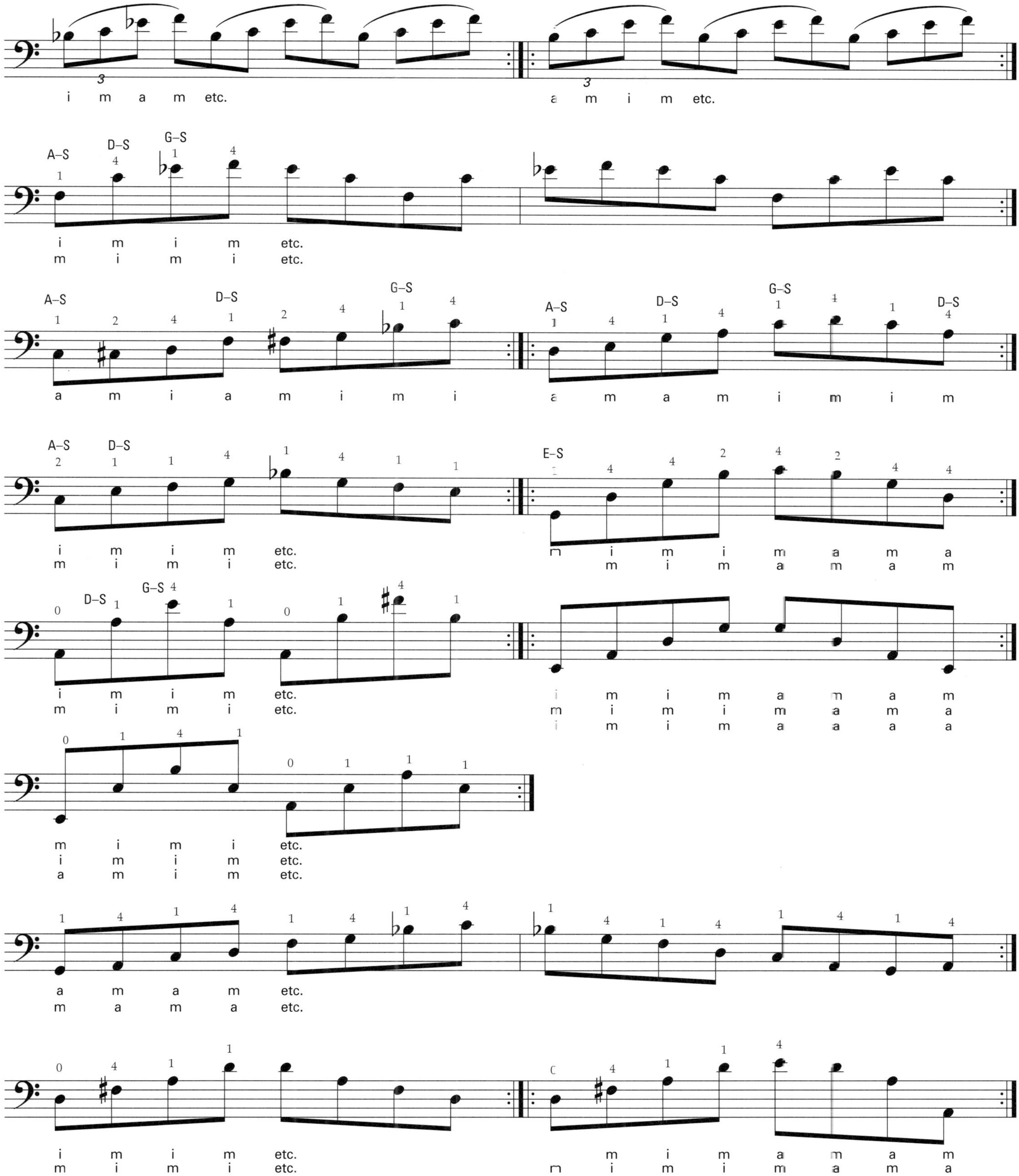

You have probably noticed by now that it is easier to change strings with the right hand when ascending than descending. Therefore many bassists use only one finger while descending. Choose the fingering that is the easiest and sounds the best.

Sie werden sicher bemerken, daß Ihnen der Wechsel des Fingersatzes der rechten Hand aufwärts leichter fällt als abwärts. Viele Bassisten benutzen daher abwärts nur einen Finger. Wählen Sie die Spielweise, die Ihnen am leichtesten fällt und gut klingt.

The exercises on this page are not altogether simple. For that reason you must begin by playing very slowly. Pay close attention to your sound and timing. Use the metronome clicks on beats 2 and 4 in 4/4 time, or as the 1st and 4th eighth-note in 6/8 time. Increase the tempo only when you have truly mastered the exercise at a slower one.

In order for you to be able to keep good track of your progress, I suggest that you keep a daily record of your tempos, practice time and how long you can play a particular exercise before your time and tone begin to suffer.

Die Übungen auf dieser Seite sind nicht ganz einfach. Spielen Sie daher alle Koordinationsübungen zuerst langsam. Achten Sie auf Sound und Timing. Benutzen Sie ein Metronom, das im 4/4 Takt auf den Zählzeiten 2 und 4 klickt, im 6/8 Takt auf dem ersten und vierten Achtel. Erhöhen Sie das Tempo erst dann, wenn Sie die entsprechende Übung sicher beherrschen.

Um einen Überblick über die fortschreitende Entwicklung der eigenen Technik zu bekommen, empfiehlt es sich, Tempo und Dauer der Übungen über einen längeren Zeitraum zu notieren. Machen Sie sich Notizen, wie schnell und wie lange Sie eine bestimmte Übung spielen können, ohne daß die anderen Elemente Klang und Timing dabei leiden.

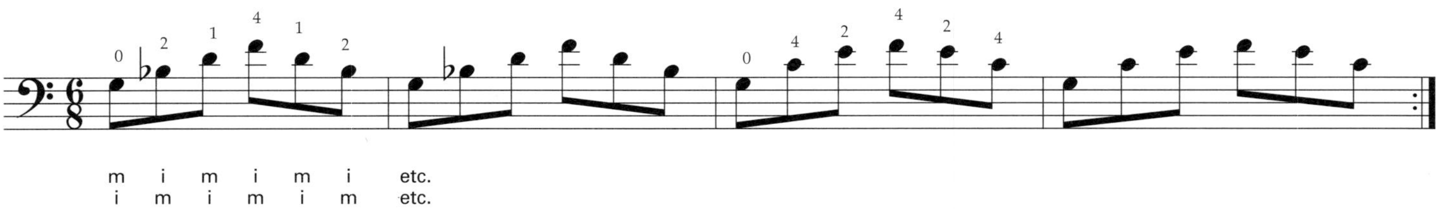

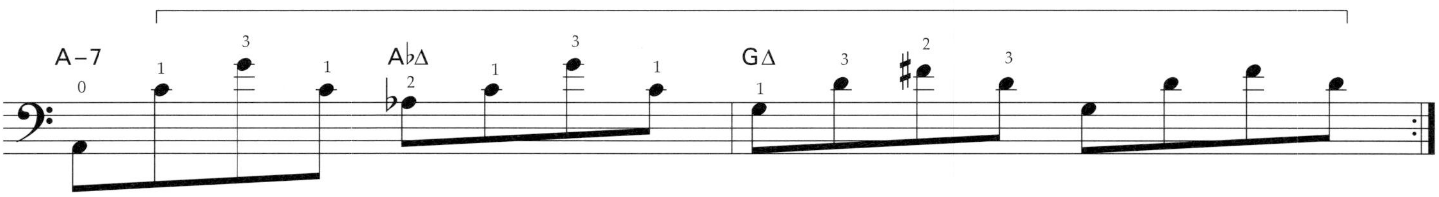

Find your own fingerings for the right hand.

Finden Sie für diese Übungen selbst Fingersätze der rechten Hand.

Here also

Hier ebenfalls

IV BASS LINES

1. General

With most of today's modern rhythm sections who play time-based jazz with triplet phrasing, for instance in bebop and hardbop compositions, it is the job of the bass to provide a so called "walking bass" line.

By analyzing bass lines from the masters like Ray Brown, Ron Carter, Rufus Reid, Dave Holland, Georg Mraz or Marc Johnson, to name just a few, one will find that they have certain things in common.

1. An exceptional rhythmic quality.
2. Clarity of the chord progression.
3. Good formal and contrapuntal construction.
4. A full, vibrant, and distinctive sound.

You will also find that the walking bass lines are improvised unless specifically written out by the arranger/composer. All the various elements of improvisation like rhythm, harmony, melody, sound, and form play an important role in the quality of a bass line as well. By further observation you will realize that the five elements are in constant interaction.

IV BASSLINIEN

1. Allgemeines

Bei den meisten modernen Rhythmusgruppen, die "Time"-bezogenen Jazz spielen, hat der Baß als Teil der Rhythmusgruppe die Aufgabe, bei Kompositionen mit "ternärer" (trioli-scher) Phrasierung wie etwa im Bebop oder Hardbop, einen sog. Walking Bass zu spielen.

Analysiert man Baßlinien solcher Meister wie Ray Brown, Ron Carter, Rufus Reid, Dave Holland Georg Mraz oder Marc Johnson, um nur einige zu nennen, wird man dabei folgende, gemeinsame Merkmale feststellen:

1. Eine außerordentlich gute rhythmische Qualität.
2. Eine harmonisch klare Gliederung.
3. Ein guter kontrapunktischer und über größere formale Abschnitte laufender Aufbau.
4. Ein voller, kräftiger, dabei prägnanter Sound.

Zu erkennen ist ebenfalls, daß Walking Baßlinien im allgemeinen improvisiert werden, es sei denn, sie werden durch einen Komponisten oder einen Arrangeur vorher festgelegt. Die für das "System" Improvisation lebenswichtigen Elemente Rhythmus, Harmonie, Melodie, Form und Klang spielen auch beim Spielen einer Baßlinie eine große Rolle. Bei eingehender Betrachtung erkennt man zudem, daß diese fünf Elemente andauernd in Wechselbeziehung zueinander stehen und miteinander vernetzt sind.

The Improvisation Network

Network Improvisation

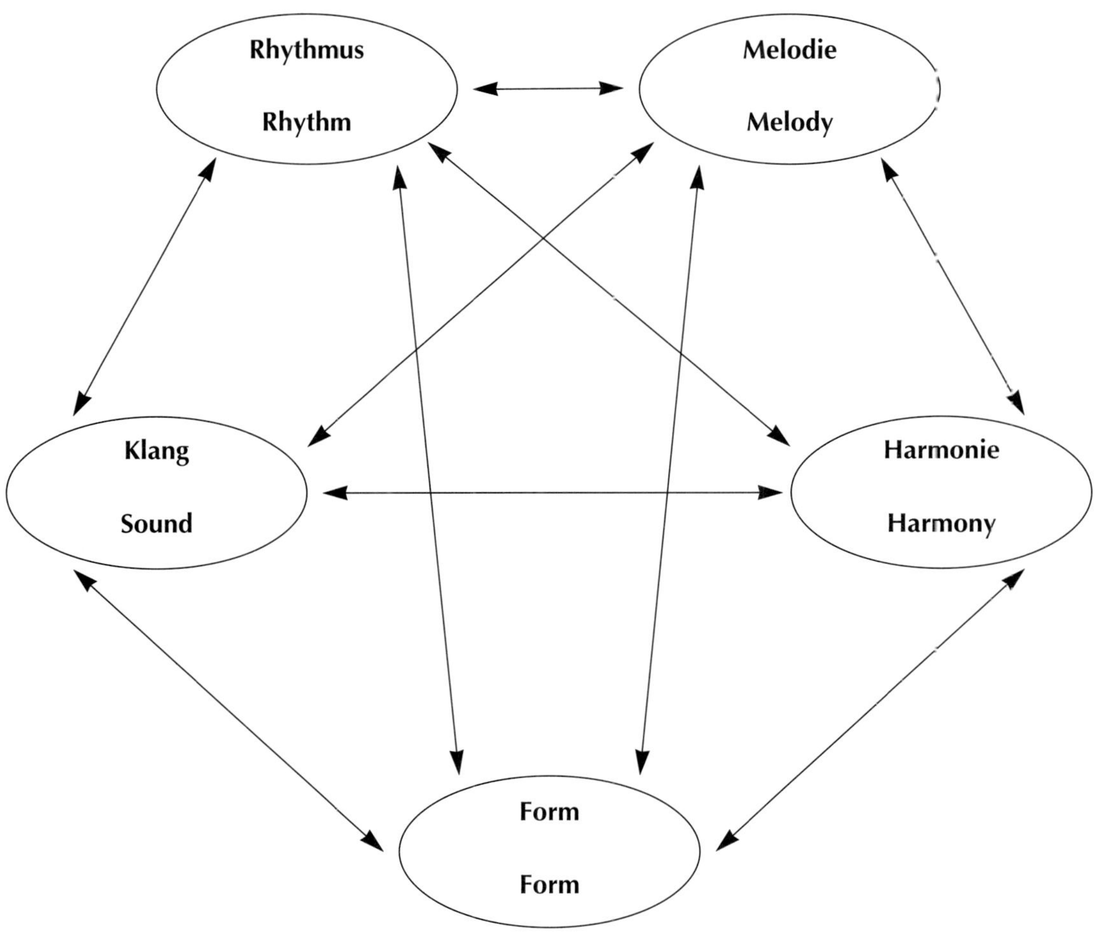

In my many years of teaching and by observing my many students, I have learned that each one's talent for using each one of the separate elements differs considerably. For that reason the learning-focus of each individual must be tailored to his own particular needs. Please refer to Chapter IX.

One who has good timing could focus more on the harmonic and melodic qualities of his practicing. It has been my experience that most young bassists (at least in Europe) are stronger in the melodic and harmonic aspects of playing. If that be the case, these individuals should then focus on improving their rhythm and timing. Some students have a clear idea about a good sound, some may need to work on this aspect of the playing.

The question is then, where are your personal strengths and weaknesses? The answer to this question will help to develop a concept of just what it is that you must learn and practice. By listening to recordings of your own practicing, you can achieve a good self-analysis in regards to the different qualities of your playing. You will also find it a great help to engage in an exchange of ideas with other musicians or a good teacher.

An old saying among piano players is also true for bassists:

"a great solo gets you applause, but great comping gets you jobs!"

Im Laufe vieler Jahre und im Umgang mit den verschiedensten Schülern/Studenten habe ich gelernt, daß die Talente bezüglich der genannten Elemente oft sehr unterschiedlich verteilt sind. Die Mischung ist bei jedem Musiker anders. Daraus folgernd sollten auch die Schwerpunkte für ein Übekonzept bei jedem anders sein (siehe Kapitel IX).

Beispielsweise müssen Bassisten mit einem bereits vorhandenen guten Timing häufig stärker an der harmonischen und/ oder melodischen Qualität arbeiten. Nach meinen Erfahrungen liegen die Talente der meisten jungen Bassisten jedoch mehr im melodischen oder harmonischen Bereich (zumindest in Europa). Bei ihnen müssen die rhythmische Qualitäten verbessert werden. Manche Studenten haben von Natur aus eine klare Vorstellung davon, was ein guter Sound ist, andere wiederum haben da ein Defizit.

Die Frage ist nun, wo Ihre ganz persönlichen Stärken und Schwächen liegen, um danach ein passendes Übekonzept zu entwickeln. Hier können eine ausführliche Selbstanalyse, am besten beim Anhören eigener Aufnahmen unter Berücksichtigung der oben genannten Qualitätsmerkmale, zudem auch ein vertrauensvolles Gespräch mit befreundeten Musikern oder auch ein guter Lehrer helfen.

Eine alte Pianistenweisheit gilt auch für Bassisten:

"Ein gutes Solo bringt den Applaus, eine gute Begleitung bringt die Jobs!"

1.1 Rhythm

As already mentioned, bass lines are mostly improvised. For this reason it would be a good idea to take a closer look at the single elements of improvisation. In doing so, you will realize that rhythm is by itself a system and that all of the different elements belonging to it are interconnected.

The different components of rhythm are:

- Pulse (the metric base). For a jazz solo it is usually the eighth-note and for a walking bass, the quarter-note;
- Timing (the proper placement of notes);
- Phrasing (the rhythmic shape of a line, either binary, ternary, or a mixture of both);
- Tempo (as a measurement of time);
- Meter (as metric divisions).

1.1 Das System Rhythmus

Weiter vorne habe ich erwähnt, daß auch Baßlinien zum größten Teil improvisiert werden. Es lohnt sich in diesem Zusammenhang, die einzelnen Elemente der Improvisation einmal genauer unter die Lupe zu nehmen, z.B. das Element Rhythmus. Dabei ist zu erkennen, daß es sich hier um ein System handelt, das aus verschiedenen Komponenten zusammengesetzt ist, die in Beziehung zueinander stehen.

Die einzelnen Teile sind

- der Puls als rhythmischer Grundwert, im Jazz beim Solo meistens Achtelnoten, beim Walking Bass meistens Viertelnoten;
- das Timing, verstanden als (exakte) Plazierung der Noten;
- die Phrasierung als rhythmische Gestaltung, entweder binär, ternär oder eine Mischform aus beiden;
- das Tempo als Zeitmaß;
- das Metrum als Zeitgliederung.

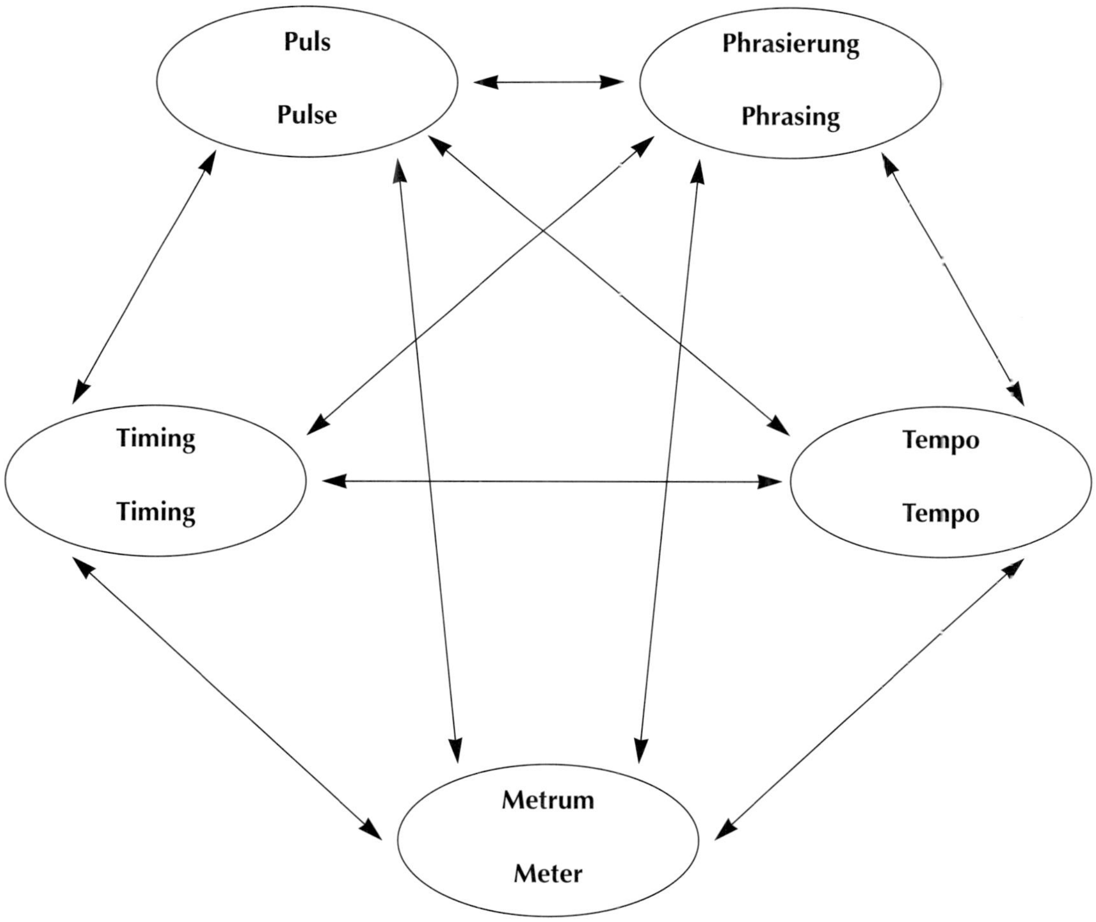

Let's take a closer look at each of these:

Auf einige Teile möchte ich näher eingehen:

1.2 Pulse

1.2 Puls

Shuffle – the rhythmic pulse is eighth note triplets

Shuffle – Puls besteht aus Achteltriolen

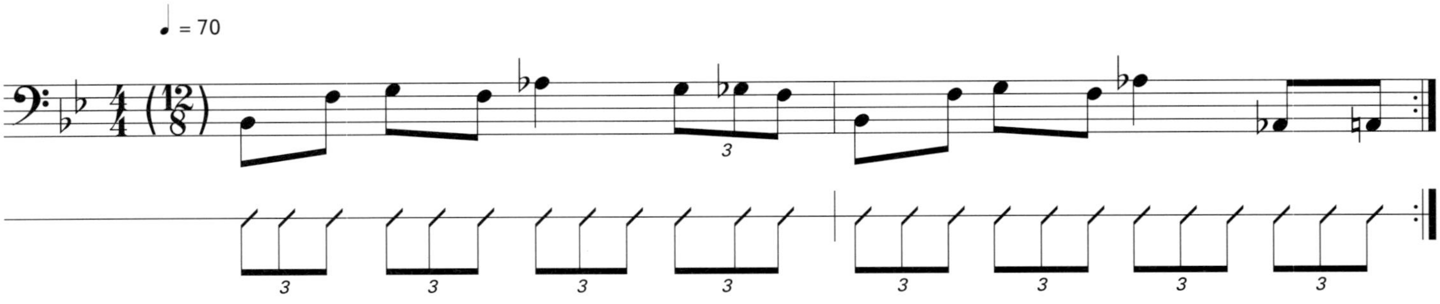

Walking bass – the rhythmic pulse is a quarter note

Walking Bass – Puls besteht aus Viertelnoten

Latin – the pulse is the eighth note

Latin – Puls besteht aus Achtelnoten

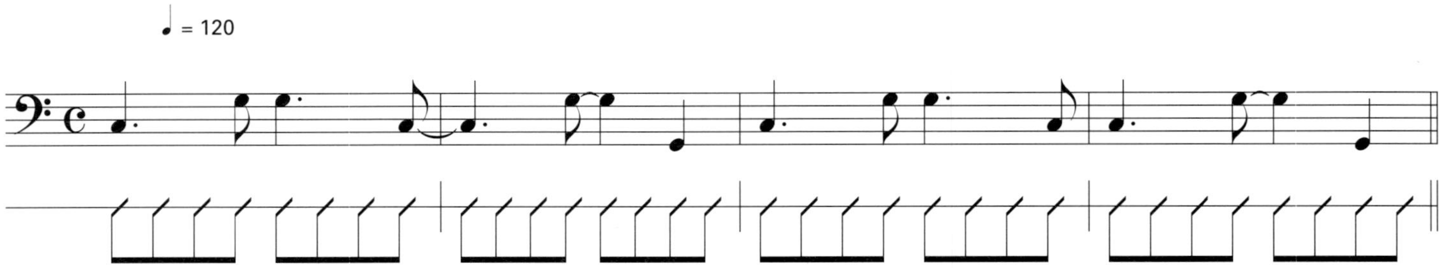

Funk, jazz rock – the pulse is the sixteenth note

Funk, Jazzrock – Puls besteht aus Sechzehntelnoten

Jazz solo – the pulse is the eighth note (see note on page 67)

Jazzsolo – Puls in Achtelnoten (ternär, s. Anmerkung S. 67)

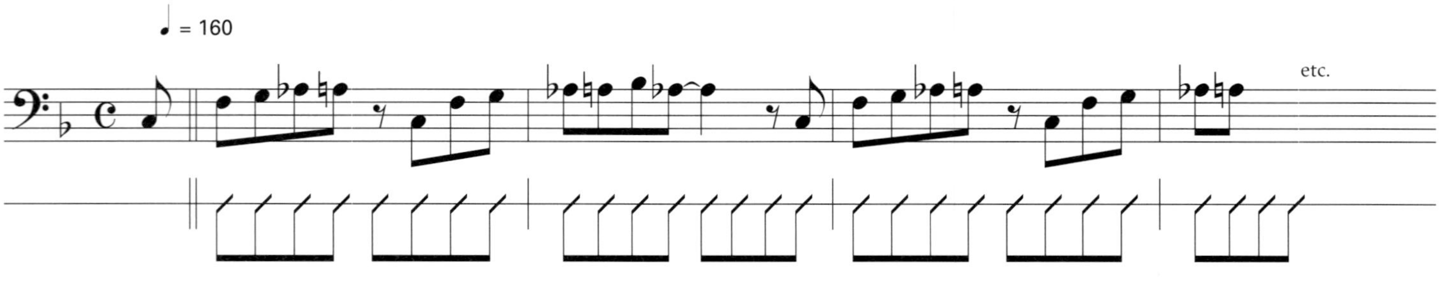

1.3 Timing

1.3.1 Definition

Generally speaking timing is defined as the "synchronized coordination of different actions".

A good bassist has the ability to

a) play the notes with constant rhythm,
b) synchronize the notes played by himself to the pulse played by the other members of the band.

As a basic exercise, play quarter-notes on the open G string while using a metronome click on beats 2 and 4 at 120 beats per minute. Record the exercise. While playing and while listening to the recording, observe the critera "a" and "b" above. If you should find that your time is uneven it could be helpful to imagine a rhythmic flow of eighth-note triplets (in faster tempos these will become straight eighth-notes). It is also helpful to sing along. Some musicians speak of "the drummer inside". With this in mind, one can think of the fingers of the right hand as being drumsticks.

When playing with a drummer listen to his pulse (usually played on the ride-cymbal) and use it to synchronize your bass line.

1.3 Timing

1.3.1 Definition

Allgemein wird Timing als synchrone Abstimmung verschiedener Aktionen bezeichnet.

Ein Bassist mit einem guten Timing ist in der Lage

a) seine Noten rhythmisch konstant zu spielen,
b) die von ihm gespielten Noten synchron zum Puls der anderen Bandmitglieder zu spielen.

Spielen Sie als Grundübung Viertelnoten auf der leeren G-Saite mit einem Metronomklick auf 2 und 4 im Tempo 120. Nehmen Sie diese Übung auf. Achten Sie sowohl beim Spielen als auch beim Abhören auf die beiden genannten Kriterien. Bei evtl. auftretenden Unregelmäßigkeiten kann es hilfreich sein, sich innerlich einen rhythmischen Fluß von Achteltriolen, bzw. in einem schnelleren Tempo Achtel, vorzustellen. Auch Mitsingen kann helfen. Manche Musiker sprechen von ihrem "Inneren Schlagzeuger". Dementsprechend kann man die Finger der rechten Hand gleichsam als Trommelstöcke ansehen.

Achten Sie beim Zusammenspiel mit einem Schlagzeuger darauf, wie er den Puls – in den meisten Fällen auf dem sog. Ride-Becken – spielt. Synchronisieren Sie Ihre Baßlinie mit diesem Puls.

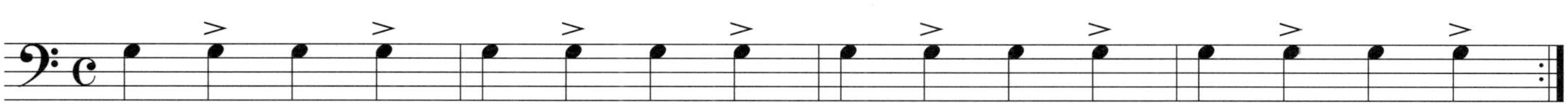

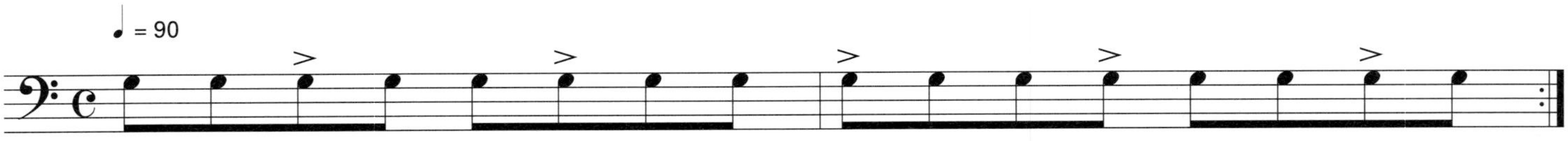

Transfer the preceding exercises to other strings and positions. Fill the eighth-note patterns with both ascending and descending scales.

Übertragen Sie die vorhergehenden Übungen auf andere Saiten, in andere Lagen, füllen Sie die Achtelketten mit Tonleitern (auf- und abwärts).

1.3.2 Micro Timing

Very important elements of creating music are the delicate nuances found in the placement of the individual notes against the rhythmic pulse. Especially in a solo you are able to create rhythmic tension and release by playing your own individual pulse which differs from that of the band by very small degrees. The following terms are commonly used.

- **laid back** – a slight delay, placing the notes behind the pulse
- **on the beat** – the notes are synchronized exactly with the beat
- **on top of the beat** – the notes are played slightly ahead of the pulse

1.3.2 Mikro-Timing

Ein wichtiges musikalisches Gestaltungsmittel ist die Nuancierung der Notenplazierung, besonders innerhalb eines Solos. Der eigene Puls wird im Verhältnis zum Puls der Band in sehr feinen Abstufungen individuell gestaltet. Auf diese Weise läßt sich eine besondere musikalische Spannung erzeugen.
Im einzelnen gibt es dafür folgende Bezeichnungen:

- **laid back** – leichte Verzögerung, hinter dem Puls
- **on the beat** – genau synchron zum allgemeinen Puls
- **on top of the beat** – etwas vor dem allgemeinen Puls

Play a theme like *Straight No Chaser* for example, and experiment with the placement of the beat by playing first behind, then ahead of the beat. Do this to the extreme. Observe how this changes your feeling toward the music. Two musicians well known for the "laid back" style of playing behind the beat are Dexter Gordon and John Scofield.

Many musicians play considerably ahead of the beat whenever they are under stress. Listen to recordings of your own playing and see how your time changes in different situations and moods.

The benchmark for excellent timing have been set by a number of famous rhythm sections throughout the history of jazz. In the legendary "John Coltrane Quartet", bassist Jimmy Garrison is the "anchor" for the band. He would play directly on the beat while the drummer, Elvin Jones, would play behind the beat and pianist McCoy Tyner would play considerably ahead. In spite of these differences, they would together produce a constant rhythmic flow to the music. Other special examples of this rhythmic-togetherness are the rhythm sections of the different Miles Davis groups – but don't limit yourself to just his recordings of the 50's and 60's.

Spielen Sie ein Thema wie z.B. *Straight No Chaser* einmal extrem hinter oder weit vor dem Beat. Beobachten Sie, welche musikalische Wirkung diese Spielweisen auf Sie haben. Berühmte Beispiele für das Spielen hinter dem Beat ("laid back") sind Dexter Gordon und John Scofield.

Vielen Musikern geht es so, daß sie unter Streß ziemlich weit vorne spielen. Hören Sie sich doch bitte darauf hin einmal eigene Mitschnitte an. In welchen Situationen haben Sie wie gespielt?

Maßstäbe in dieser Richtung wurden natürlich von einigen berühmten Rhythmusgruppen der Jazzgeschichte gesetzt, z.B. durch die des legendären John Coltrane Quartetts. Bassist Jimmy Garrison ist der "Anker" der Band. Er spielt meistens genau auf dem Beat. Drummer Elvin Jones spielt dahinter, Pianist McCoy Tyner häufig davor, aber alle spielen in einem gleichmäßig laufenden, rhythmischen Fluß. Sie bilden ein organisches Ganzes. Auch die Rhythmusgruppen von Miles Davis, nicht nur die aus den fünfziger und sechziger Jahren, sind in diesem Zusammenhang besonders hörenswert.

2. Walking Bass

2.1 Basic Rules

In pieces based on chord progressions, a walking bass line should reflect the harmony very clearly. The bass player communicates in this respect with the piano (keyboard), the guitar (when used), and the soloist as well.

Such bass lines can be developed by using:

- digital patterns
- a two-beat feel
- arpeggios
- leading tones
- diatonic passing notes
- chromatic approach notes
- scales and tetrachords
- rhythmical embellishment

2. Walking Bass

2.1 Grundregeln

Walking Bass Linien, die zu harmonisch gebundenen Stücken gespielt werden, sollten die Harmonien dieser Stücke deutlich erkennen lassen. Innerhalb einer Band findet die Kommunikation in dieser Beziehung sowohl mit den Harmonieinstrumenten Piano bzw. Keyboard oder Gitarre (falls vorhanden) als auch dem Solisten statt. Baßlinien mit klarer harmonischer Konzeption bieten die beste Voraussetzung dazu.

Solche Baßlinien können entwickelt werden

- mit digitalen Patterns
- im Two-Beat Feel
- mit Akkordbrechungen
- mit Leittönen
- mit diatonischen Nachbar– und Durchgangstönen
- mit chromatischen Annäherungen
- mit Skalen und Tetrachorden
- mit rhythmischen Verzierungen

2.2 Crash Course Utilizing Digital Patterns

The following is based on chord-scales.
Example: The Dorian scale is used with a II–7 chord (a minor chord built on the second degree of a major scale).

2.2 Schnellkurs mit Digital-Patterns

Grundlage hierfür ist die Akkord/Skalentheorie. So paßt z.B. zu einem Mollakkord auf der II. Stufe die dorische Skala:

The Mixolydian scale is used with a V7 (dominant seventh) chord.

F mixolydisch zu F7

You can apply numbers to the scale degrees to help you to quickly transpose each scale in relation to the root of the present chord.

Jede Stufe dieser Skalen kann man mit den entsprechenden Zahlen versehen, die man schnell und leicht transponieren kann, immer in Relation zum jeweiligen Grundton des entsprechenden Akkordes (bzw. der I. Stufe der dazu passenden Skala).

Example: *Just Friends*; the digital patterns are
1 2 3 5, 1 2 3 1 from C Ionian, 1 7 6 5 from C Dorian, 1 5 6 5 from F Mixolydian.

Beispiel: *Just Friends* mit den Digital-Patterns
1 2 3 5 , 1 2 3 1 von C Dur, 1 7 6 5 von C dorisch, 1 5 6 5 von F mixolydisch.

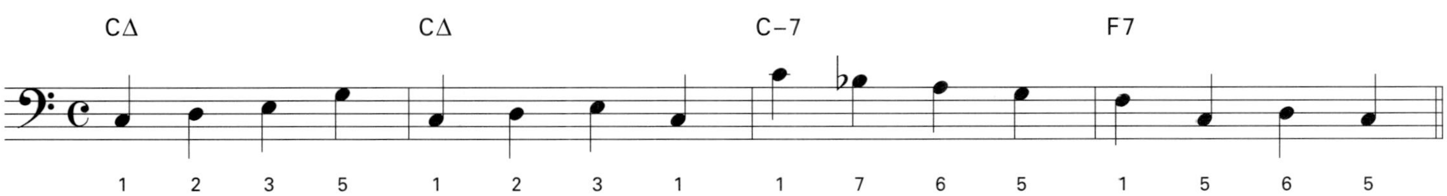

Example: ***Autumn Leaves***

Beispiel: ***Autumn Leaves***

Use these digital patterns with the following exercises on the II V progression.

Spielen Sie verschiedene Digital-Patterns über die unten stehenden II V Verbindungen:

	Minor seventh	Dominant seventh
a)	1 2 1 2	1 2 1 2
b)	1 3 4 5	1 5 6 5
c)	1 2 3 1	1 2 3 1
d)	1 3 4 5	1 7 6 5
e)	1 3 4 5	1 2 3 5
f)	1 2 3 5	1 7 6 5
g)	1 7 6 5	1 5 3 2
h)	1 3 1 7	3 2 1 3

	Mollseptakkord	Dominantseptakkord
a)	1 2 1 2	1 2 1 2
b)	1 3 4 5	1 5 6 5
c)	1 2 3 1	1 2 3 1
d)	1 3 4 5	1 7 6 5
e)	1 3 4 5	1 2 3 5
f)	1 2 3 5	1 7 6 5
g)	1 7 6 5	1 5 3 2
h)	1 3 1 7	3 2 1 3

Find more combinations yourself!

Practice these exercises also along with Jamey Aebersold's play-along recordings, vol. 3, "The II-V-I Progression", (side A, track 2).

Finden Sie selber andere Kombinationen!

Diese Übungen können Sie auch zu Jamey Aebersold's "Play-Along CD Vol. 3, The II-V7-I Progression" (2. Stück) mitspielen.

These patterns are often used with the IIø V progressions:

minor seventh chord, ♭5 (half-diminished) seventh chord	altered dominant
a) 1 ♭3 4 ♭5	1 ♭2(♭9) ♭3(♯9) 3
b) 1 ♭7 ♭6 ♭5	1 ♭7 ♯5(♭6) ♭5

Bei II V Verbindungen in Moll hört man öfter diese Patterns:

Mollseptakkord, ♭5 (halbvermindert)	alterierter Dominantseptakkord
a) 1 ♭3 4 ♭5	1 ♭2(♭9) ♭3(♯9) 3
b) 1 ♭7 ♭6 ♭5	1 ♭7 ♯5(♭6) ♭5

Example: Dø - G7♭9 to C– 6^{9}

Beispiel: Dø - G7♭9 nach C– 6^{9}

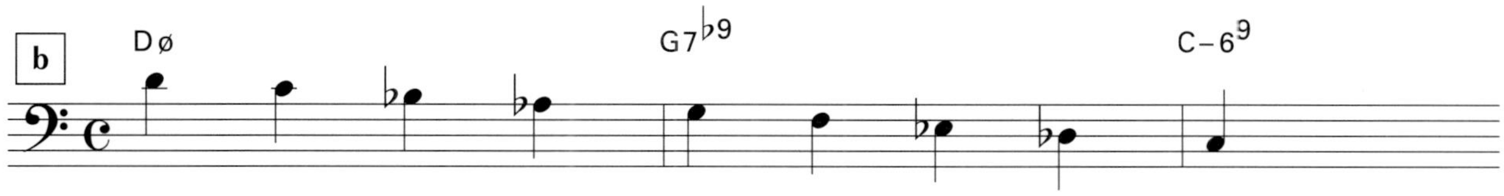

2.3 The Two-Beat Feel

The "two-beat" style dates from the early days of jazz. The bass plays in a tuba style on only two beats in a bar. For a jazz standard a good sounding accompaniment is for the bass to play two-beat for the "A" section, and walking bass for the bridge. Where there is only one chord per measure, the bass usually plays the root of the chord on the first beat and the fifth of the chord on the third beat.

Example: *Mack The Knife* by Kurt Weill

2.3 "Two-Beat Feel"

Bei dieser Spielweise, die ihren Ursprung in den frühen Tagen des Jazz hat, spielt man ähnlich wie eine Tuba nur zwei "Beats" per Takt. Gut klingt das als Baßbegleitung beim Vorstellen eines Standard-Themas, wobei meistens die A-Teile im "Two-Beat Feel" und der Mittelteil mit durchlaufenden Vierteln als Walking Bass gespielt werden; bei eintaktigen Akkordwechseln auf die Zählzeit 1 den Grundton, auf 3 die Quinte.

Beispiel: *Mack The Knife* von Kurt Weill

With two chord symbols in one bar you would play their respective roots on the first and third beat:

Man spielt bei halbtaktigen Akkordwechseln auf 1 den Grundton des ersten Akkordes, auf 3 den Grundton des folgenden Akkordes:

Example: *"Rhythm Changes"*, bars 1-16 (note the ascending bass line in measures 5-7 (see Chapter IV.2.11, page 62)).

Beispiel: *"Rhythm Changes"*, Takt 1-16 (beachten Sie die aufsteigende Baßlinie in den Takten 5-7 (siehe IV.2.11, Seite 62)).

PRACTICE TIP:
The previous exercises are can be used best as "timing" exercises. In the beginning, use only your index finger to pluck the strings while being careful to keep the dynamics and duration of the notes constant. Let the notes flow into each other. See if your time varies whenever you change strings or play a tone on the E string. Record the exercises and listen very carefully to your own playing. See if you can determine if you are concentrating too much on any one aspect of your playing at the expense of another. Is your intonation bad because you concentrate only on timing? Perhaps the other way around? See if you can identify the problem and find a possible solution.

Isolate the problem and invent appropriate exercises.

ÜBEHINWEIS:
Die beiden vorausgegangenen Übungen sind auch bestens als Timing-Übungen geeignet. Zupfen Sie die Töne zu Beginn nur mit dem Zeigefinger der rechten Hand und achten Sie bitte auf eine gleichmäßige Dynamik und eine gleichbleibende Dauer der Noten. Lassen Sie die Töne ineinander fließen. Beobachten Sie, ob bei einem Saitenwechsel oder beim Anschlagen der Töne auf der E-Saite evtl. Unregelmäßigkeiten im Timing entstehen. Machen Sie von diesen Übungen eine Aufnahme, und hören Sie sich sorgfältig Ihr eigenes Spiel an. Können Sie feststellen, ob durch eine zu starke Konzentration auf eine Sache wie z.B. Intonation oder Ausdauer ein anderes Element wie z.B. das Timing möglicherweise leidet, oder umgekehrt? Stellen Sie gegebenenfalls die möglichen Ursachen fest und suchen Sie eine Lösung. Isolieren Sie das Problemfeld und überlegen Sie sich entsprechende Übungen.

2.4 Arpeggios

In order to create walking bass lines you can play arpeggios of four-note seventh chords along with their inversions and octave shifts (see page 106ff). The root is most often played on the the first beat of the bar. The third of the chord is usually included somewhere in the measure to help define the quality of the chord.

2.4 Akkordbrechungen

Man spielt Akkordbrechungen vierstimmiger Septakkorde (siehe Seite 106ff.). Dabei sind verschiedene Umkehrungen und Oktavierungen möglich. Häufig wird auf der Zählzeit 1 der Grundton und im weiteren Verlauf des Taktes auch die Terz gespielt, um so die Qualität des Akkordes (Dur oder Moll) zu verdeutlichen.

Example: ***Mack The Knife***

Beispiel: ***Mack The Knife***

2.5 Diatonic Neighboring And Passing Tones

Here the diatonic (scale) tones are used along with the chord tones (marked by an asterisk). In slow tempo progressions that follow the cycle of fifths, the forth degree of a scale, especially on major and dominant seventh chords (e.g. the note F in a C major scale) must be used carefully as it gives the impression that the next chord is beeing played too soon.

2.5 Diatonische Nachbar- und Durchgangstöne

Hierbei werden Akkordtöne mit diatonischen (tonleitereigenen) Tönen verbunden oder umspielt (gekennzeichnet mit *). Vorsicht bei der Verwendung der leitereigenen Quarte in Durakkorden, vor allem bei langsamen Tempi. Es könnte der Eindruck entstehen, daß bei Akkordfolgen im Quintfall zu früh zum nächsten Akkord gewechselt wird.

Example ***Autumn Leaves,*** **bars 1-8**

Beispiel: ***Autumn Leaves,*** **Takt 1-8**

Further examples:

Weitere Beispiele:

b

c

d

2.6 Leading Tones

The use of leading-tones make possible a smooth voice leading from one chord to another, especially in the following examples:

V7 I – the 3 of V leads up to the root of I
II–7 V7 – the ♭7 of II leads up to the 3 of V
IIø V7 – the ♭5 of the II half-diminished chord leads down to the root of the V

2.6 Leittöne

Leittöne ermöglichen eine fließende, logische Stimmführung von einem Akkord zum anderen, bevorzugt bei Akkordverbindungen von der V. zur I. Stufe und von der II. zur V. Stufe. Dabei leiten große Terzen zum Grundton des nächsten Akkordes, kleine Septimen zur folgenden Terz, verminderte Quinten (vor allem bei halbverminderten Akkorden der II. Stufe) ebenfalls zum folgenden Grundton.

Example: *What Is This Thing Called Love,* bars 1-16

Beispiel: *What Is This Thing Called Love,* Takt 1-16

Example: ***Confirmation*****, bars 1-16**

Beispiel: ***Confirmation*****, Takt 1-16**

Note:
These types of bass lines are especially good for backing a soloist when there is no other harmony instrument playing. It makes the harmony clear and easy to be heard. Typical situations would be a trio with sax, bass and drums, or with a piano/guitar trio, whenever the soloist is playing "single-note lines".

Anmerkung:
Baßlinien dieser Art eignen sich besonders gut für die Begleitung eines Solisten, wenn kein weiteres Harmonieinstrument mitspielt, da die Akkorde und deren Wechsel deutlich zu hören sind. Typische Spielsituationen: Trio mit Sax, Drums und Baß oder Piano- bzw. Gitarrentrio, wenn der Solist sog. "Single-Note Lines" spielt.

2.7 Chromatic Lines

Here we have two possibilities:

a) the next chord tone is approached by half-step chromatically;
b) the first tone of the next chord is approached chromatically.

2.7 Chromatik

Hierbei gibt es zwei Möglichkeiten:

a) der nächste Ton wird chromatisch von unten oder oben angesteuert,
b) der erste Ton des folgenden Akkordes wird chromatisch angesteuert.

Example: B♭ Blues

Beispiel: Blues in B♭

Further examples:

Weitere Beispiele:

2.8 Scales And Tetrachords

Play the appropriate scales and tetrachords for each chord symbol. In progressions using the cycle of fifths, the lines are frequently connected over two bars. A short analysis follows each example.

2.8 Skalen und Tetrachorde

Man spielt die zu den Akkorden passenden Skalen und Tetrachorde (Viertongruppen), bei Akkordverbindungen im Quintfall häufig über zwei Takte. Den folgenden Beispielen ist immer eine kurze Analyse nachgestellt, um dies zu verdeutlichen.

Example: ***Autumn Leaves*****, bars 1-8**

Beispiel: ***Autumn Leaves*****, Takt 1-8**

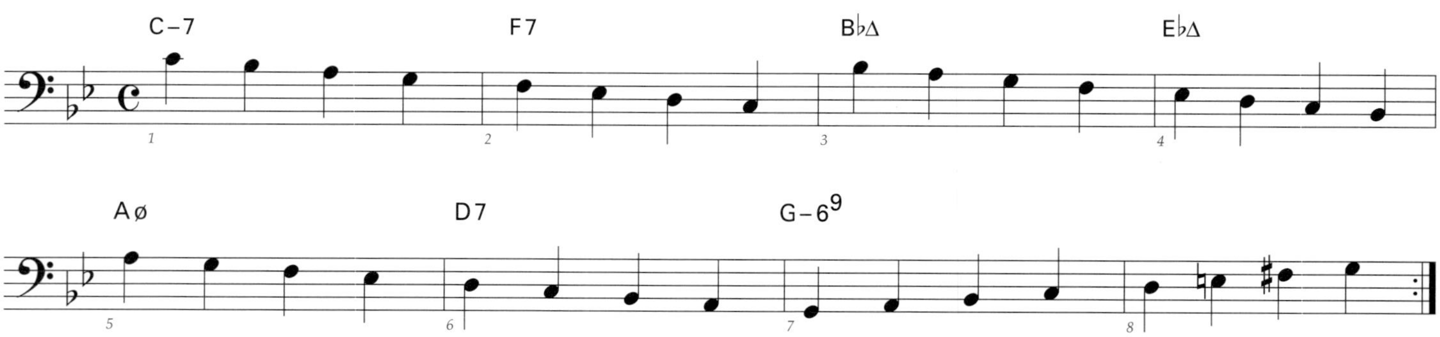

Analysis:

Bars 1 and 2: C Dorian, descending
Bars 3 and 4: B♭ major (Ionian), descending
Bars 5 and 6: A Locrian, descending
Bars 7 and 8: G melodic minor, ascending

Analyse:

Takt 1 und 2: C dorisch abwärts
Takt 3 und 4: B♭ Dur (ionisch) abwärts
Takt 5 und 6: A lokrisch abwärts
Takt 7 und 8: G melodisch Moll aufwärts

Example: B♭ Blues, bars 1-4

Beispiel: Blues in B♭, Takt 1-4

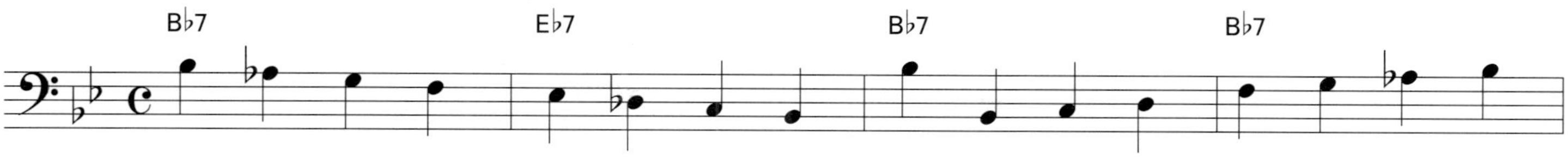

Analysis:

Bars 1 and 2: B♭ Dorian
Bars 3 and 4: B♭ Mixolydian

Analyse:

Takt 1 und 2: B♭ dorisch
Takt 3 und 4: B♭ mixolydisch

Example: ***Just Friends*****, bars 1-16**

Beispiel: ***Just Friends*****, Takt 1-16**

Analysis:

Bars 1 and 2:	C Lydian
Bars 3 and 4:	C Dorian (with octave shift)
Bars 5 and 6:	B Phrygian
Bars 7 and 8:	B♭ Dorian descending (with octave shift)
Bars 9 and 10:	A Dorian
Bars 11 and 12:	B Dorian
Bars 13 and 14:	A Mixolydian ♯11
Bar 15:	chord notes
Bar 16:	D Dorian ascending

Analyse:

Takt 1 und 2:	C lydisch
Takt 3 und 4:	C dorisch (mit Oktavverschiebung)
Takt 5 und 6:	B (H) phrygisch
Takt 7 und 8:	B♭ dorisch abwärts mit Oktavverschiebung
Takt 9 und 10:	A dorisch
Takt 11 und 12:	B dorisch
Takt 13 und 14:	A mixolydisch ♯11
Takt 15:	Akkordtöne
Takt 16:	D dorisch aufwärts

Example: Reharmonisation of *Stella By Starlight*

Beispiel: Reharmonisation von *Stella By Starlight*

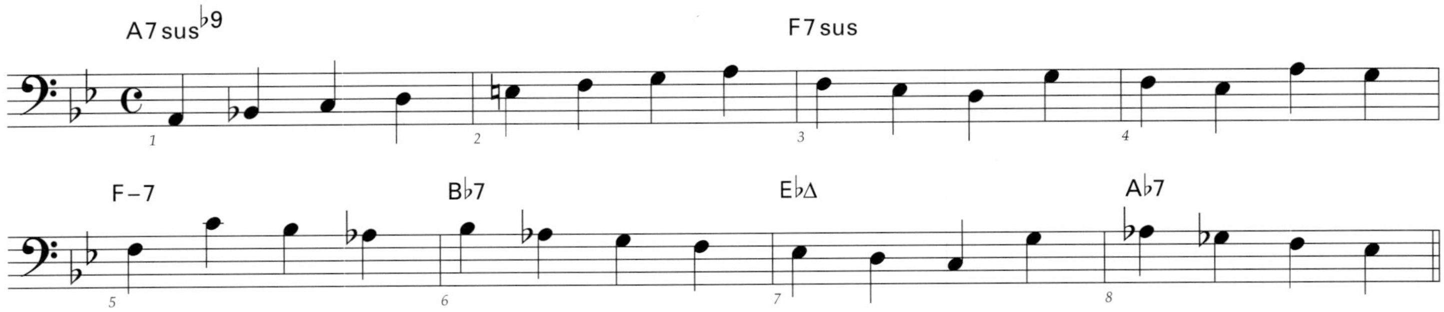

Analysis:

Bars 1 and 2:	A Phrygian
Bars 3 and 4:	F Mixolydian
Bars 5 and 6:	F Dorian
Bar 7:	E♭ major (Ionian)
Bar 8:	A♭ Mixolydian

Analyse:

Takt 1 und 2:	A phrygisch
Takt 3 und 4:	F mixolydisch
Takt 5 und 6:	F dorisch
Takt 7:	E♭ Dur (ionisch)
Takt 8:	A♭ mixolydisch

Example: *What Is This Thing Called Love?*

Beispiel: *What Is This Thing Called Love?*

Analysis:

Bar 1:	G Locrian descending
Bar 2:	C altered scale
Bars 3 and 4:	F Dorian
Bars 5 and 6:	D Locrian
Bars 7 and 8:	C major (Ionian), scale fragments
Bars 9 and 10:	C altered scale
Bars 11 and 12:	F Dorian
Bars 13 and 14:	D Locrian
Bars 15 and 16:	E Phrygian

Analyse:

Takt 1:	G lokrisch abwärts
Takt 2:	C alterierte Skala
Takt 3 und 4:	F dorisch
Takt 5 und 6:	D lokisch
Takt 7 und 8:	Skalenfragmente von C Dur (ionisch)
Takt 9 und 10:	C alterierte Skala
Takt 11 und 12:	F dorisch
Takt 13 und 14:	D lokrisch
Takt 15 und 16:	E phrygisch

This type of bass line is well suited for fast tempos. A comprehensive knowledge of the relationship of scales and chords and a well-trained ear are necessary to enable one to respond quickly to the piano or guitar voicings. Carefully study the relationship between chords and scales (see Chapter VIII).

Baßlinien dieser Art passen besser zu schnellen Tempi. Voraussetzung für ihre "Konstruktion" sind sehr gute Kenntnisse in der Akkord/Skalentheorie sowie ein gutes Gehör für die vom Pianisten oder Gitarristen gespielten Voicings. Studieren Sie bei den vorstehenden Analysen genau, welche Skalen bei welchen Akkorden verwendet wurden (s. Kapitel VIII).

2.9 Pentatonic Scales

Pentatonic scales lend themselves to modal compositions like *Windows* by Chick Corea

Example: *Windows*

2.9 Pentatonische Tonleitern

Pentatonische Tonleitern bieten sich bei einer modalen Komposition an, wie z.B. *Windows* von Chick Corea.

Beispiel: *Windows*

Analysis:

Bars 1-4:	B♭ minor pentatonic
Bars 5-8:	G minor pentatonic ♭5
Bars 9-12:	F minor pentatonic
Bars 13-16:	A♭ minor pentatonic

Analyse:

Takt 1-4:	B♭ Moll-Pentatonik
Takt 5-8:	G Moll-Pentatonik mit ♭5
Takt 9-12:	F Moll-Pentatonik
Takt 13-16:	A♭ Moll-Pentatonik

2.10 Bass Lines For II V Progressions

The following study is comprised of walking bass lines on the four-bar progression C– 7 / F 7 / D– 7 / G 7 .

Practice the exercise:

1. In a moderate tempo as a reading exercise. Find fingerings that include open strings to use as an intonation help.
2. Decide which lines sound good to you and which don't.
3. Observe the transitions from one measure to another and decide which you like best and which ones you like the least.
4. Compare these lines with others that you have already heard? Do you recognize certain lines or fragments of lines? Consider under what conditions walking bass lines were performed (instrumentation, tempo, style, etc.).

2.10 Baßlinien über II V Verbindungen

Hier eine Walking Baßlinie über die viertaktige Akkordverbindung C– 7 / F 7 / D– 7 / G 7 .

Üben Sie schrittweise:

1. Als Leseübung im mittleren Tempo. Finden Sie eigene Fingersätze mit Leersaiten als Intonationshilfe.
2. Beurteilen Sie die Linien. Welche finden Sie gut und welche gefallen Ihnen weniger?
3. Beobachten Sie die Übergänge von einem Takt zum nächsten. Welche klingen gut, welche weniger gut?
4. Vergleichen Sie diese Baßlinien mit Linien, die Sie schon einmal irgendwo gehört haben. Erkennen Sie einzelne Linien oder Teile daraus? Unter welchen Gegebenheiten (Tempo des Stücks, Besetzung der Band, Stilistik etc.) hat der Bassist/die Bassistin den Walking Bass gespielt?

Bass lines on a four-bar II V7 progression

Baßlinien über eine viertaktige II V7 Verbindung

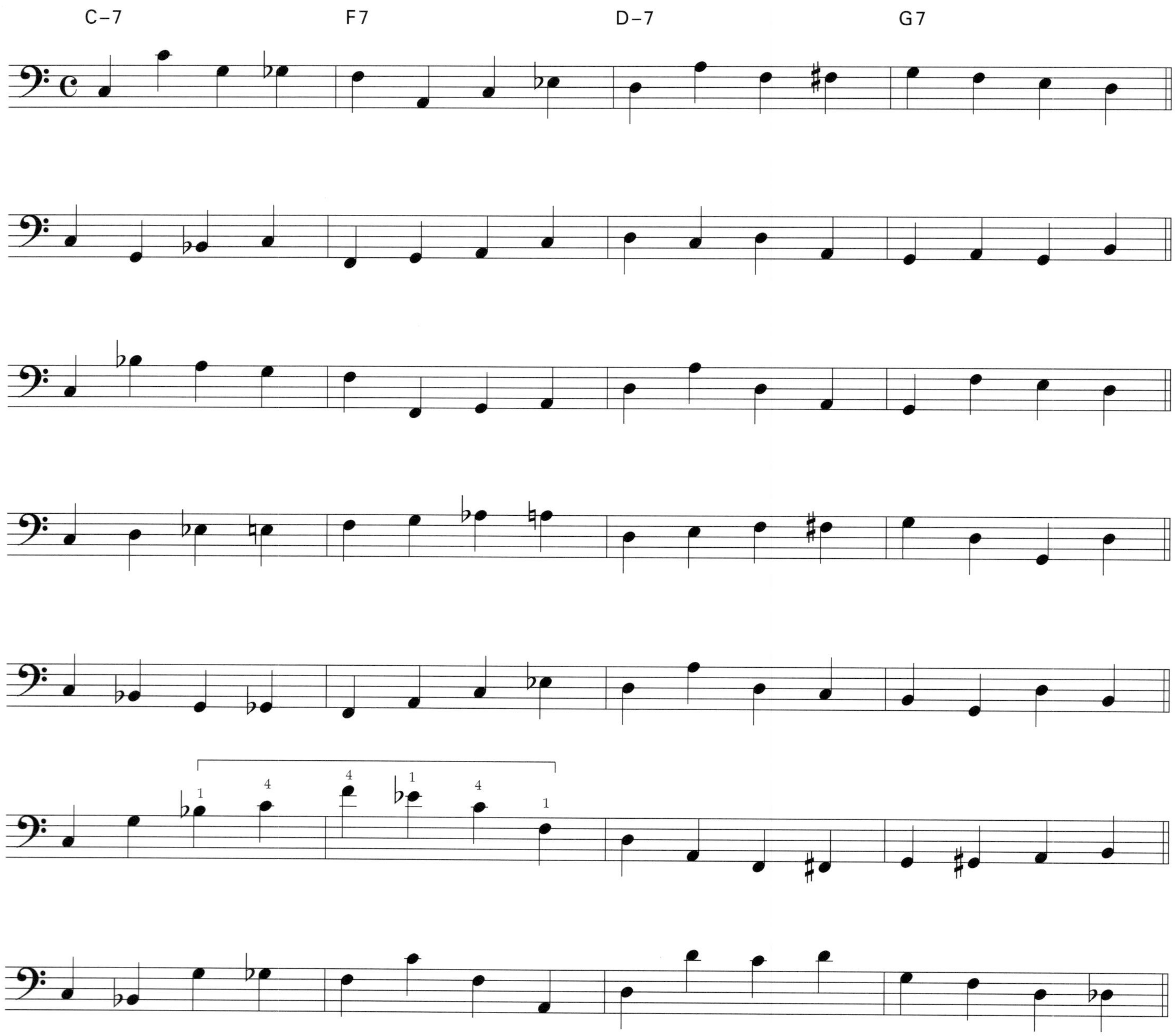

Combine the first and second measures from any line with the third and fourth measures from any other.

Kombinieren Sie beliebig Takt 1 und 2 aus einer Zeile mit Takt 3 und 4 aus einer anderen Zeile.

2.11 Harmonic Clichés

Certain chord progressions have been so often used that they have become clichés. One example of this is the so-called "Rhythm Changes", named after the chord progression found in the George Gershwin song *I've Got Rhythm*. The experienced bass player realizes immediately that a specific kind of voice-leading is required.

This progression is the basis for many other songs. Some examples from the "Swing" era are *Lester Leaps In, Cottontail, Every Tub, The Lunceford Special,* and *The Jeep Is Jumpin.*

From the "Bebop" era are such examples as *The Theme, One Bass Hit, Thriving From A Riff, Dexterity, Crazeology, Rhythm-A-Ning, Shaw 'nuff, Fifty-second Street Theme, Moose The Mooche, Cheers,* and later *Oleo, The Flintstones,* and *Rocky And His Friends.*

In some instances only the "A" section is used and something else used for the bridge. In *Good Bait*, the bridge is the same as the "A" section except transposed to E♭. A few of the many examples of this are *Blue Moon, Tuxedo Junction, Brilliant Corners,* and *Christopher Columbus.*

Transposed to F major, the Rhythm Changes are used as the basis for a number of other compositions like *Salt Peanuts* by Dizzie Gillespie, *Marmaduke* by Charlie Parker, *Fingers* by Thad Jones, and *Funghi Mama* by Blue Mitchell.

Some pieces use the Rhythm Changes "A" section in F and a different progression for the middle section: *Mean To Me, Between The Devil And The Deep Blue Sea, You Took Advantage Of Me, Parisian Thoroughfare* from Bud Powell, and others.

The following is the most frequently played version of the Rhythm Changes.

2.11 Harmonische Klischees

Manche Akkordverbindungen sind als fester Bestandteil des allgemeinen harmonischen Repertoires zu harmonischen Klischees geworden. Jeder erfahrene Bassist erkennt bei ihnen, daß in diesen Fällen eine bestimmte Art der Linienführung zu spielen ist.

Dazu gehören auf jeden Fall die sog. "Rhythm Changes", benannt nach der George Gershwin Komposition *I've Got Rhythm.* Auf dieser Harmoniefolge basieren sehr viele Stücke. In der Swing-Ära z.B. *Lester Leaps In, Cottontail, Every Tub, The Lunceford Special, The Jeep Is Jumpin.*

In der Bebop-Ära Stücke wie *The Theme, One Bass Hit, Thriving From A Riff, Dexterity, Crazeology, Rhythm-A-Ning, Shaw 'nuff, Fifty-second Street Theme, Moose The Mooche, Cheers,* und später *Oleo, The Flintstones, Rocky And His Friends.*

Bei manchen Stücken wurden nur die A-Teile übernommen, der Mittelteil jedoch verändert, so z.B. *Good Bait* (hier hat der Mittelteil die gleichen Harmonien wie ein A-Teil, jedoch nach E♭ Dur transponiert), *Blue Moon, Tuxedo Junction, Brilliant Corners,* und *Christopher Columbus* u.a.

Transponiert nach F Dur sind die "Rhythm Changes" die harmonische Basis für eine Reihe von weiteren Kompositionen wie *Salt Peanuts* von Dizzy Gillespie, *Marmaduke* von Charlie Parker, *Fingers* von Thad Jones, *Funghi Mama* von Blue Mitchell.

Manchen Stücken liegt der "Rhythm" A-Teil in F zugrunde, die Mittelteile haben andere Harmonien: *Mean To Me, Between The Devil And The Deep Blue Sea, You Took Advantage Of Me, Parisian Thoroughfare* von Bud Powell u.a.

In dieser, gegenüber dem Original von George Gershwin schon leicht modifizierten Version werden die Rhythm Changes vielfach gespielt:

Example: Rhythm Changes

Beispiel: Rhythm Changes

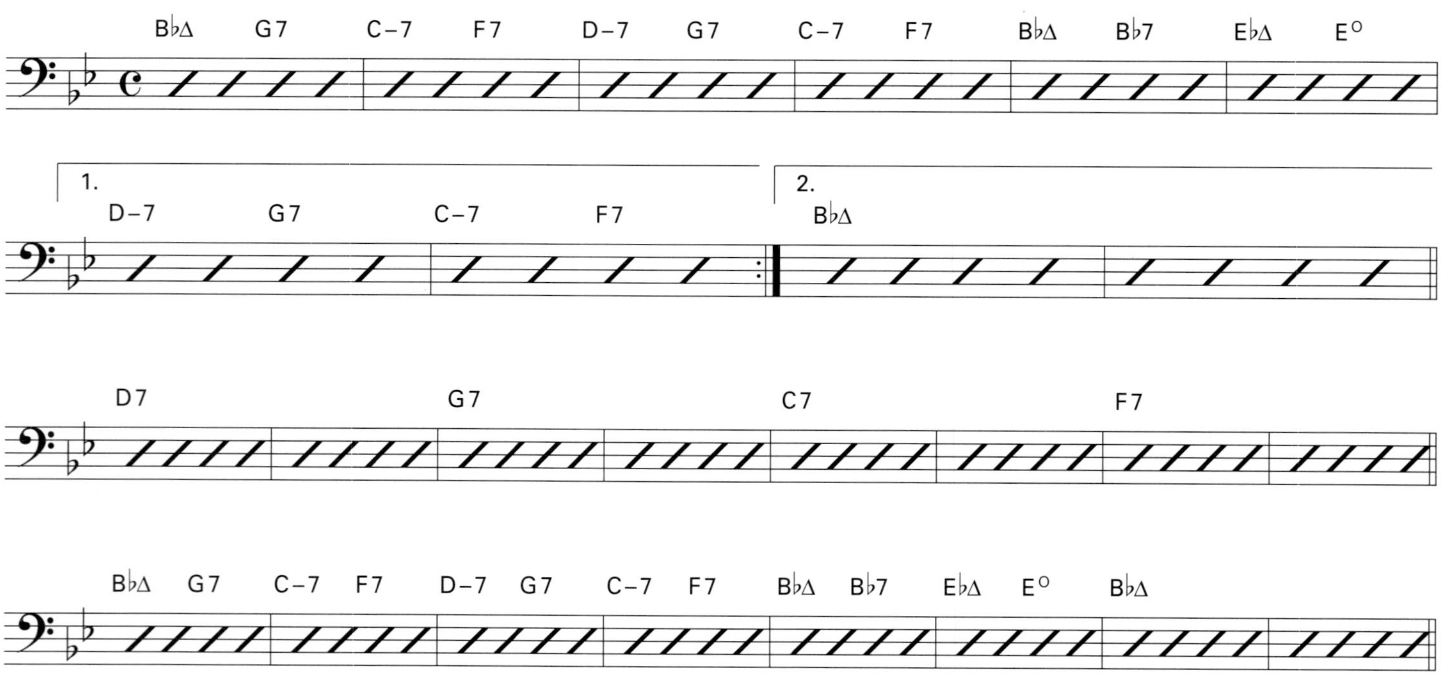

2.11.1 Ascending Voice Leading

The following chords from measures 5-7 of the Rhythm Changes are very often used as an ascending line.

2.11.1 Aufsteigende Stimmführung

Die harmonische Wendung von Takt 5-7 der "Rhythm Changes" wird sehr häufig mit folgender aufsteigender Stimmführung gespielt:

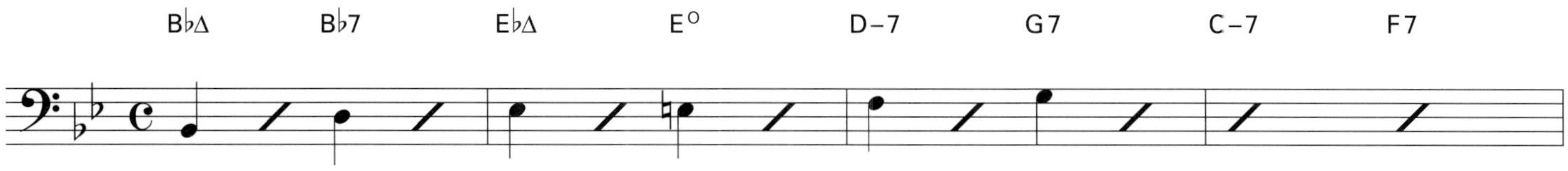

Similar progressions surface in many standards.
A few examples:

Ähnliche Akkordfolgen tauchen in zahlreichen Standards auf.
Einige Beispiele:

Someday My Prince Will Come

Someday My Prince Will Come

***St. Thomas* last 4 measures (here in C major)**

***St. Thomas* (hier in C Dur), vier Takte vor Schluß**

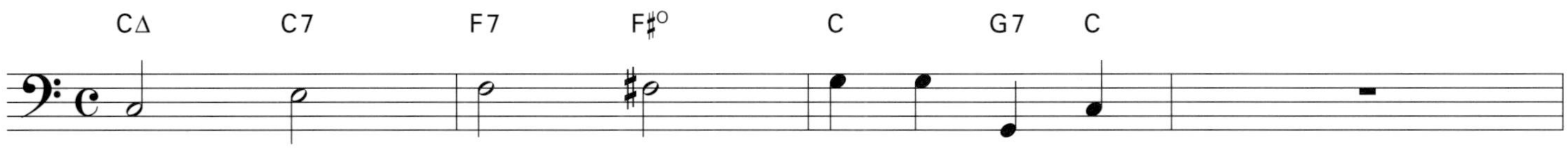

***The Preacher* last 4 measures**

***The Preacher*, ebenfalls vier Takte vor Schluß**

The ascending chromatic voice leading found in the first four measures of the Rhythm Changes is also a commonly used device.

Allgemein üblich ist auch die chromatische Linienführung in den ersten vier Takten der Rhythm Changes:

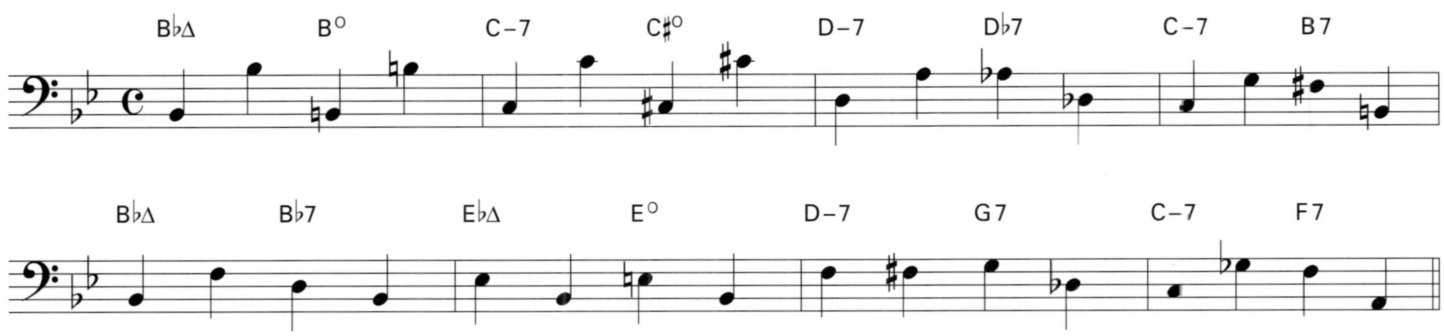

2.11.2 Descending Voice Leading

The decending line like the one found in *My Funny Valentine* is another important harmonic cliché that the bassist can use to provide a more interesting voice leading to a static progression.

2.11.2 Absteigende Stimmführung

Ein weiteres, für den Bassisten wichtiges harmonisches Klischee sind Akkordverbindungen, bei denen eine absteigende Stimmführung die ansonsten statisch wirkenden Harmonien lebendiger klingen läßt, z.B. bei der Ballade *My Funny Valentine*.

Example: ***My Funny Valentine***

Beispiel: ***My Funny Valentine***

Example: ***Here's That Rainy Day***

Beispiel: ***Here's That Rainy Day***

Some other examples of the descending bass line are *In A Sentimental Mood, Like Someone In Love, The Song Is You* (beginning at measure 9 in the bridge), *Round Midnight, Someone To Watch Over Me, This Masquerade* and *What Are You Doing The Rest Of Your Life?*.

Weitere Stücke, in denen sich diese Art der abwärts geführten Baßlinie anbietet, sind z.B. *In A Sentimental Mood, Like Someone In Love, The Song Is You* (ab Takt 9 im Mittelteil), *Round Midnight, Someone To Watch Over Me, This Masquerade* und *What Are You Doing The Rest Of Your Life?*.

2.12 Pedal Point

In the following progression the bass plays a single tone (pedal point) for a number of measures. Two good examples are *Dolphin Dance* by Herbie Hancock and *Naima* by John Coltrane. Pedal point is a popular device often used to freshen up and give a "modal" touch to old standards in moderate or faster tempos. In a II V I progression – either major or minor – this can be easily accomplished by playing a rhythmic line using just the root of the dominant (V7) chord.

2.12 Akkorde mit Pedaltönen

Bei diesen Akkordverbindungen spielt der Baß einen Pedalton über mehrere Takte, z.B. bei *Dolphin Dance* von Herbie Hancock oder *Naima* von John Coltrane. Pedaltöne sind aber auch ein beliebtes Mittel, um ältere Jazzstandards aufzufrischen und ihnen so einen "modalen Touch" zu verpassen, bevorzugt in mittleren und schnellen Tempi. Um das zu erreichen, wird bei einer II V I Verbindung (Dur und Moll sind möglich) der Grundton der V. Stufe (Dominantpedal) rhythmisiert.

Example: *I Love You*

Beispiel: *I Love You*

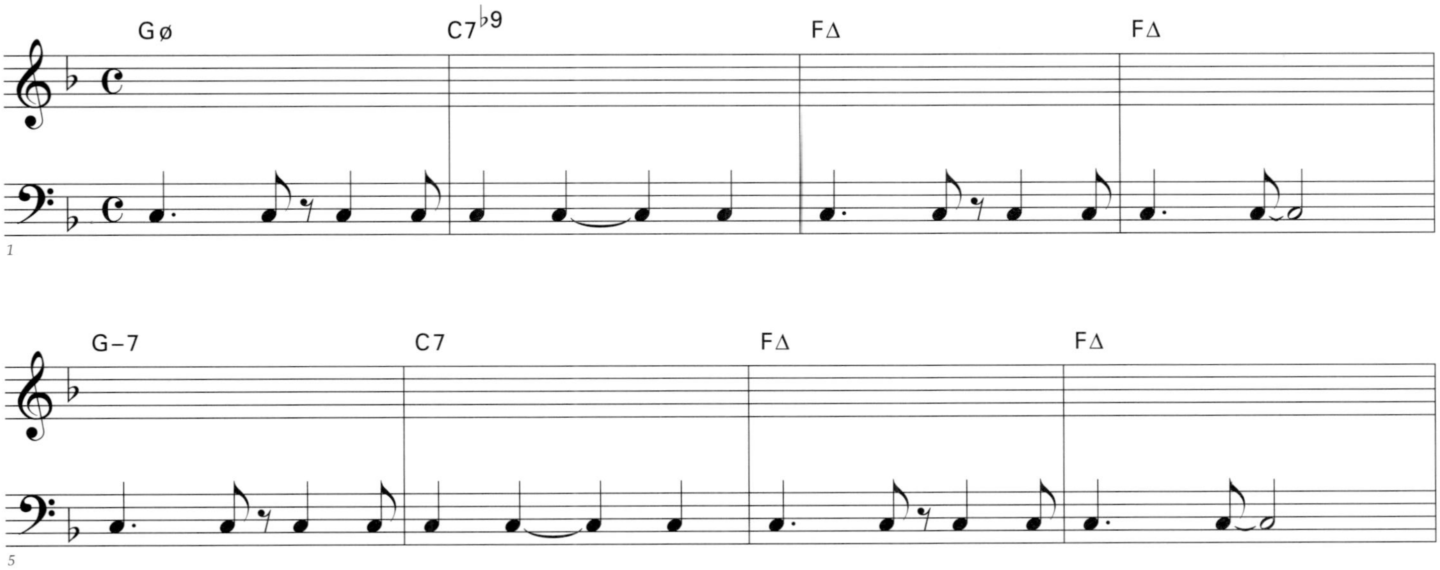

Example: *Dearly Beloved*

Beispiel: *Dearly Beloved*

Example: ***Joy Spring,*** **bars 1-16**

Beispiel: ***Joy Spring,*** **Takt 1-16**

Recommended listening: "The Dolphin" recorded by the Stan Getz Quartet (Concord CJ-158).

Two more examples of dominant pedals are the last four bars of both *The Night Has A Thousand Eyes* or *The Way You Look Tonight.*

Hören Sie dazu die LP bzw. CD "The Dolphin" mit dem Stan Getz Quartett auf Concord CJ-158.

Weitere Stücke mit Dominantpedalen sind z.B. *The Night Has A Thousand Eyes* oder *The Way You Look Tonight* (jeweils die vier letzten Takte der A-Teile).

3. Rhythmic Embellishments

Until now we have been dealing mostly with bass lines composed primarily of quarter-notes. These are appropriate for very fast tempi and allow you to maintain control of the rhythmic flow and micro timing.

However in slow to medium you might want to play in a more rhythmic and active manner but you have to make sure that the timing does not suffer.

To do this you could use anticipated notes, dotted eighth notes, triplets (drops), pulling off notes with your left hand, or combinations of these devices.

3. Rhythmische Verzierungen

Bisher haben wir uns hauptsächlich mit Baßlinien beschäftigt, die aus einfachen Viertelnotenketten bestanden. Bei schnellen bis sehr schnellen Tempi ist es auch sehr sinnvoll, so zu spielen; der rhythmische Fluß bleibt gleichmäßig und stabil, das Mikro-Timing kann gut kontrolliert werden.

Bei langsamen und mittleren Tempi gibt es darüber hinaus die Möglichkeit, rhythmisch aktiver und variabler zu spielen, immer unter der Voraussetzung, daß die Qualität des Timings nicht leidet.

Rhythmisch lebendigere Linien entstehen durch vorgezogene Noten, punktierte Achtel, durch Triolen (Drops), durch abziehen einer Note mit der linken Hand oder durch verschiedene Kombinationen von Effekten.

NOTE:
A walking bass line is usually played with a swing feel. The quarter-note which is normally divided into two eighth-notes is not (straight or binary), but instead gives a relationship of 2:1 (triplet or ternary).

ANMERKUNG:
Ein Walking Bass wird bekanntlich im Swing Feel gespielt, d.h. die Unterteilung einer Viertelnote in zwei Achtelnoten ist nicht gleichmäßig (binär) sondern steht im Verhältnis 2 zu 1 (ternär).

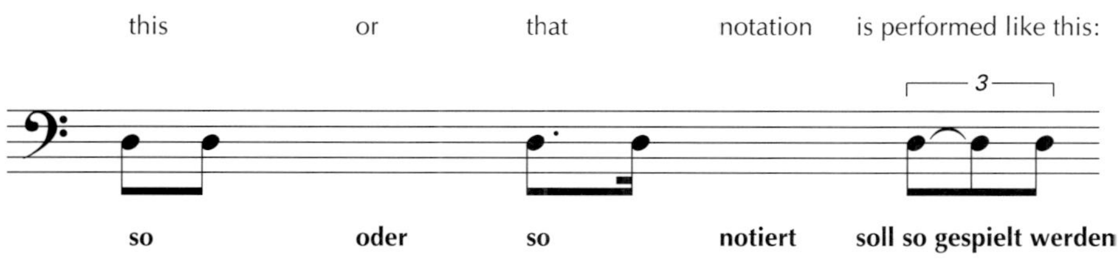

That's what it says in most books.

However, the pure mathematical quantization of 2 : 1, or 66 2/3 : 33 1/3 (assuming a value of 100 for a quarter note) is not altogether realistic. It depends on tempo, type of music, and personal style.

As the tempos become faster, the equation is gradually extended from 66/23 : 33 1/3 through 60/40, 55/45 all the way to 50/50. As the tempo increases the triplet phrasing becomes more closer to that of the straight-eighth.

The reality is that each performer will gravitate to his own personal feel of the timing.

With this in mind, it is interesting to listen to the differences between the two vibraphonists Lionel Hampton and Milt Jackson. Even at fast tempos, Hampton plays the eight with a triplet feel, while on the other hand Jackson plays them straight at even middle and slow tempos.

Looking back to the styles of the swing era, one can find examples like that of saxophonist Coleman Hawkins. In medium tempos he played the eighth notes much more as triplets than does Randy Brecker today.

Genau so steht es auch in (fast) allen Büchern. Nur...

Diese reine Form der Quantisierung von 2 : 1 oder 66 2/3 zu 33 1/3 (wenn man für eine Viertelnote den Wert von 100 annimmt) sieht in der Praxis häufig anders aus. Sie ist abhängig vom Tempo, von der Stilistik und vom persönlichen Stil.

Bei schneller werdenden Tempi verlagert sich die Quantisierung häufig graduell von 66 2/3 : 33 1/3 über 60/40, 55/45 allmählich zu 50/50. Die Phrasierung wird also bei zunehmendem Tempo immer gerader.

Relativiert wird diese Beobachtung dadurch, daß jeder Musiker, jede Musikerin bewußt oder unbewußt eine eigene Quantisierungsweise bevorzugt.

In diesem Zusammenhang ist es interessant, sich die unterschiedliche Auffassung der beiden Vibraphonisten Lionel Hampton und Milt Jackson anzuhören. Hampton spielt auch im Up Tempo die Achtel triolisch, Jackson spielt auch bei langsamen und mittleren Tempi die Achtel gerade.

Im Hinblick auf die Stilistik kann man z.B. feststellen, daß der Saxophonist Coleman Hawkins im Swing bei einem mittleren Tempo die Achtel viel triolischer phrasierte als es Randy Brecker heute macht.

All of what we have just discussed will have an effect on the entire rhythmic concept, whether it be walking bass, interpretation, or improvisation.

Das oben Gesagte betrifft die rhythmische Konzeption insgesamt: beim Walking Bass, bei der Interpretation und bei der Improvisation.

3.1 Anticipations

The note which is to be played on the downbeat is anticipated by playing it an eighth-note sooner.

3.1 Vorgezogene Noten

Die eigentlich auf dem Beat fällige Note wird um ein Achtel vorgezogen.

Examples:

Beispiele:

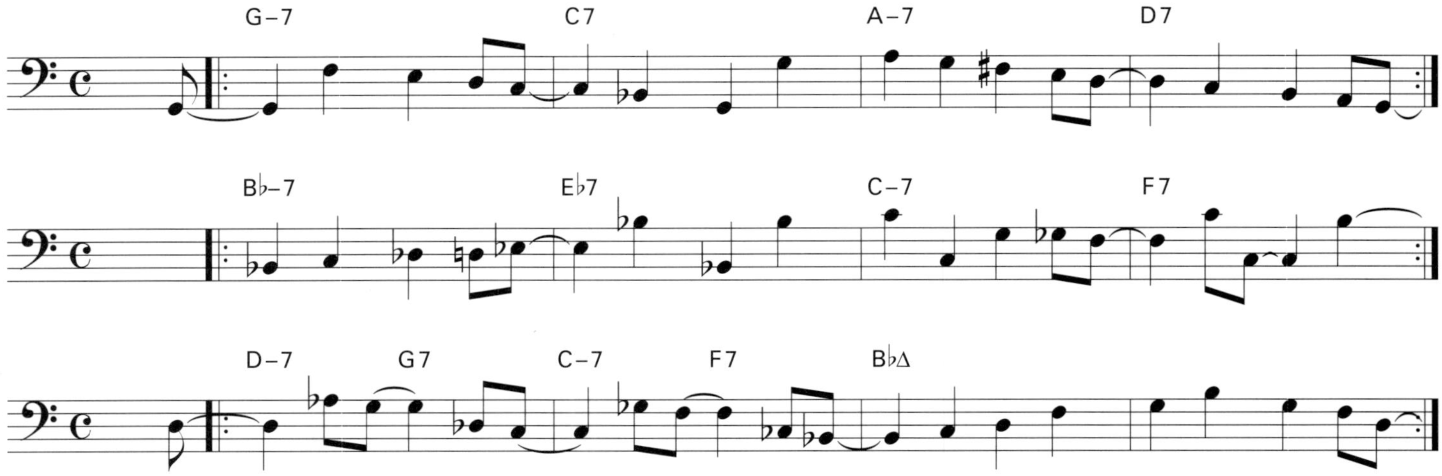

3.2 Dotted Eighth Notes

A combination of dotted eighth and sixteenth-notes would appear to be a more correct notation of the common eighth-note swing feel. They are usually notated as straight-eighth notes for legibility and the triplet interpretation is left to the player. Practice the following examples at different tempos.

3.2 Punktierte Achtel

Obwohl im Jazz, wie schon erwähnt, Achtel ternär phrasiert werden und man deshalb eigentlich die Achtel punktiert notieren müßte, werden sie aus Gründen der besseren Lesbarkeit nur als zwei normale Achtel notiert. Spielen Sie die folgenden Beispiele jeweils in mehreren unterschiedlichen Tempi.

Examples:

Beispiele:

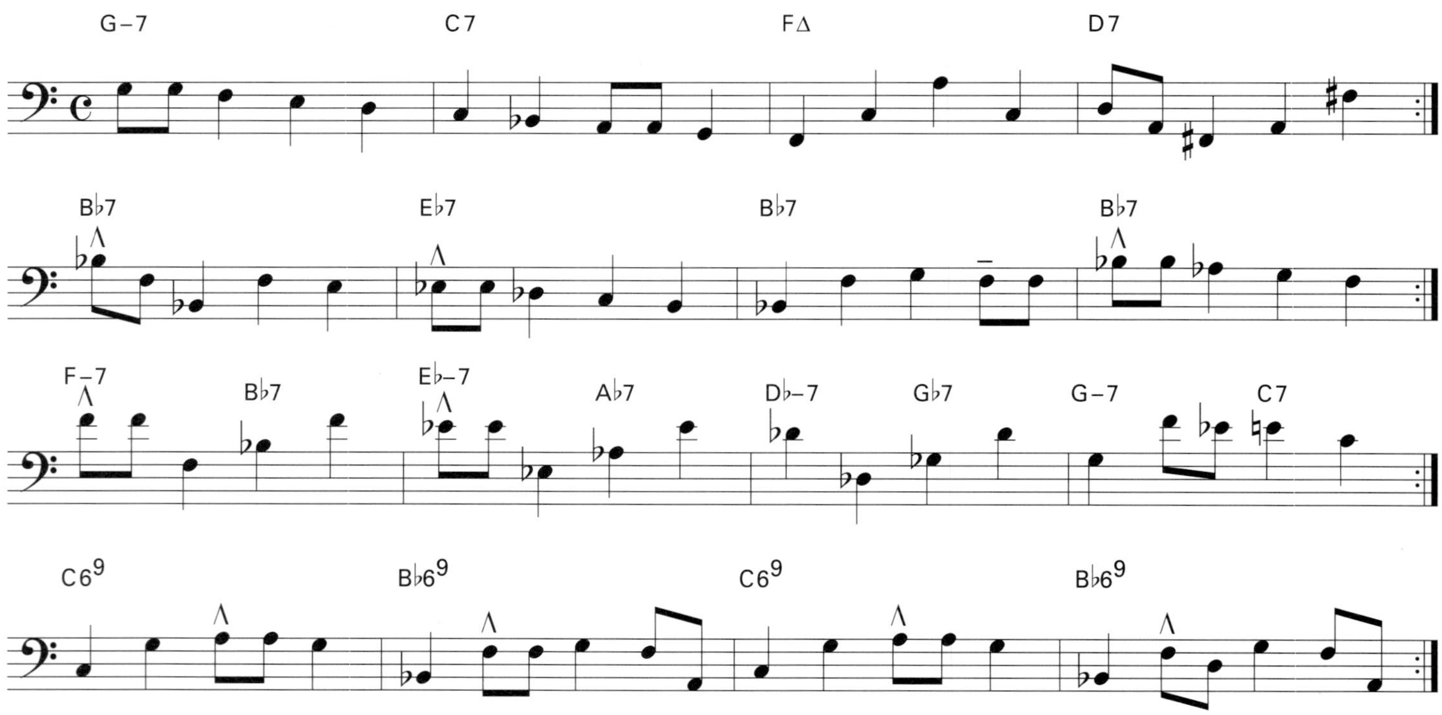

3.3 Drops

Eighth-note triplet groups are often used in addition to anticipations and dotted-eighths. Although there is no hard rule, they often appear on the last beat of a measure including a tone leading into the next chord. They are called "Drops" since these figures are usually played descending. There are countless variations of drops, and every bass player has his favorites.

3.3 "Drops"

Zusätzlich zu den vorgezogenen Vierteln und/oder den punktierten Achteln werden häufig Achteltriolen gespielt. Sie erscheinen auf allen möglichen Zählzeiten, oft auf dem letzten Viertel eines Taktes mit einem Leitton zum nächsten Akkord. Da sie größtenteils von oben nach unten "fallen", heißen sie "Drops". Unzählige Varianten sind möglich und jeder Bassist hat seine eigenen Vorlieben.

Examples:

Beispiele:

3.4 Various Exercises

3.4 Verschiedene Übungen

Repeat each exercise until it has a very high rhythmic quality. You should have the feeling that it starts to "swing".

Spielen Sie jede Übung solange, bis Sie mit ihrer rhythmischen Qualität zufrieden sind. Sie sollten das Gefühl haben, daß die Übung "swingt".

3.5 Percussive Effects

There are more possibilities for one to give the bass line a stronger rhythmic accent other than the anticipations and dotted note devices we have just covered. A type of percussive effect can be added by pulling the string away from the fingerboard with the fingers of the left hand.

3.5 Perkussive Effekte

Um einer Baßlinie starke rhythmische Akzente zu geben, haben Sie außer den bisher gezeigten vorgezogenen und punktierten Noten noch einige weitere Möglichkeiten. Eine Art perkussiver Effekt entsteht dadurch, daß Finger der linken Hand das *Pizzicato* ausführen. Dabei wird die Saite gleichsam vom Griffbrett "abgezogen".

Examples:

Beispiele:

The notes that are marked with "x" are to be plucked with the left hand. In exercises "e" and "f" the open G string is also to be pulled off with the left hand.

Preparatory exercises can be found in Chapters II and III.

Die mit "x" gekennzeichneten Noten werden mit der linken Hand gezupft. Bei den Übungen "e" und "f" wird die leere G-Saite mit links abgezogen.

Vorübungen dazu finden Sie in den Kapiteln II und III.

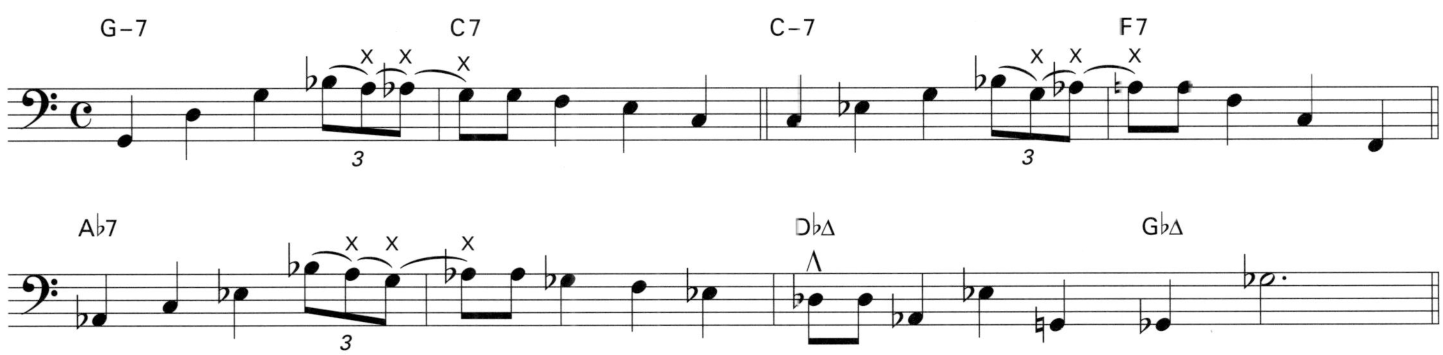

These effects must be performed with the utmost precision. They are intended to add to, and not to distract from the rhythmic flow of the music.

Nochmals: Effekte dieser Art klingen nur dann gut, wenn sie rhythmisch sicher gespielt werden. Durch sie muß der rhythmische Fluß gestärkt und nicht gestört werden.

3.6 Muffled Strings

The following effect is known as "muffled strings".

The left hand deadens the string for the off-beat eighth-notes which creates a percussive effect of indefinite pitch. These notes are marked "x" in the example.

3.6 Abgedämpfte Saiten

Der folgende Effekt ist unter der Bezeichnung "muffled strings" bekannt. Die zwischen das Metrum fallenden Achtel werden nur leicht mit der linken Hand heruntergedrückt. Es entsteht so ein von der Tonhöhe her nicht definierter Ton mit perkussivem Charakter. Die betreffenden Noten sind mit einem "x" auf der Notenlinie gekennzeichnet.

Example:

Beispiel:

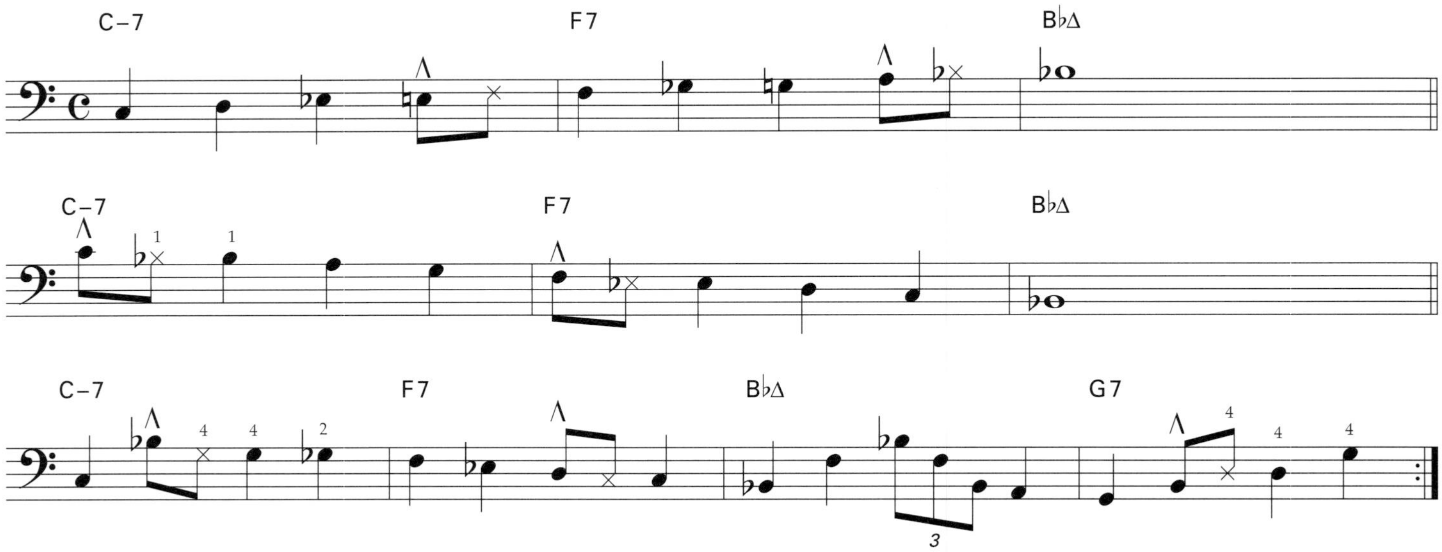

This next percussive effect is achieved by letting the right hand finger that plucked the downbeat eighth-note slide to the next open string and pluck it shortly. These notes are also marked in the following example with "x".

Beim nächsten Effekt rutscht der Finger der rechten Hand, der die Achtelnote auf dem Beat gespielt hat, auf die nächsttiefere leere Saite und zupft sie kurz an. Dadurch entsteht auch hier ein perkussiver Effekt. Die betreffenden Noten sind wiederum mit einem "x" gekennzeichnet.

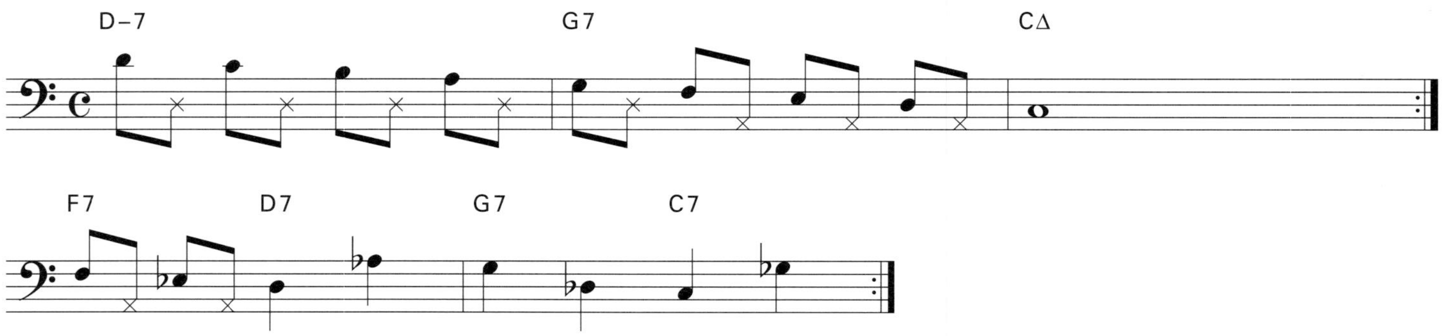

The following exercise combines the three percussive effects.

Bei dieser Übung werden die drei verschiedenen Effekte miteinander gemischt.

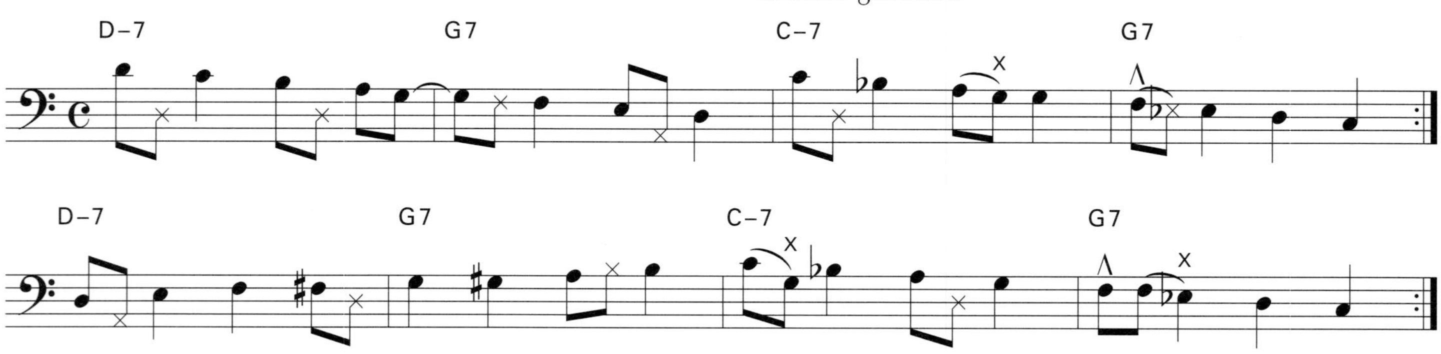

All of the above effects only sound good when your time is absolutely strong and consistent. Listen extremely critically and remember the Miles Davis quote: "Less is more."

Alle oben gezeigten Effekte klingen nur dann gut, wenn sie rhythmisch absolut sicher gespielt werden. Seien Sie extrem kritisch. Auch hier gilt das Zitat von Miles Davis:" Weniger ist mehr".

4. Various Bass Lines

4.1 Sixteen-Bar Progressions

The following bass line is typical of one that Niels Henning Œrsted Pedersen might play:

4. Verschiedene Baßlinien

4.1 Baßlinie über eine 16taktige Akkordfolge

Das hier ist eine Baßlinie wie sie vielleicht Niels Henning Œrsted Pedersen spielen würde:

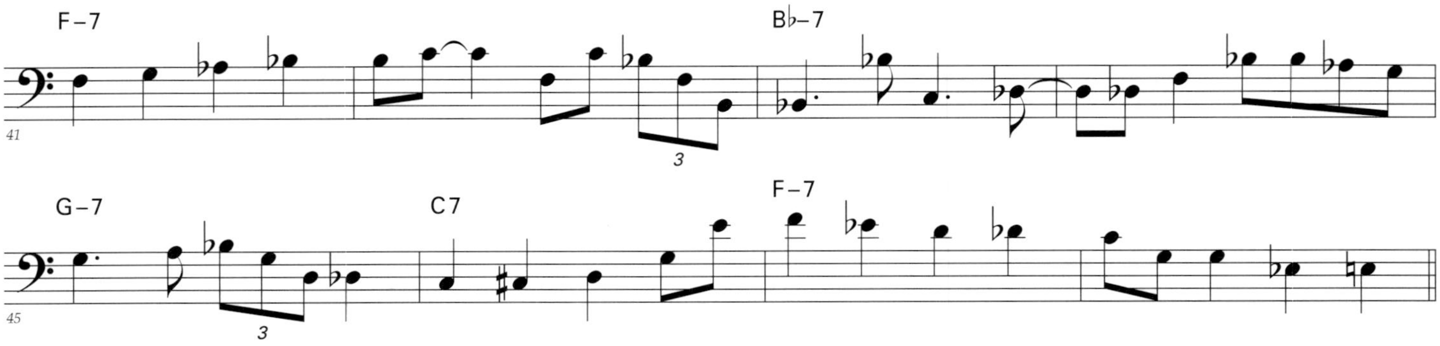

4.2 Half-Time Feel, etc.

At this time it would be helpful to define some terms like *half time, half-time feel, double time* and *double-time feel* first:

- **Straight**
  The rhythmic flow is provided by all rhythm instruments using the quarter note as the basic beat value.
- **Half-time feel**
  One rhythm instrument uses the half note as the basic beat value while the others use the quarter note.
- **Double-time feel**
  One instrument of the rhythm sectionuses the eighth note as the basic beat value while the others use the quarter note.
- **Real half-time**
  All instruments half the tempo (augmentation).
- **Real double-time**
  All instruments double the tempo (diminution).

Common Situations:

- The theme is stated in a slow to medium tempo with the bass playing half-notes on beats 1 and 3 resulting in half-time feel, also called two-beat feel in early jazz styles.
- In a slow to medium tempo: Only the drummer doubles the tempo by playing the the hi-hat on beats 2 and 4 of the new tempo, giving the music a double-time feel. If the band follows the tempo will actually be doubled and becomes real double-time.
- The bass player alone doubles the tempo by playing a walking bass line which gives the music a double-time feel. The band either follows the bass player's lead switching to real double-time, or the bass player returns to the basic (straight) tempo.

Listen to famous rhythm sections and observe the manner in which they combine the different time-divisions and make the transitions from one level to the other. Practice these different playing situations with your band.

4.2 Half-Time Feel u.s.w.

Eine Erklärung der Begriffe *half time, half-time feel, double time* und *double-time feel* ist an dieser Stelle sicher hilfreich:

- **Straight**
  Die gesamte Rhythmusgruppe spielt gemeinsam Viertel als rhythmischen Fluß.
- **Half-time feel**
  Ein Instrument der Rhythmusgruppe spielt Halbe als rhythmischen Grundwert, die anderen "straight".
- **Double-time feel**
  Ein Instrument spielt Achtel als rhythmischen Grundwert, die anderen "straight".
- **Real half-time**
  Alle Instrumente spielen im halben Tempo.
- **Real double-time**
  Alle Instrumente spielen im doppelten Tempo.

Häufige Spielsituationen:

- Beim Vorstellen eines Themas spielt die Band im langsamen oder mittleren Tempo, der Bassist spielt Halbe als Grundwert. Es ergibt sich ein Half-Time Feel, im frühen Jazz auch Two-Beat Feel genannt.
- Der Drummer (nur er) spielt nach einiger Zeit bei einem Stück im langsamen oder mittleren Tempo die Hi-Hat im doppelt so schnellen Tempo auf 2 und 4. Es entsteht ein Double-Time Feel. Erst wenn die gesamte Band ebenfalls im doppelten Tempo spielt, ergibt sich die Double Time.
- Der Bassist (nur er) spielt nach einiger Zeit im doppelt so schnellen Tempo einen Walking Bass. Auch hier entsteht ein Double-Time Feel, das so lange bestehen bleibt, bis entweder die gesamte Band folgt (Real Double-Time) oder der Bassist wieder zum ursprünglichen Tempo zurückkehrt (Straight).

Achten Sie bei berühmten Rhythmusgruppen darauf, wie die verschiedenen Ebenen miteinander verbunden werden. Falls möglich, üben Sie Übergänge von einer Ebene zur anderen mit Ihrer eigenen Band.

In almost every instance the actual length of time a given chord is played within the "harmonic" rhythm of the music remains the same as it did in real-time, whether in half-time or double-time. If a chord is played 4 seconds in 4/4 real-time at 60 beats per minute, it will also be played 4 seconds in double-time at 120 beats per minute. (If one wishes to change this rule it would be advisable to make it known to the others in the group before beginning the piece.)

In fast allen Fällen bleibt die absolute Dauer der Akkorde, der sog. "harmonische Rhythmus" gleich. Dauert ein Akkord z.B. im Tempo 60 über einen 4/4 Takt vier Sekunden, dauert er im Double Time bei Tempo 120 über zwei 4/4 Takte ebenfalls vier Sekunden. Will man von dieser Faustregel abweichen, ist es ratsam, vor Beginn des Stücks etwas anderes zu verabreden.

Example: Half-time feel on *Stella By Starlight*, bars 25-32

Beispiel: Half-Time Feel über *Stella By Starlight*, Takt 25-32

a

b

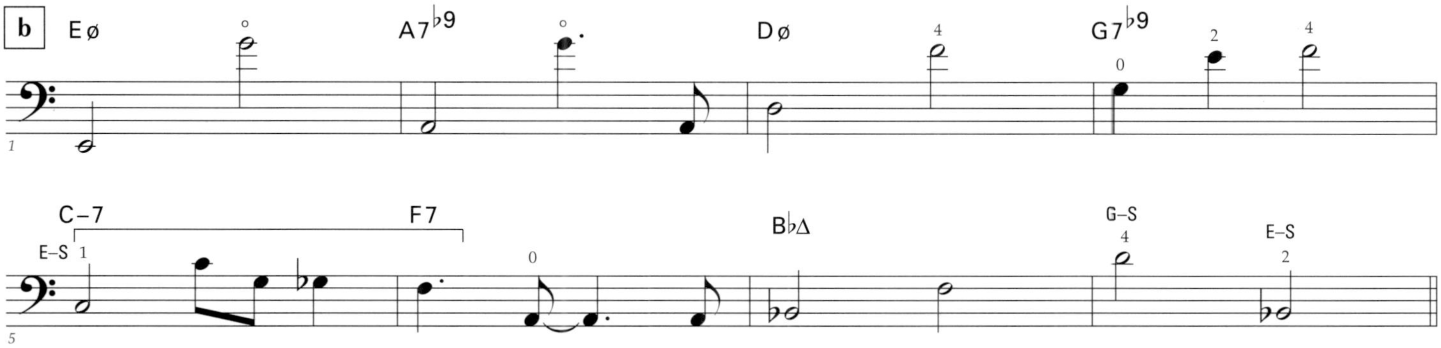

c

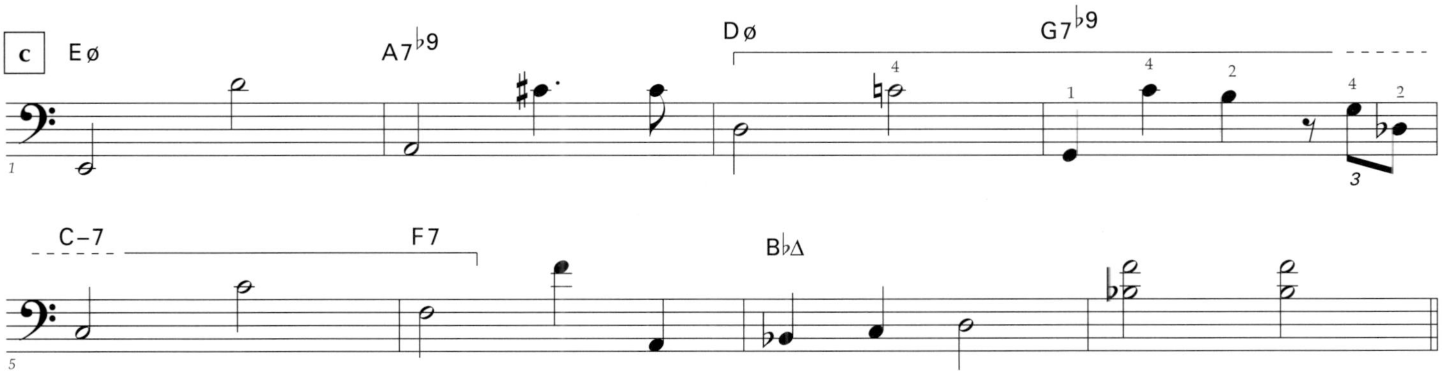

d

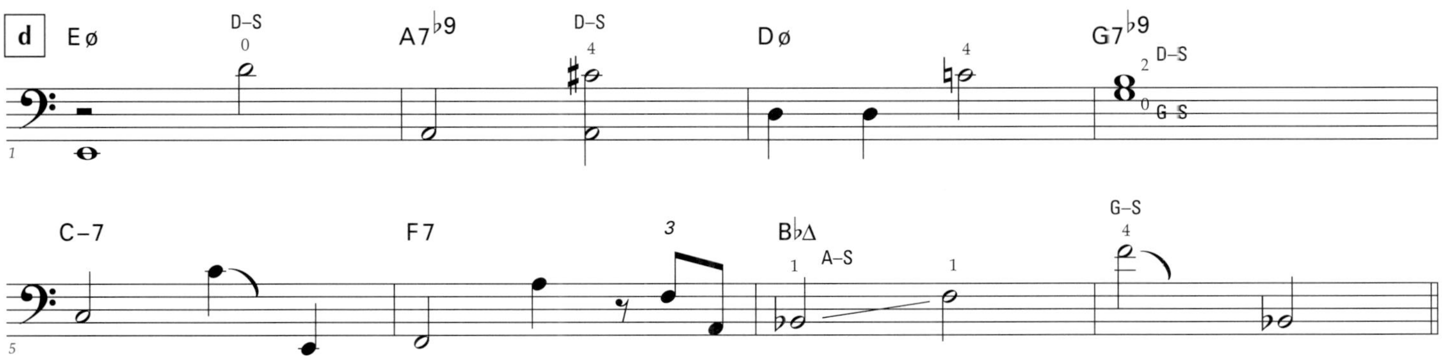

4.3 Bass Lines For A Ballad

The following is a typical example for a Ballad. I have taken the liberty to make a few simple changes in the harmony of *Lover Man* in the "bridge" section (bar 17 etc.). (See Chapter 2.11.2)

4.3 Baßlinie über eine Ballade

Das folgende Beispiel ist typisch für eine Ballade, hier *Lover Man*. Der Mittelteil ist von mir leicht reharmonisiert worden (siehe 2.11.2).

Example: ***Lover Man***

Beispiel: ***Lover Man***

4.4 Turnarounds

4.4 Turnarounds

4.5 Various Blues Progressions

The following bass lines are examples of how one can make a blues progression more complex.

In the first example this is achieved by inserting a II V progression in bars 4 and 8 and a turnaround in the last two measures.

4.5 Verschiedene Blues-Versionen

Die Baßlinien über diese Akkorde sind Beispiele dafür, wie man einen Blues harmonisch komplexer gestalten kann.

Beim ersten Beispiel geschieht das durch eine II V Verbindung im 4. und 8. Takt, sowie durch einen Turnaround in den letzten beiden Takten.

Example 1:

Beispiel 1:

In example 2 one will find a series of II V progressions. Three of them lead to the characteristic subdominant chord in bar 5. Beginning in measure 8 the II V progressions moves down chromatically until the beginning to the turnaround in measure 11. Harmonizing the often stereotyped progression in this manner can make a blues more interesting and fresher. Certain uses of chords are a necessary part of a good back-up musician's vocabulary. In spontaneous performances, e.g. a jam session, it is always very interesting, how the other members of the band respond to the bass players suggestions. Or on the other hand, is the bass player able to follow the suggestions of his colleagues?

Numerous different blues progressions are to be found in David Baker's book "Jazz Improvisation".

Beim zweiten Beispiel sind gleich eine ganze Reihe von II V Verbindungen zu erkennen. Drei davon sind der IV. Stufe in Takt 5 "vorgeschaltet". Ab dem 8. Takt gehen die II V Verbindungen chromatisch abwärts bis zum 11. Takt, in dem dann wiederum ein Turnaround anfängt. Durch diese Reharmonisation von simplen, manchmal leicht stereotypen Changes kann ein Blues interessanter und frischer klingen. Bestimmte Akkordwendungen gehören zum allgemeinen Vokabular eines guten Begleiters bzw. einer guten Rhythmusgruppe. Beim spontanen Zusammenspiel, z.B. bei einer Session, ist es immer spannend zu erleben, ob und wie die Mitspieler auf Vorschläge des Bassisten eingehen. Oder ob umgekehrt der Bassist auf die Vorschläge seiner Mitspieler eingehen kann.

Eine Reihe von sehr unterschiedlichen Blues Changes stellt David Baker in seinem Buch "Jazz Improvisation" vor.

Example 2:

Beispiel 2:

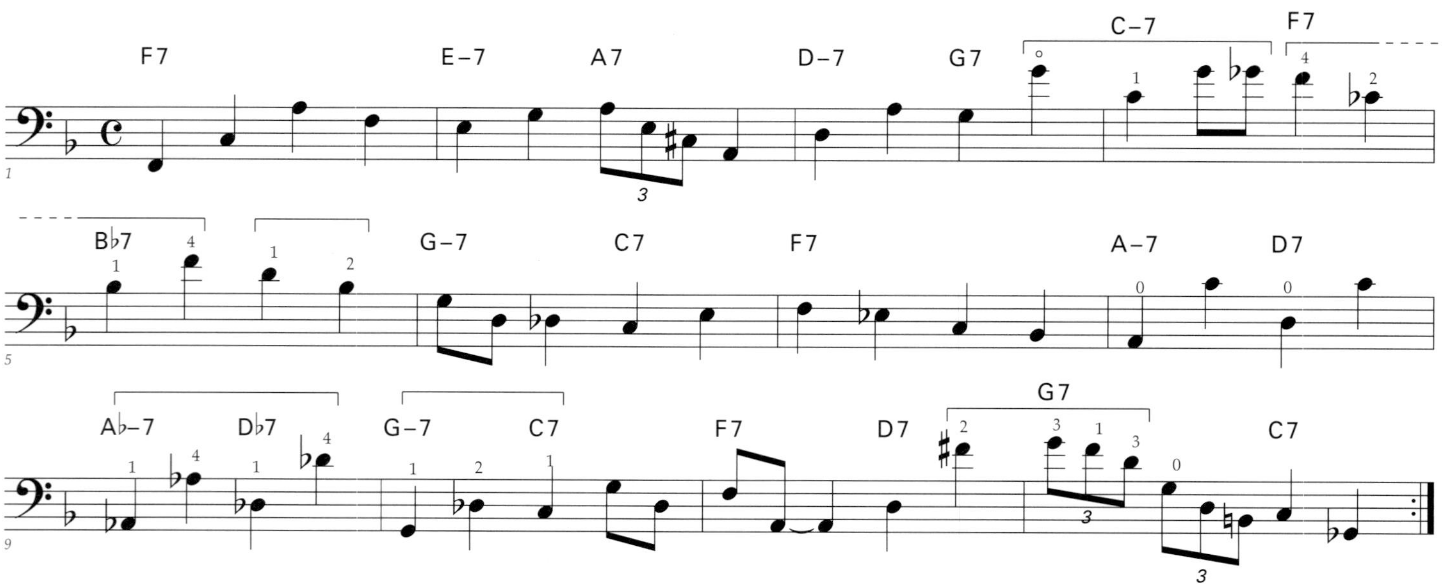

Example 3:

Beispiel 3:

These bass lines for a blues in F are based on the following...

Measures	**The Devices**
4, 5, 6, 7, 8, 11, 12:	arpeggios
18-20, 24:	arpeggios
1, 3, 9, 13, 15,17:	neighboring and passing notes
9, 10, 11, 12,16:	leading tones
18 to 19:	leading tones
21-22:	scales
1, 2, 6, 8, 9:	chromatic passing tones
8, 16, 20, 23, 24:	chromatic approach tones

Diese Baßlinie über einen Blues in F basiert auf den folgenden Vorgaben:

Takt	
4, 5, 6, 7, 8, 11, 12:	Akkordbrechungen
18-20, 24:	Akkordbrechungen
1, 3, 9, 13, 15,17:	Nachbar- und Durchgangstöne
9, 10, 11, 12,16:	Leittöne
18 nach 19:	Leittöne
21-22:	Skalen
1, 2, 6, 8, 9:	chromatische Durchgangstöne
8, 16, 20, 23, 24:	chromatische Annäherung

4.6 Bass Line For *Satin Doll*

I wrote down a complete chorus over the chord changes of *Satin Doll* by Duke Ellington to illustrate some of the above mentioned principles.

4.6 Baßlinie über *Satin Doll*

Hier habe ich Ihnen einen kompletten Chorus über die Changes von *Satin Doll* von Duke Ellington ausnotiert, in dem Sie viele der in diesem Kapitel besprochenen Prinzipien wiederfinden.

4.7 Bass Line For *All The Things You Are*

Here is a suggestion as to how one could play a chorus of *All The Things You Are*.

4.7 Baßlinie über *All The Things You Are*

Dies ist ein Vorschlag, wie man einen Chorus über *All The Things You Are* gestalten könnte.

4.8 Voice-Leading Over A Number Of Measures

Observe the "anchor" notes that provide a descending or an ascending voice- leading over groups of 4 to 8 measures. (The root of the chord must not always be used for the first beat of the measure.) The bass lines will be composed in a contrapuntal style. The empty spaces can be notated as you wish.

4.8 Stimmführung über mehrere Takte

Bitte beachten Sie die durch die "Stütznoten" erkennbare ab- und aufsteigenden Stimmführung über acht bzw. vier Takte. (Dabei muß nicht unbedingt der Grundton des Akkordes auf 1 gespielt werden.) Es entstehen so größere Zusammenhänge. Die Baßlinie wird kontrapunktisch gestaltet. Notieren Sie in den Zwischenräumen Noten Ihrer Wahl.

4.9 Bass Line For *Giant Steps*

This harmonically complex piece is a challenge, not just for the bass player. This example should help you in learning to deal with these changes.

4.9 Baßlinie über *Giant Steps*

Dieses Stück ist harmonisch nicht ganz einfach und eine Herausforderung - nicht nur für den Bassisten. Das folgende Beispiel soll Ihnen einige Hinweise geben, wie Sie mit den Changes umgehen können.

"Compose" your own version. Memorize both the example given along with your own version.

An often used "trick" to simplify of the changes in *Giant Steps* is to substitute a II–7 chord for the V7 chords.

For instance:

B A–7 / G F–7 / E♭ / A–7 D7 /
G F–7 / E♭ D♭–7 / B / F–7 B♭7 usw.

"Komponieren" Sie eine eigene Version. Lernen Sie dann die vorgegebne und Ihre eigene Version auswendig!

Ein beliebter Kunstgriff zur Vereinfachung der Improvisation über die *Giant Steps* Changes besteht darin, die Dominantseptakkorde durch Mollseptakkorde der II. Stufe zu ersetzen, so z.B. :

B A–7 / G F–7 / E♭ / A–7 D7 /
G F–7 / E♭ D♭–7 / B / F–7 B♭7 usw.

Here is the resulting bass line for measures 1-8:

Die daraus resultierende Baßlinie klingt für Takt 1-8 so:

4.10 Bass Lines In A Single Position

Both of the following examples can be played in one position. The advantage is that they can very easily be transposed to another key simply by shifting the hand position. In order to play a blues in D♭, simply move the hand position from C up 1/2 step. For a B♭ blues, the hand is moved down a whole step. The fingerings will remain the same, the hand stays in one position, and the intonation will be stable.

4.10 Baßlinien ohne Lagenwechsel

Die beiden folgenden Baßlinien werden ohne Lagenwechsel nur in einer Lage gespielt. Der besondere Effekt dieser Linien liegt darin, daß sie sich leicht in einer anderen Lage und damit in einer anderen Tonart spielen lassen. Verschieben Sie die Baßlinie in C um eine halbe Lage nach oben, erhalten Sie eine Baßlinie in D♭. Bei einem Blues in B♭ schieben Sie die linke Hand um eine ganze Lage nach unten, u.s.w. Der Fingersatz bleibt gleich, die Hand bleibt in einer Position und die Intonation bleibt stabil.

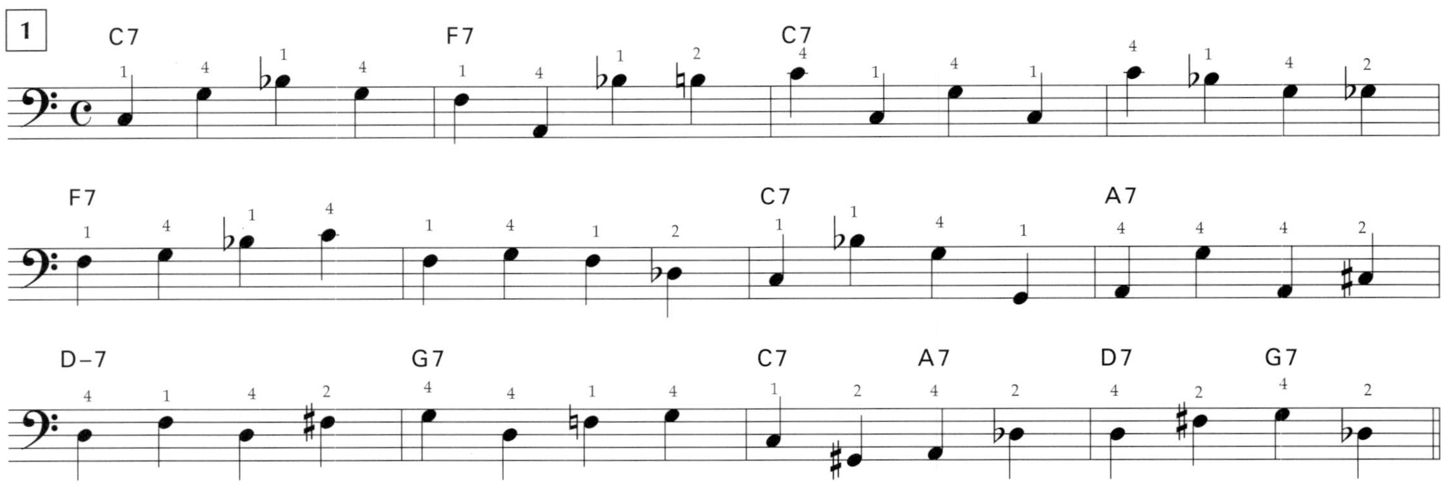

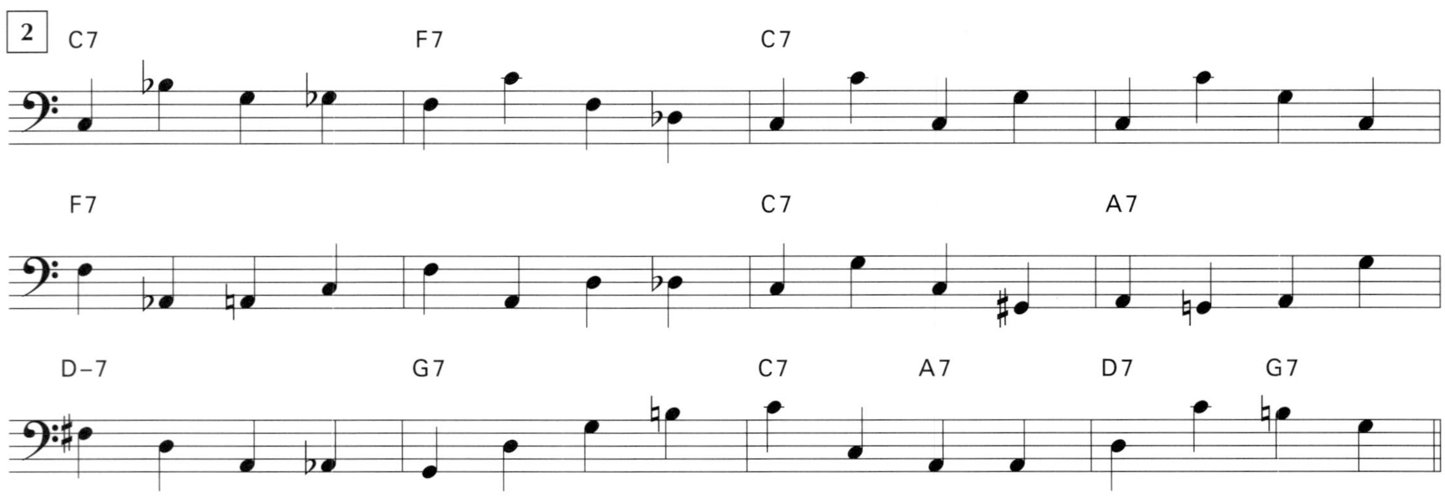

3

For bass lines such as this, it is very important that you know all the notes in each position on all four strings. You have to be able to think "across the strings".

A good exercise for this is to memorize all the notes in each position by saying them out loud while playing them. Begin with the note F on the E string, and move up chromatically to D♭ on the same string.

Eine ganz wichtige Voraussetzung für Baßlinien dieser Art ist, daß man alle Töne kennt, die sich auf den vier Saiten in der gleichen Lage befinden. Man muß im eigentlichen Sinne des Wortes "querdenken" können.

Eine gute Übung dafür besteht darin, in jeder einzelnen Lage die jeweiligen Noten auf allen vier Saiten zu spielen und laut zu benennen. Beginnen Sie mit der Note F auf der E-Saite und bewegen Sie sich chromatisch nach oben bis zum D♭ auf der E-Saite.

This is also a good "mental-training" exercise. By that I mean that you must imagine yourself doing the exercise.

This will accelerate your improvement. Position shifts on all four strings will become second nature. These are not limited to just the G string, which is most likely the case with beginners.

Create your own "single position bass lines". Learn them by heart thus building a repertoire of easy transposable bass lines for different types of songs.

Diese Übung läßt sich auch sehr gut als "mentales Training" durchführen. Das heißt, daß Sie die Übung allein in Ihrer inneren Vorstellung und ohne Instrument durchführen.

Sie werden schon bald einen enormen Zuwachs an spieltechnischen Möglichkeiten feststellen. Lagenwechsel werden auf allen Saiten zur Selbstverständlichkeit. Diese sind nicht nur, wie so häufig vor allem bei Anfängern festzustellen, allein auf die G-Saite beschränkt.

Erfinden Sie auf der Grundlage der Übungen 1, 2 und 3 selbst noch weitere Linien (auch über andere Harmonien und Stücke) dieser Art. Lernen Sie verschiedene Linien auswendig.

4.11 Modal Bass Lines

This is an example of a chord progression from the early days of "Modal Jazz".

4.11 Modale Baßlinien

Dieses Beispiel ist an Harmoniefolgen aus den frühen Tagen des modalen Jazz angelehnt.

Please analyze this. Which scales are used? Listen to John Coltrane's *Impressions* and Miles Davis' *So What*.

Bitte analysieren Sie diese Version. Welche Skalen wurden verwendet? Hören Sie dazu auch John Coltranes *Impressions* und Miles Davis' *So What*.

4.12 Often Used Bass Patterns

4.12 Häufig gespielte Baß Patterns

Example: ***Equinox*** **(John Coltrane) medium tempo**

Beispiel: ***Equinox*** **(John Coltrane) mittleres Tempo**

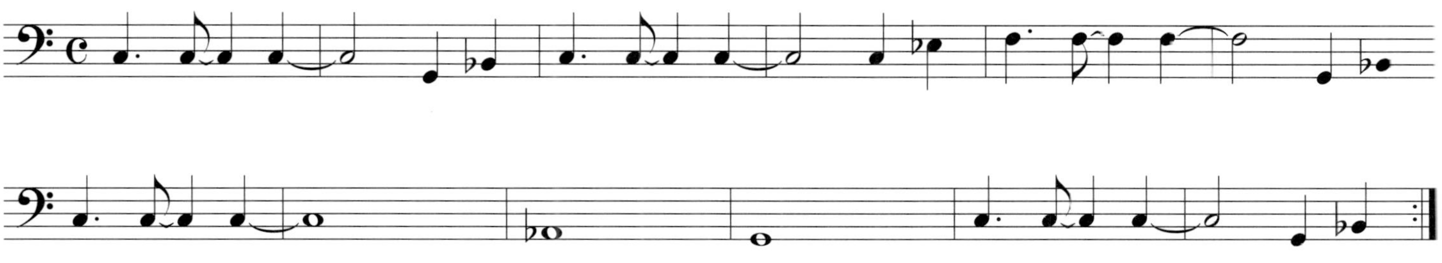

Example: ***Footprints*** **(Wayne Shorter)**

Beispiel: ***Footprints*** **(Wayne Shorter)**

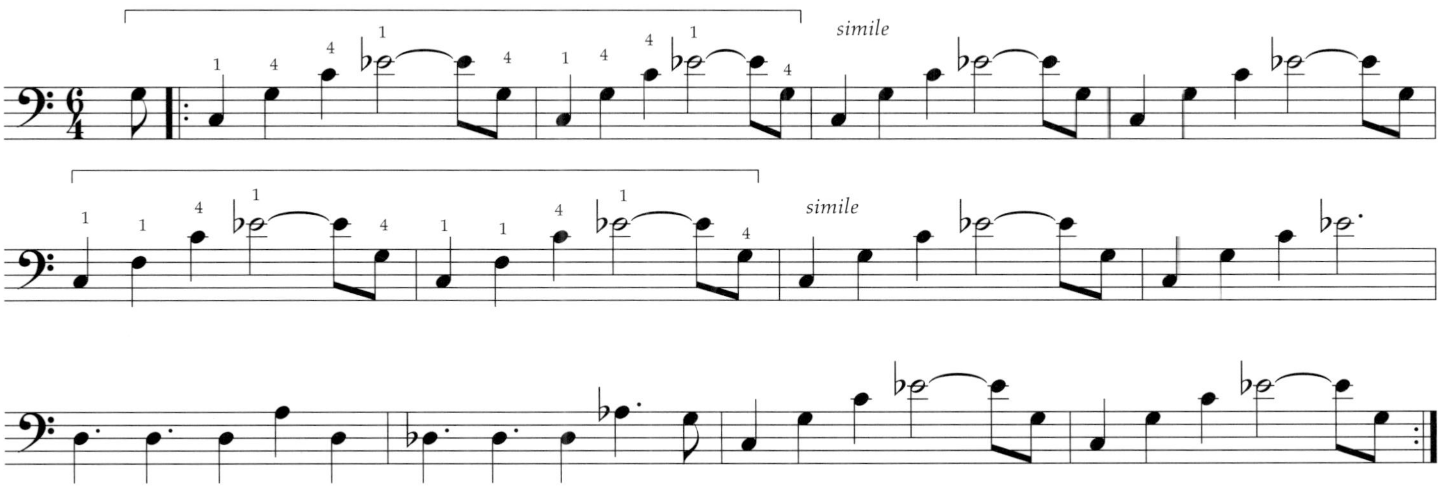

Example: ***All Blues*** **(Miles Davis)**

Beispiel: ***All Blues*** **(Miles Davis)**

Example: ***All The Things You Are*** **(Jerome Kern) Intro**

Beispiel: ***All The Things You Are*** **(Jerome Kern) Intro**

5. Straight-Eighth Bass Lines

In contrast to the "triplet" phrasing of the eighth notes used in bebop and hardbop, in the mid sixties, jazz was influenced by rock and Latin-American music and took on a more "straight-eight" feel (evenly divided quarter-note). Typical examples of music from this time are Herbie Hancock's *Maiden Voyage*, or Joe Zawinul's *Mercy, Mercy, Mercy*. The Latin-American rhythms most frequently used in jazz are the samba and the bossa nova from Brazil, and the salsa and the calypso from the Carribean.

5. Binäre Baßlinien

Im Unterschied zur Spielweise im Bebop oder Hardbop, wo die Phrasierung auf triolischer Basis (ternär) abläuft, wird im Jazz ab Mitte der sechziger Jahre beeinflußt vom Rock und der lateinamerikanischen Musik auch im sog. "Achtelfeeling", also binär phrasiert. Typische Beispiele aus dieser Zeit sind Herbie Hancocks *Maiden Voyage* oder Joe Zawinuls *Mercy, Mercy, Mercy*. Aus Brasilien wurden insbesondere Bossa Nova und Samba übernommen, aus der Karibik vorwiegend Salsa und Calypso.

5.1 Straight-Eighths

Examples:

5.1 "Gerade Achtel"

Beispiele:

c
C∆
B♭∆
C∆
B♭∆
d
D7 sus 4
F7 sus 4
E♭7 sus 4
E7 sus 4
D7 sus 4
F7 sus 4
E♭7 sus 4
E7 sus 4

Descending bass line

Absteigende Baßlinie

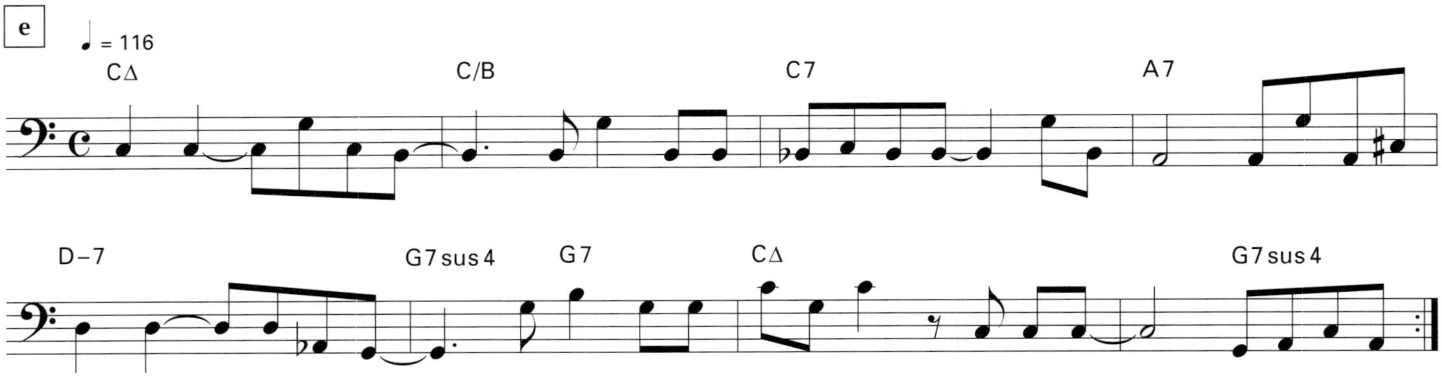

You can hear other good bass line examples of this style by listening to the recordings of Cannonball Adderley, Horace Silver, and Ahmad Jamal from the 60's and 70's.

Hören Sie in diesem Zusammenhang als Quelle guter Baßlinien Aufnahmen der Gruppen um Cannonball Adderley, Horace Silver oder Ahmad Jamal aus den sechziger und siebziger Jahren.

5.2 Jazz-Rock Patterns

The following exercise is an example of a common jazz-rock pattern. The notation of so many sixteenth notes look complicated at first, but to simplify and learn such lines one can notate them with all the note values doubled and then play them *alla breve* (2/2 time). In the first version (f1) the tempo is ♩ = 76 for the quarter-note , and in the second (f2), *alla breve* version, the tempo is 𝅗𝅥 =76 for the half-note. When played properly, both versions will sound the same.

5.2 Jazz-Rock Patterns

Bei der folgenden Übung handelt es sich um ein gebräuchliches Jazz-Rock Pattern. Die Notation erscheint auf den ersten Blick durch die vielen Sechzehntelnoten sehr kompliziert. Um sich an ein solches Notenbild zu gewöhnen, gibt es folgende Hilfe: Man notiert alles noch einmal mit verdoppelten Notenwerten wie im danach folgenden Beispiel und spielt dann *alla breve,* d.h. im 2/2 Takt. Bei der ersten Version ist das Tempo ♩ = 76. Bei der *alla breve* Version ist das Tempo 𝅗𝅥 = 76. Beide Notationsarten klingen im Endergebnis genau gleich.

Examples:

Beispiele:

The patterns can also be played in a more triplet feel, which is what is sometimes played in a "Funk" style. The pulse will then be the sixteenth-note triplet instead of the straight-sixteenth.

Die Patterns können auch mehr ternär phrasiert werden, so wie sie in der Funk Musik öfter gespielt werden. Als Puls liegen dann Sechzehntel-Triolen statt gleichmäßig gespielter Sechzehntel zugrunde.

Examples:

Beispiele:

g

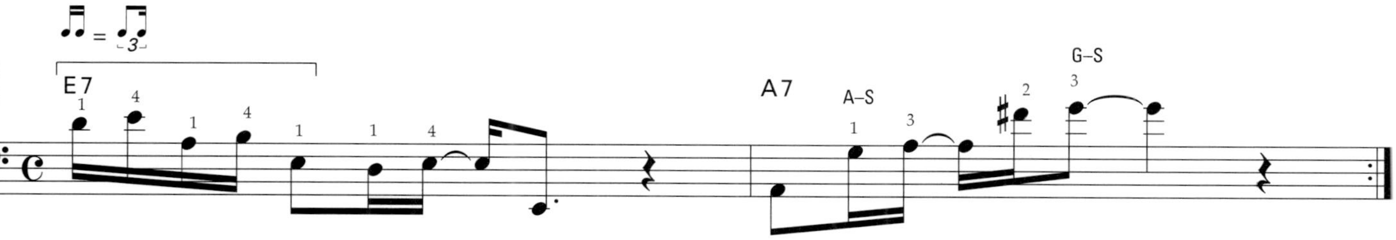

h

i

Bass lines of this style are in principle built the same way as the walking bass lines in the previous chapter. Here too precision plays a very important role. In rock and pop music in contrast to jazz the rhythm section very often is expected to play more specified parts. During the performance spontaneous variations are less important. In most cases the parts are worked out before hand, especially in funk and fusion. The goal is to create a characteristic mood by playing a "catchy groove" throughout the song.

Baßlinien solcher Art sind im Prinzip ähnlich aufgebaut wie die Walking Bass Lines im vorigen Kapitel. Und auch hierbei spielt die rhythmische Präzision selbstverständlich eine sehr große Rolle. In der Rock- und Popmusik ist es oft so, daß von den Mitgliedern der Rhythmusgruppe erwartet wird, mehr spezifizierte, vorgegebene Parts zu spielen. Häufige Variationen sind weniger wichtig. Meistens sind die Patterns vorher ausgearbeitet, vor allem bei Funk und Fusion Musik. Das Ziel besteht darin, eine bestimmte Groove (charakteristische Stimmung) zu schaffen, die dann meistens während des gesamten Stücks beibehalten wird.

5.3 Funk-Rock Patterns

One can find many common phrases and patterns in funk and rock that are often used by bass players, such as found in exercises "f1" (ascending chromatic passing-tones between the 3rd and 5th, and descending between the minor 7th and 5th.) (See page 90)

Rhythmic patterns like the ones in exercise "h" are also very common. These are what are called "3 in 4" patterns. (The examples here are repeated groups of 4 x 3 and 1 x 4 sixteenth-notes in a measure.)

5.3 Funk-Rock Patterns

Auch im (Funk-) Rock haben sich einige sehr gebräuchliche Phrasen und Patterns herausgebildet, die von vielen Bassisten gespielt werden, so z.B. chromatische Durchgänge zwischen Terz und Quinte aufwärts und kleiner Sept und Quinte abwärts, wie in Übung "f1" (siehe S. 90).

Rhythmische Patterns wie in Übung "h" oder ähnlich sind ebenfalls sehr häufig. Es sind dies die sog. "3 in 4" Patterns (hier: viermal 3 und einmal 4 Sechzehntelnoten).

Weitere Patterns dieser Art sind:

Examples:

Beispiele:

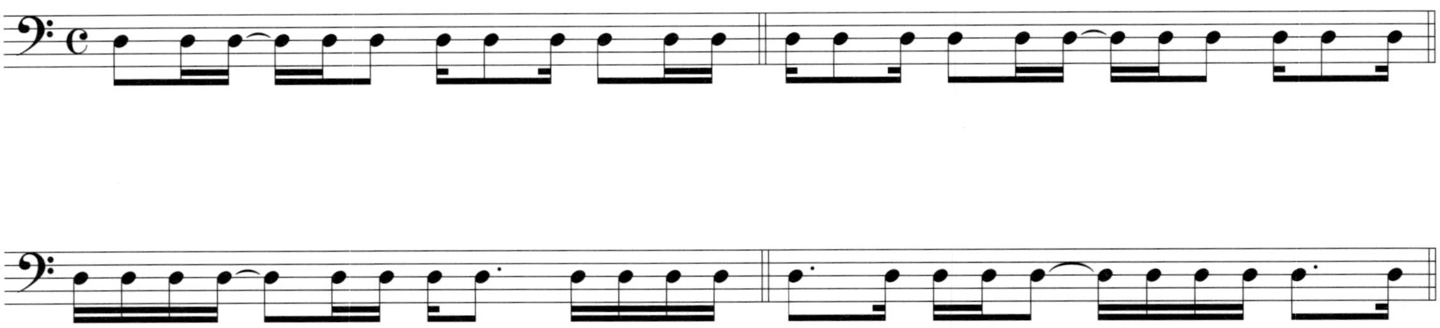

Finish this example with notes similar to those found in exercise "h" and create more funk-rock patterns.

Füllen Sie diese Beispiele mit Tönen nach Art der Übung "h" und bilden Sie so weitere Funk-Rock Patterns.

Frequently used rhythm patterns:

Häufig benutzte Rhythmus Patterns:

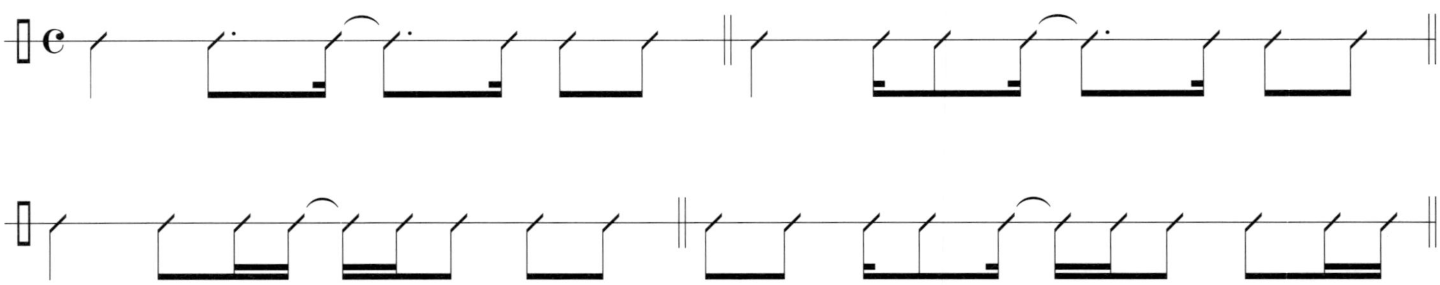

NOTE:
An inexhaustible source for good bass "licks" is the book dedicated to legendary bassist James Jamerson, "Standing In The Shadows Of Motown" (Dr. Licks Publishing, Wynnewood, Pa., 19096 U.S.A. with 2 CD's)

ANMERKUNG:
Eine unerschöpfliche Quelle für gute Bass Licks ist das Buch (mit 2 CD's) "Standing In The Shadows Of Motown", das dem legendären Bassisten James Jamerson gewidmet ist (Dr. Licks Publishing, Wynnewood, Pa., 19096 U.S.A).

6. Latin-American Jazz Bass Lines

6.1 Standard Patterns

In the 50's (and in some cases earlier) Latin-American music already had a large influence on jazz. I have chosen here two famous examples of Latin jazz bass lines; *A Night In Tunesia* (example "a") and two different bass lines to *Manteca* (examples "b" and "c").

6. Lateinamerikanische Jazz-Baßlinien

6.1 Standard Patterns

Die lateinamerikanische Musik hat den Jazz schon in den vierziger Jahren (teilweise schon früher) beeinflußt. Aus dieser Zeit habe ich zwei bekannte Latin-Jazz Baßlinien ausgewählt: Die Baßfigur zu *A Night In Tunesia* (Beispiel "a") und zwei Baßlinien zu *Manteca* (Beispiel "b" und "c").

Examples:

Beispiele:

a

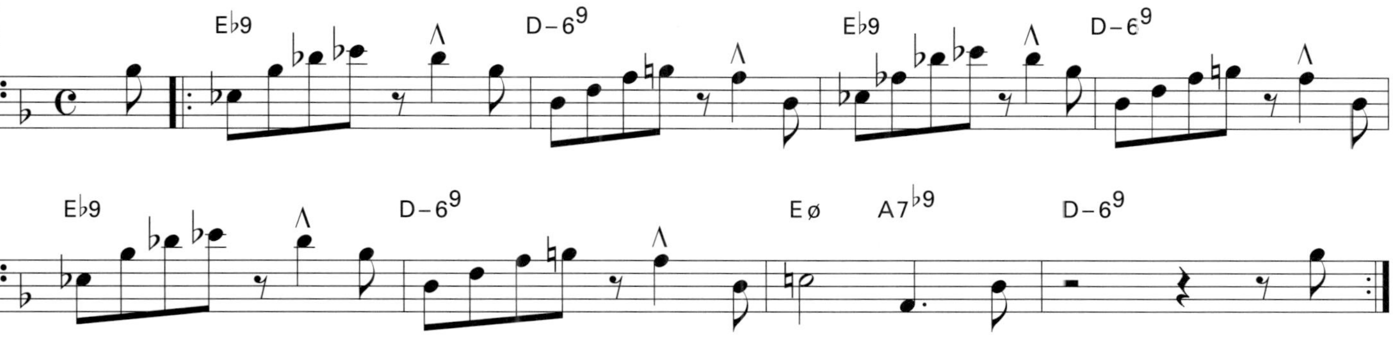

b

c

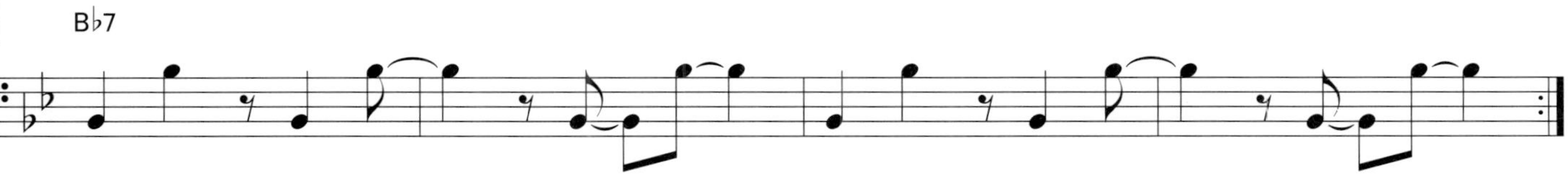

I have marked the following examples as "Latin jazz standard patterns 1 and 2". The first figure fits compositions like *I'll Remember April,* or *Love For Sale.* The second is better for pieces like *On Green Dolphin Street,* or *My Little Suede Shoes.*

Die folgenden Beispiele habe ich als Latin Jazz Standard Pattern 1 und 2 bezeichnet. Eine Figur wie die erste paßt zu Kompositionen wie *I'll Remember April* oder *Love For Sale,* die zweite besser zu Stücken wie *On Green Dolphin Street* oder *My Little Suede Shoes.*

Latin jazz standard pattern 1

Latin Jazz Standard Pattern 1

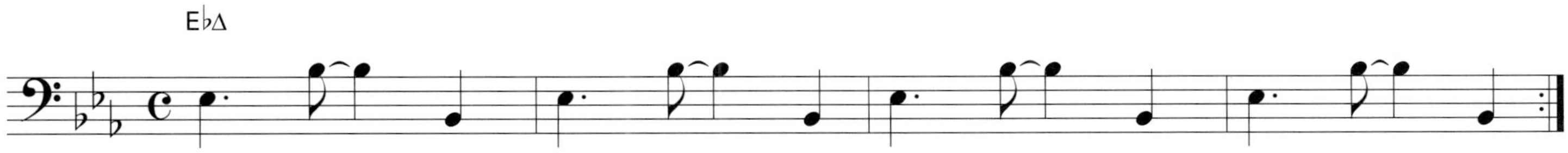

Latin jazz standard pattern 2

Latin Jazz Standard Pattern 2

An example of a useful voice-leading:

Beispiel über eine gebräuchliche Akkordverbindung:

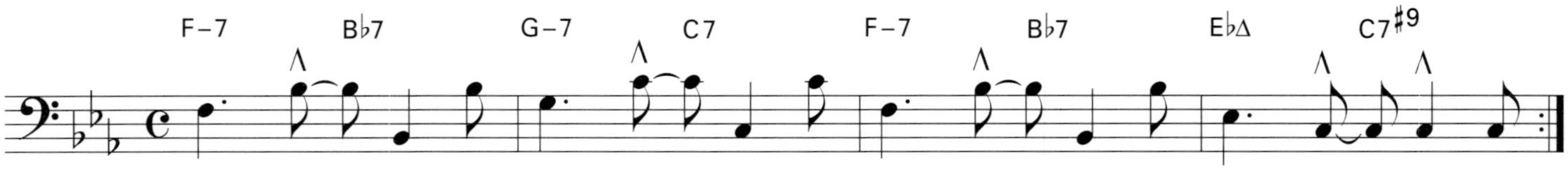

6.2 Bossa Nova

The bossa nova is generally played at a moderate tempo, and in an "easy" style. The following example shows the characteristic rhythm in the first measure, variation, and voice-leading between the chord changes.

6.2 Bossa Nova

Die Bossa Nova wird meist im Medium Tempo gespielt, also eher etwas ruhiger. Charakteristisch ist die rhythmische Figur im ersten Takt und die kleinen Variationen und Überleitungsfloskeln zwischen Harmoniewechseln.

Example:

Beispiel:

6.3 Samba

The first example is based on the harmony from *Energia,* a composition from the famous Brazilian musician Sivuca. Observe the notation in 2/4, and the continuing accent given to the second beat.

6.3 Samba

Das erste Beispiel basiert auf den Harmonien von *Energia,* einer Komposition des bekannten brasilianischen Musikers Sivuca. Beachten Sie die Notation im 2/4 Takt und die durchlaufende Betonung auf der 2:

Example 1:

Beispiel 1:

***Energia,* variation "a"**

***Energia,* Variation "a"**

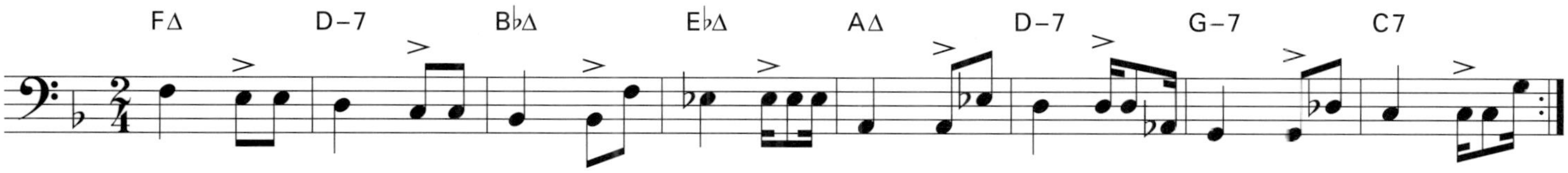

***Energia,* variation "b"**

***Energia,* Variation "b"**

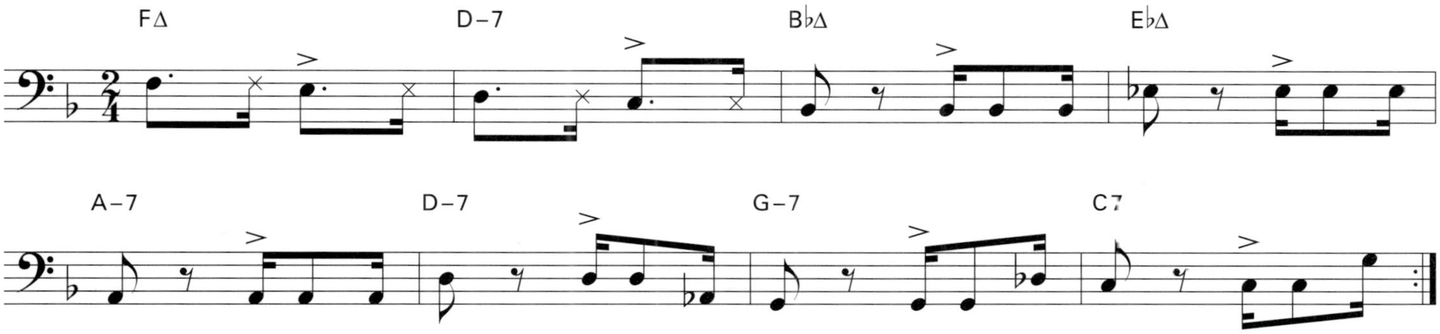

Example 2:

Beispiel 2:

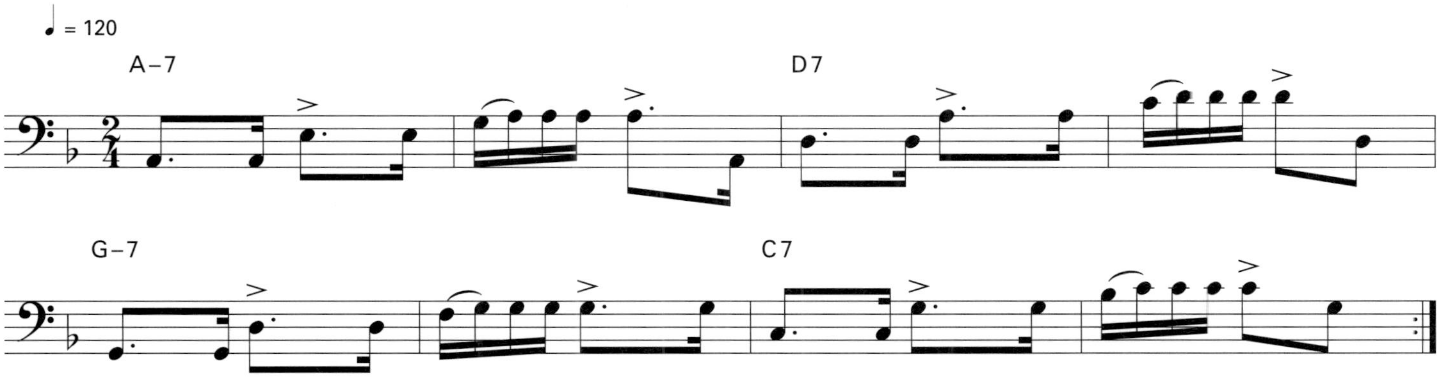

Samba: further examples

Samba: weitere Beispiele

6.4 Afro-Cuban and Salsa

6.4 Afro-Cuban und Salsa

Example: Afro-Cuban

Beispiel: Afro-Cuban

Example: Salsa, with a typical clave and piano pattern

Beispiel: Salsa, mit typischer Clave und Piano Figur

Beginners will learn the figure easier if they at first practice leaving out the ties between beats "4" to "1"

Anfänger lernen die Figur schneller, wenn sie zu Beginn die Bindebögen von Zählzeit "4" zur nächsten "1" noch nicht spielen.

Salsa: Bass line variation

Salsa: Variation der Baßlinie

NOTE:

An excellent source for good bass lines (jazz, rock, and latin) is "The New Real Book" Vols. 1 and 2, published by Bassist Chuck Sher.

Another valuable addition to the bass player's library as a source for many examples of Latin-American and funk is the "Groove Piano Buch" (German text) from Philipp Moehrke, (Advance Music 1995.)

ANMERKUNG:

Eine ausgezeichnete Quelle für gute Baßlinien (Jazz, Rock und Latin) ist "The New Real Book" (Vol. 1, 2 und 3), herausgegeben von unserem Baßkollegen Chuck Sher.

Insbesondere lateinamerikanische Stile und Funkpatterns werden im "Groove Piano Buch" von Philipp Moehrke (Advance Music 1995) ausführlich mit zahlreichen Beispielen erläutert, die auch für den Bassisten brauchbar sind.

V ELEMENTS OF SOUND

1. General

There are six elements that play a large role in the production of a contrabass sound. These are...

1. The instrument
2. The right hand
3. The left hand
4. The strings
5. The electronic pick up
6. The amplifier

The following illustration shows the relationships of these elements.

V WIRKUNGSGEFÜGE SOUND

1. Allgemeines

Bei der Entstehung von Sound auf dem Kontrabaß spielen vor allem sechs Elemente eine große Rolle:

1. Das Instrument
2. Die rechte Hand
3. Die linke Hand
4. Die Saiten
5. Der Tonabnehmer
6. Der Verstärker

Anhand der nachstehenden Graphik sind die Beziehungen der einzelnen Elemente gut zu erkennen.

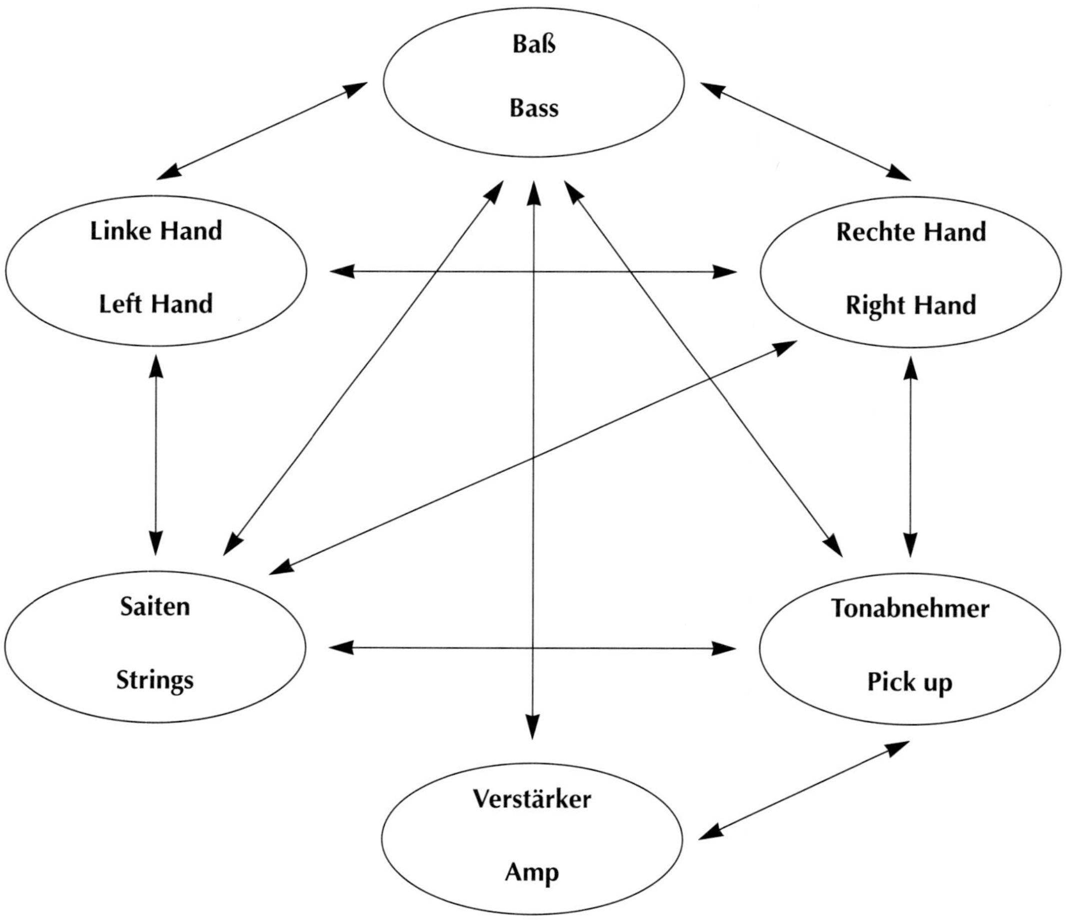

1.1 Description Of The Relationships

The instrument quality and condition has an effect on

- the left hand; (the condition of the fingerboard, the thickness of the neck and the height of the bridge in relation to the strings)
- the right hand; (the string height, the distance between the strings, the length of the fingerboard and position of the bridge.)
- the string vibrations; (some instruments may have a dead spot, where a particular note sounds weak and does not sustain.)
- the electronic pickup; (the placement of the electronic pickup will produce a different tone quality or change the vibrations of the bridge.)
- the amplifier; (through unevenly amplified frequencies. A bad bass wont be made to sound much better just by using a good amplifier.)

The right hand position, and the way the hand is used has an effect on

- the strings; (where can we pluck the string to make a *pizzicato* sound softer, or louder? Which hand position works best for walking bass? Which is better for playing solos?)
- the left hand; (good coordination between both hands make possible the smooth changing of positions and crossing the strings which further results in better timing.)
- the dynamics, phrasing and articulation.

The left hand technique has an impact on the

- string vibration; (pressing the string properly results in a long sustained tone.)
- right hand (in terms of coordination.)
- overall tone; (pulling off, hammering, glissando, and muting.)

String quality, condition, and position effect

- the right hand; (position, strength, dexterity, smoothness of string crossing and position changes.)
- left hand; (strength, smoothness of string crossing and position changes, dexterity, and intonation.)
- instrument; (through the pressure of the strings on the bridge and body.)
- sustaining of the tone
- tone quality; (gut strings give a completely different tone quality as do steel strings.)

Amplifier quality and technical features are considerations for

- the choice of the pickup. (Some of the pickups sound different when used with different amps.)
- the strength of the right hand; (the amplifier cannot compensate for a weak right hand.)
- the instrument; (care must be taken in choosing the correct amplifier for your bass. As an example, choosing an amplifier with a built-in equalizer can be a definite advantage.)
- tone effects; (echo, reverb, compression, chorus, etc.)

1.1 Beschreibung der Wechselbeziehungen

Qualität und Beschaffenheit des Instruments haben Einfluß auf

- die linke Hand, z.B. der Zustand des Griffbretts, die Dicke des Halses, die Höhe des Stegs in Verbindung mit der Saitenlage.
- die rechte Hand, z.B. Saitenlage, Saitenabstand zueinander, Länge des Griffbretts, Position des Stegs.
- die Schwingungen der Saiten, z.B. beim sog. "Wolf" (einzelne Töne klingen schwach und dumpf).
- den Tonabnehmer, z.B. unterschiedliche Plazierungen verändern den Klang oder verändern die Schwingungen des Stegs.
- den Verstärker, z.B. durch Hervorheben oder Abschwächen bestimmter Frequenzbereiche (Formanten). Ein schlechter Baß wird auch mit einem guten Verstärker nicht viel besser klingen.

Spielweise und Position der rechten Hand haben Einfluß auf

- die Saiten. An welcher Stelle klingt ein *Pizzicato* weicher, wo klingt es härter? Welche Handstellung eignet sich besser für den Walking Bass, welche besser für das Solospiel?
- die linke Hand. Eine gute Koordination zwischen beiden Händen ermöglicht flüssige Lagen- und Saitenwechsel und ein gutes Timing.
- Dynamik, Phrasierung und Artikulation.

Die Technik der linken Hand beeinflußt

- die Schwingungsdauer der Saiten, kräftiges Drücken ermöglicht längeres Sustain.
- die rechte Hand im Hinblick auf die Koordination. (s. oben).
- den Klang im allgemeinen, z.B. durch Abziehen, Aufschlagen, Glissandi, Dämpfen.

Qualität, Beschaffenheit und Lage der Saiten haben Wirkung

- auf die rechte Hand, deren Position, den erforderlichen Kraftaufwand, die erreichbare Schnelligkeit, flüssige Saiten- und Lagenwechsel.
- auf die linke Hand, den erforderlichen Kraftaufwand, Lagen- und Saitenwechsel, die mögliche Schnelligkeit, die Intonation.
- auf den Baß, z.B. durch den Druck der Saiten auf Steg und Decke.
- auf das Sustain der Töne.
- auf den Sound im allgemeinen: Darmsaiten ergeben eine völlig andere Klangfarbe als Stahlsaiten.

Qualität und Ausstattung eines Verstärkers stehen im Zusammenhang mit

- der Wahl des Pick Ups. Manche Tonabnehmer klingen mit verschiedenen Amps sehr unterschiedlich.
- dem erforderlichen Kraftaufwand der rechten Hand. Aber – mangelnde Intensität der rechten Hand kann man durch mehr Volumen am Amp nicht ausgleichen.
- dem Instrument. Die sorgfältige Auswahl des Amps

The quality and position of the electronic pickup effects the

- choice of strings (electromagnetic pickups require the use of steel strings);
- choice of amplifier (see above);
- vibration of the bridge, body, and fingerboard will change according to the placement of the pickup;.
- amplification of individual frequencies (for instance, a bad amplifier can cause feedback).

A closer look at these influences will help you to more clearly understand their relationships to one another.

Each individual element can be controlled and/or changed up to a certain degree at will. The individual mechanical controls, instrument, strings, pickup, or amplifier can be varied. The manner in which the hands are used is another variable.

There are variables over which the player has no control that also influence the tone, such as the performers own physical attributes (nature of the skin, soft or callouse or sweaty for example, and the size of the fingers or hands). These effect the sound in different ways. For instance, have you ever listened to someone else play your instrument?

The acoustics of each individual room will also have an influence on the sound of your instrument. It often takes some time in order for one to get used to a room's particular acoustics.

A chapter of an entirely different kind is the relationship between the bassist and the sound engineer. Even if one has quality amplification, he is still dependent on the P.A. and the engineer. A clear and precise idea of the desired sound worked out in a friendly and respectful manner between the bassist and the engineer is most helpful.

ermöglicht unter Umständen, eventuelle Schwächen des Instruments, z.B. in den tiefen Frequenzen,mit Hilfe eines evtl. eingebauten Equalizers auszugleichen.

- möglichen Klangerweiterungen wie z.B. Hall, Kompression, Chorus, etc.

Qualität, Beschaffenheit und Position des Tonabnehmers bestimmen

- die Wahl der Saiten (bei elektromagnetischen Pick Ups sind Stahlsaiten erforderlich);
- die Auswahl des Amps (s. dort);
- das Schwingungsverhalten des Stegs, der Decke oder des Griffbretts (je nachdem, wo der Tonabnehmer befestigt wird);
- die Verstärkung oder Absenkung bestimmter Frequenzen im Amp (Extrembeispiel Rückkopplung).

Eine genauere Betrachtung dieses Wirkungsgefüges Sound ermöglicht das Erkennen von Zusammenhängen, die einem sonst vielleicht nicht so klar erscheinen würden.

Die oben genannten Elemente lassen sich in gewisser Weise steuern oder verändern. Instrument, Saiten, Tonabnehmer oder Verstärker lassen sich austauschen. Spielweisen der rechten und der linken Hand können entwickelt oder verändert werden. Darüber hinaus gibt es jedoch einige Faktoren, die ebenfalls Einfluß auf den Sound haben, die sich aber der Veränderung durch den Musiker weitgehend entziehen.

Damit meine ich die physischen Voraussetzungen, die man von Natur aus mitbringt, wie z.B. die Beschaffenheit der Haut oder die Größe der Hände/Finger. Beides hat bis zu einem gewissen Grad Einfluß auf den Sound. Haben Sie schon einmal einen anderen Musiker Ihren Baß spielen gehört?

Überdies spielen die Bedingungen eine Rolle, die bei einem Auftritt durch die mehr oder weniger gute Akustik des betreffenden Raumes vorgegeben sind. Manchmal dauert es ziemlich lange, bis man sich daran gewöhnt hat.

Ein Kapitel ganz besonderer Art ist die Beziehung zwischen Bassist und Mischer. Selbst bei einer guten P.A. ist man vom Mischer weitestgehend abhängig. Klare und präzise Vorstellungen über den gewünschten Sound, dabei behutsam und freundlich geäußert, sind bei der Kommunikation zwischen beiden äußerst hilfreich.

1.2 Example: Groove Pattern

The following examples should help to make clear the influence of articulation, dynamics and hand positions.

Play the following figure.

1.2 Beispiel: Groove Pattern

Hierbei soll der Einfluß von Artikulation, Dynamik und Lagenspiel verdeutlicht werden.

Spielen Sie bitte die folgende Figur:

In the first measure, using the "hammer-on" effect with the left hand, slur from the notes D to E and G to A. In the second measure slur D to E. On the repeat in the second measure and on the last eighth-note of the triplet, the E is sustained into the next measure.

Use the following articulations:

- = play the note long

∧ = play the note short

Play an accent on the off-beats.

Binden Sie nun durch Aufschlagen der linken Hand die Töne D nach E im 1. Takt, G nach A und wieder D nach E im zweiten Takt. Bei der Wiederholung bleibt das E im zweiten Takt auf dem letzten Triolenachtel der Zählzeit vier liegen und klingt so in den nächsten Takt hinein.

Spielen Sie die Artikulation wie eingezeichnet:

- bedeutet lang,

∧ bedeutet kurz.

Betonen Sie die Off-beats.

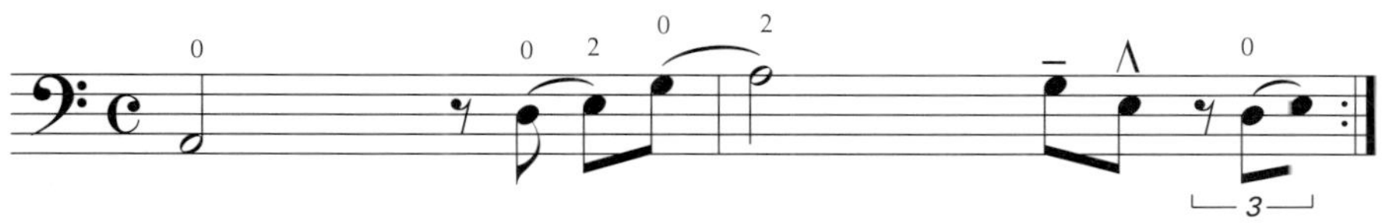

Now play the third version using the written fingerings.

Spielen Sie nun die dritte Version mit dem eingezeichneten Fingersatz.

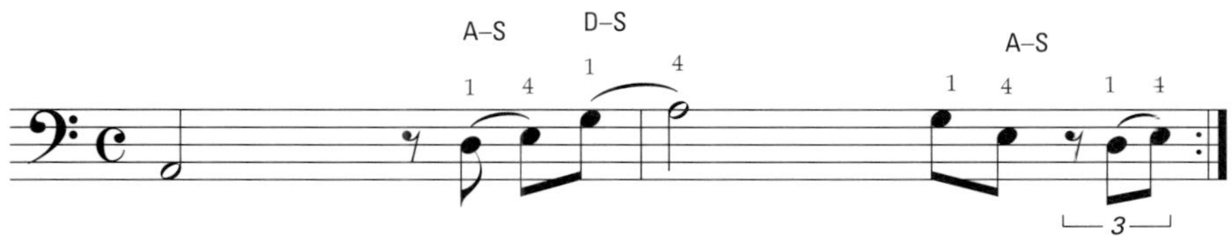

Compare all three versions and decide for yourself which sounds best.

Vergleichen Sie die drei Versionen und entscheiden Sie, welche für Sie am besten klingt.

1.3 Example Of Tone Control: *Like Someone In Love*

The following example using the first 16 measures of *Like Someone In Love* is notated in two different ways. The first is that of a normal walking bass line, as one would often find it notated. The second version is more strongly focused on sound.

Ties indicate where one can sustain longer tones. The finger is to remain on the string. Open strings are not to be dampened. (For instance in bar 16 the G on the first beat will be sustained until the end of the measure. That applies also to the D on 2, the B on 3, and the low G on 4.) The result of this is a fuller, rounder, chord-like sound. Prerequisites for this are good quality instrument and strings, and advanced performance techniques. Bass lines such as these are recommended whenever there is no other harmony instrument playing. (For example, a saxophone, drums, and bass trio.)

Any wide intervals between the 5th and 10th are advised. The interval of the second in bar 6 of the second example stands out as a special effect.

1.3 Klanggestaltung am Beispiel von *Like Someone In Love*

Die folgende Baßlinie über die ersten 16 Takte von *Like Someone In Love* ist auf zwei Arten notiert: Beim ersten Mal ganz normal als einstimmiger Walking Bass, wie man es in vielen Notenbeispielen findet. Die zweite Version orientiert sich am Klang.

Haltebögen zeigen an, wo und wie lange Töne weiterklingen. Dabei bleiben die Finger der linken Hand liegen, leere Saiten werden nicht abgedämpft. So z.B. in Takt 16: Das auf Zählzeit 1 gespielte G klingt weiter bis zum Ende des Taktes, das auf 2 gespielte D ebenfalls, genau so das B auf 3 und schließlich auf 4 das tiefe G. Das Ergebnis ist ein voller, runder, akkordischer Klang. Voraussetzung dafür sind eine gute Qualität von Instrument und Saiten und eine entsprechende, fortgeschrittene Spieltechnik, die sich aber mit einigem Üben schnell erreichen läßt. Baßlinien dieser Art empfehlen sich als Begleitung, wenn kein weiteres Harmonieinstrument vorhanden ist, z.B. für die Besetzung Sax, Drums und Baß.

Der Lage des Instruments entsprechend werden weite Intervalle zwischen Quinte und Dezime bevorzugt. Die Sekunde in Takt 6 des zweiten Beispiels sticht schon als besonderer Effekt hervor.

Example 1:

Beispiel 1:

Example 2:

Beispiel 2:

VI ARPEGGIOS

1. General

Functional harmony plays an important role in jazz improvisation with perhaps the exceptions of "Free" and some of the "Avant garde" jazz. Most of the communication within an ensemble is in the element of harmony. It is therefore important for the bassist to have a concrete knowledge of chords, how they are constructed, their relationships, their sounds, and harmonic progressions.

A basic ability in piano playing is especially helpful, and for this I would like to recommend "The Jazz Piano Book" by Mark Levine, published by Advance Music. (English edition published by Sher Music Co.)

2. Major Triads

Examples:

VI AKKORDBRECHUNGEN

1. Allgemeines

Bei der Improvisation im Jazz, ausgenommen der sog. Free Jazz und Teile des Avantgarde Jazz, spielt die funktionelle Harmonik eine wichtige Rolle. Innerhalb einer Band findet ein großer Teil der musikalischen Kommunikation im harmonischen Bereich statt. Für den daran interessierten Bassisten ist die genaue Kenntnis von Aufbau, Klang und Beziehungen der Akkorde untereinander unbedingt erforderlich.

Grundkenntnisse im Pianospiel sind äußerst hilfreich. In diesem Zusammenhang möchte ich das "Jazz Piano Buch" von Mark Levine empfehlen, das ebenfalls bei Advance Music erschienen ist.

2. Durdreiklänge

Beispiele:

NOTE:
In order to avoid unnecessary changing of position, it is recommended to chose positions that allow at least two of the chord notes to be played.

ANMERKUNG:
Um unnötige Lagenwechsel zu vermeiden, ist es ratsam, möglichst die Lage so zu wählen, daß immer mindestens zwei Töne in der gleichen Lage gegriffen werden können.

2.1 Inversions

Begin each arpeggio with:

1. the root of the chord
2. the third of the chord
3. the fifth of the chord
4. the octave

2.1 Umkehrungen

Beginnen Sie nun jede Akkordzerlegung wie im folgenden Beispiel:

1. mit dem Grundton
2. mit der Terz
3. mit der Quinte
4. mit der Oktave (= Grundton)

Example: Arpeggios

Beispiel: Akkordzerlegungen

2.2 Minor Triads

A minor triad is made by substituting the minor third for the major third of a triad.

2.2 Molldreiklänge

Verwenden Sie die kleine statt der großen Terz, so erhalten Sie Molldreiklänge:

Example: A minor

Beispiel: A Moll

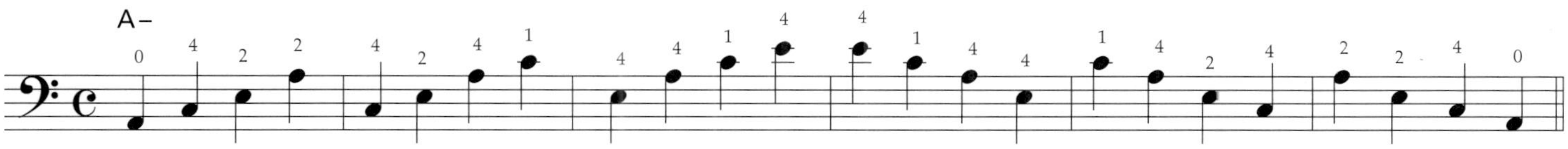

3. Major Seventh Chords

The major seventh chords is a chord with a major 3rd, and major 7th. Practice all arpeggios from E∆ to E♭∆ in the root position first, then practice the inversions.

Exercise: Major seventh chords

3. Durseptakkorde

Spielt man Akkorde mit großer Terz und großer Septime, erhält man Durseptakkorde ("Major 7"). Üben Sie zunächst alle Akkordbrechungen chromatisch von E∆ bis E♭∆ in der Grundstellung und dann ihre Umkehrungen.

Übung: Durseptakkorde

4. Dominant Seventh Chords

The dominant seventh chord is a chord with a major 3rd, and minor 7th. The following example is that of an E dominant seventh chord chord in root position and three inversions.

4. Dominantseptakkorde

Vierklänge mit großer Terz und kleiner Septime heißen Dominantseptakkorde. Im folgenden Beispiel finden Sie die Grundstellung von E7 und die drei möglichen Umkehrungen.

Example: E7

Beispiel: E7

Practice moving chromatically from E7 to E♭7. Play all chords in root position and all three of their inversions.

Üben Sie auch hier wieder chromatisch von E7 bis E♭7 alle Akkorde in Grundstellung und Umkehrungen.

Exercise: Dominant seventh chords

Übung: Dominantseptakkorde

5. Minor Seventh Chords

The minor seventh chord is a chord with a minor third (♭3) and minor seventh (♭7). Complete the following exercises by filling in the proper chord tones for the arpeggios.

5. Mollseptakkorde

Mollseptakkorde sind Akkorde mit kleiner Terz (♭3) und kleiner Septime (♭7). Führen Sie die folgenden Übungen selbst weiter und füllen Sie die Leertakte mit den richtigen Akkordbrechungen aus.

Exercises: Minor seventh chords

Übungen: Mollseptakkorde

6. "sus4" Chords

A chord where the 4th degree of the scale is substituted for the 3rd degree (A V7 with the 3rd of the chord raised 1/2 step.)

6. "sus4" Akkorde

Spielt man bei einem Dominantseptakkord statt der Terz die Quarte, erhält man "sus 4" Septakkorde.

Example: sus 4 chords and their inversions

Beispiel: sus 4 Akkorde und ihre Umkehrungen

Study

Studie

7. Diminished Chords

Diminished chords consists of superimposed minor thirds. One chooses either the diminished triad (1, ♭3, ♭5) as shown in example 1, the diminished seventh chord (1, ♭3, ♭5, ♭♭7) as shown in example 2, or the half-diminished chord (1, ♭3, ♭5, ♭7) as illustrated in example 3.

7. Verminderte Akkorde

Verminderte Akkorde bestehen aus übereinandergeschichteten kleinen Terzen. Man unterscheidet zwischen verminderten Dreiklängen (Beispiel 1), verminderten Septakkorden (Beispiel 2) und halbverminderten Akkorden (Beispiel 3).

Example 1: diminished triad

Beispiel 1: verminderter Dreiklang

Example 2: diminished seventh chord

Beispiel 2: verminderter Septakkord

Example 3: half-diminished seventh chord

Beispiel 3: halbverminderter Septakkord

Since the structure of the diminished seventh chord is comprised of three superimposed minor thirds, the inversions of the chord will have the same notes as found in root position. For that reason only three different diminished seventh chords exist.

Der verminderte Septakkord besteht aus drei übereinander liegenden kleinen Terzen. Da die Umkehrung eines solchen Akkords wieder die gleiche Struktur aufweist und aus denselben Tönen besteht, gibt es eigentlich nur drei verschiedene verminderte Septakkorde.

Example: diminished seventh chords

Beispiel: verminderte Septakkorde

The diminished seventh chord is also to be found in the V7♭9 (1, 3, 5, ♭7, ♭9).

Ein verminderter Septakkord ist auch im Dominantseptakkord mit hinzugefügter kleiner None enthalten.

Example:

Beispiel:

8. Augmented Chords

The augmented chord is comprised of two superimposed major thirds.

8. Übermäßige Akkorde

Übermäßige Akkorde erhält man durch Schichtung von großen Terzen.

Example: augmented chord

Beispiel: übermäßige Akkorde

The dominant seventh with the raised fifth is related to this family of augmented chords. A good example can be found in the first measure of the bridge of *Stella By Starlight*.

Verwandt mit diesen Akkorden ist der Dominantseptakkord mit übermäßiger Quinte, wie Sie ihn z.B. im ersten Takt des Mittelteils von *Stella By Starlight* finden.

Example:

Beispiel:

9. Two-Octave Arpeggios

Begin each of the two-octave arpeggios from a different chord tone. Observe the four-note pattern and play all six inversions of the exercise chromatically. Do this using all the major and minor triads.

9. Akkordzerlegungen über zwei Oktaven

Beginnen Sie die Akkordzerlegungen über zwei Oktaven jeweils von einem anderen Akkordton. Behalten Sie immer das viertaktige Schema bei. Spielen Sie alle 6 Umkehrungen der folgenden Übung auch wieder chromatisch über alle Dur- und Molldreiklänge.

Exercise: E major

Übung: E Dur

The challenge with arpeggios (also called "broken chords") lies in the necessary position shifts and intonation. Find the positions that include as many chord-tones as possible. Exercises such as these are also included in the "classical" training for bassists.

Instruments used in classical music often have a large distance between the strings and the fingerboard requiring position shifts mostly on the G and D strings. By using steel strings and less string heigth one has the possibility of using fingerings that can include all the strings. The bass line of. *Footprints* by Wayne Shorter (s. p. 87) is a good example. This is played across all the strings.

Die Herausforderung bei Akkordzerlegungen (auch Akkordbrechungen genannt) liegt im Lagenwechsel und in der Intonation. Entscheiden Sie sich bei mehreren Möglichkeiten für die, bei der möglichst mehrere Töne in einer Lage gespielt werden können. Übungen dieser Art gehören auch in der "klassischen" Ausbildung zur allgemeinen Überoutine. Die dabei erforderlichen Lagenwechsel finden dort meist auf der D- und G-Saite statt, wahrscheinlich aus klanglichen und grifftechnischen Gründen (hohe Saitenlage). Stahlseiten und eine niedrigere Saitenlage ermöglichen jedoch ein Lagenspiel, das alle Saiten einbezieht. Ein gutes Beispiel ist die die Baßlinie zu *Footprints* von Wayne Shorter (s. S. 87) Es wird also eher quer über die Saiten gespielt.

For the following exercises write in your own fingerings wherever there are no fingerings shown. Take your time and try different possibilities. Choose the one possibility that suits you best and stay with it. This will keep you from having to make snap decisions for the fingerings during a performance. In my experience this leads to many mistakes.

Notieren Sie im folgenden da, wo keine Fingersätze angegeben sind, Ihre eigenen Vorschläge. Probieren Sie in aller Ruhe mehrere Möglichkeiten. Wenn Ihnen nach eingehender Prüfung eine der Versionen am besten gefällt, sollten Sie bei dieser bleiben. Sie vermeiden so die Gefahr, sich erst während des Spielens für einen bestimmten Fingersatz entscheiden zu müssen. Erfahrungsgemäß führt das häufig zu Fehlern.

Example: Fingerings and positions

Beispiel: Fingersätze und Lagen

9.1 Rhythm Patterns For Two-Octave Arpeggios

9.1 Rhythmus-Patterns für Arpeggios über 2 Oktaven

Exercise:

Übung:

So as not to fill these chapters with exercises that you should be able to work out for yourself, I am including the following exercises only as examples to help you on your way to inventing your own.

Examples:

Um nicht die Seiten dieses Kapitels mit Übungen zu füllen, die Sie sich auch selbst erarbeiten können, sind die folgenden Beispiele als Anregung gedacht.

Beispiele:

10. Arpeggios For II V Progressions

10. Akkordzerlegungen über II V Verbindungen

Exercises:

Exercises:

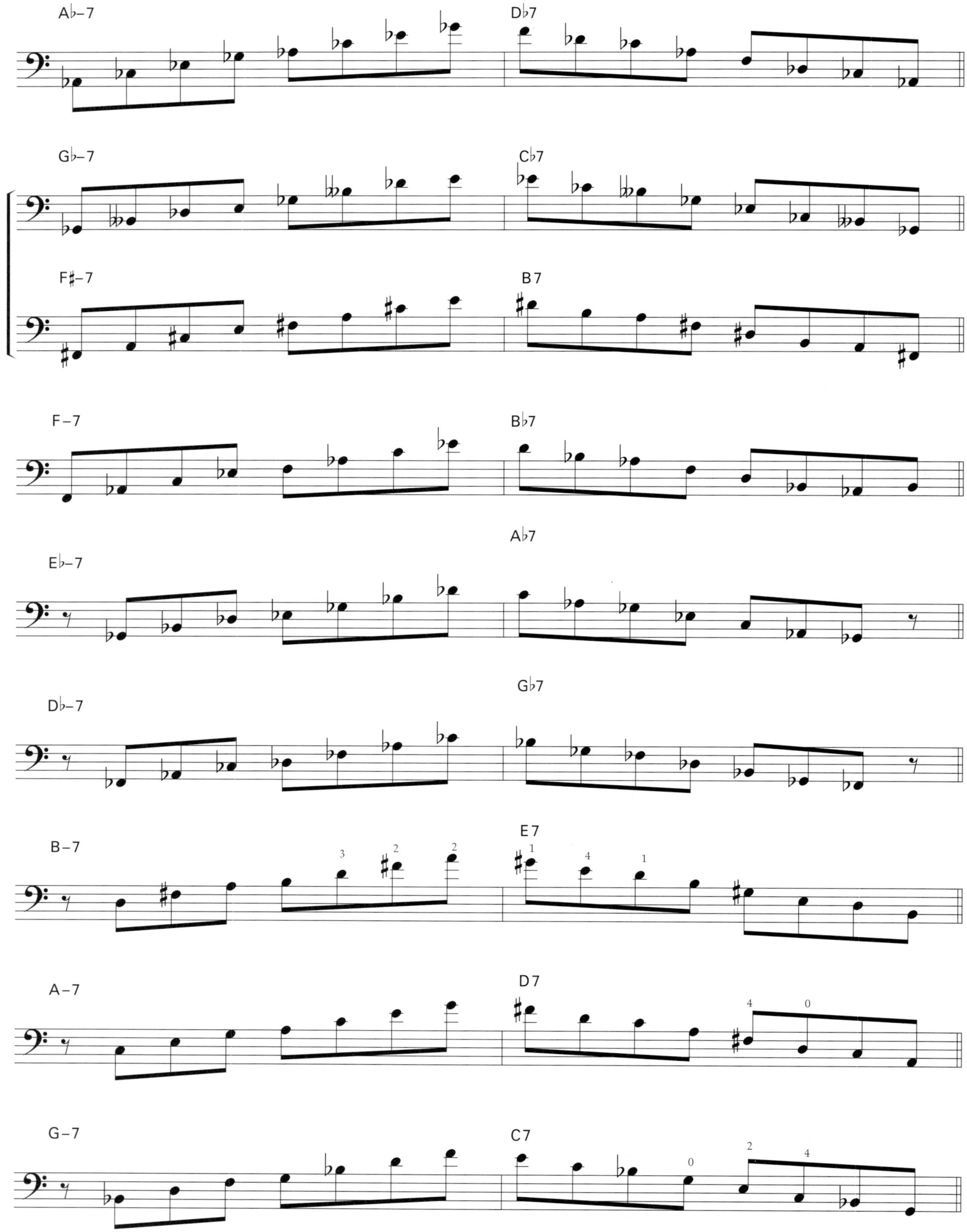

Exercises:
Also play the exercises with a triplet swing feel. (See Chapter VII "Phrasing and Articulation")

Übungen:
Spielen Sie die Übungen auch als punktierte Achtel im "Triolenfeeling" (ternär, siehe Kapitel VII "Phrasierung und Artikulation").

11. Chord Extensions

Until now we have been working with chords that are built up in thirds, the root (1), third (3), fifth (5), and seventh (7). By further use of superimposed thirds, we can add the ninth (9), eleventh (11), and the thirteenth (13), thus exhausting the tones of a common scale. Although the function of the chord remains the same, through the use of these so called "tension-tones" the color of the chord can be changed. Listen to the piano introduction of the Miles Davis version of *Bye Bye Blackbird*.

11. Akkorderweiterungen

Bisher haben wir uns mit einfachen Akkorden beschäftigt, die in Terzen aufgebaut sind: Grundton (1), Terz (3), Quinte (5), Septime (7). Durch weitere Terzschichtungen erhält man die None (9), die Undezime (11) und die Tredezime (13) – damit ist das Repertoire einer üblichen siebenstufigen Skala erschöpft. Durch diese sog. Spannungstöne verändert sich zwar die Farbe der Akkorde, nicht aber ihre Funktion. Hören Sie sich daraufhin z.B. die Piano Einleitung zu *Bye Bye Blackbird* in der Version von Miles Davis an.

Example: G–7 with the added 9, 11 and 13:

Beispiel: G–7 mit hinzugefügter 9, 11 und 13:

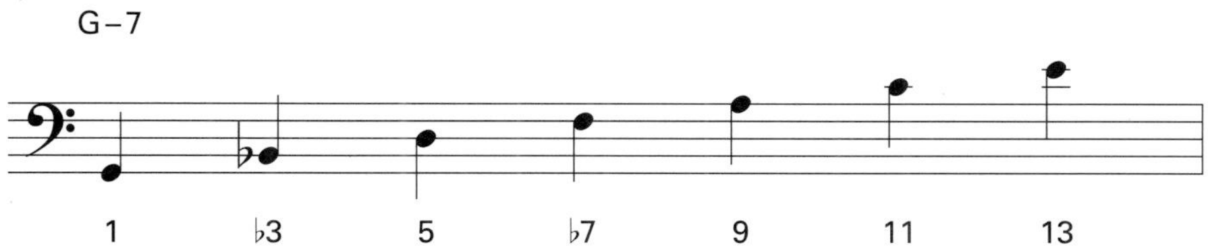

With chords that include the major 3rd, (major or V7 chords) the ♯11 is most often used. The interval of a minor ninth between the third and the eleventh of the chord is changed to a major ninth resulting in a "cleaner" sound. The chord-scales are the Lydian for the major seventh and Mixolydian ♯11 for the dominant scale. More detailed information about chord-scales is to be found in Chapter VIII.

Bei Akkordschichtungen mit großer Terz (Dur- oder Dominantsept) wird meistens die ♯11 statt der 11 verwendet, da sie zur großen Terz eine große statt einer kleinen None bildet und somit etwas "cleaner" klingt. Passende Skalen wären Lydisch und Mixolydisch ♯11. Im Kapitel VIII über Skalen finden Sie nähere Erläuterungen.

Examples:

Beispiele:

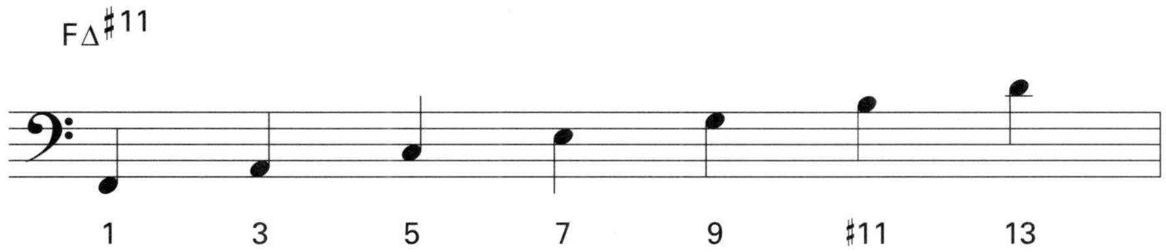

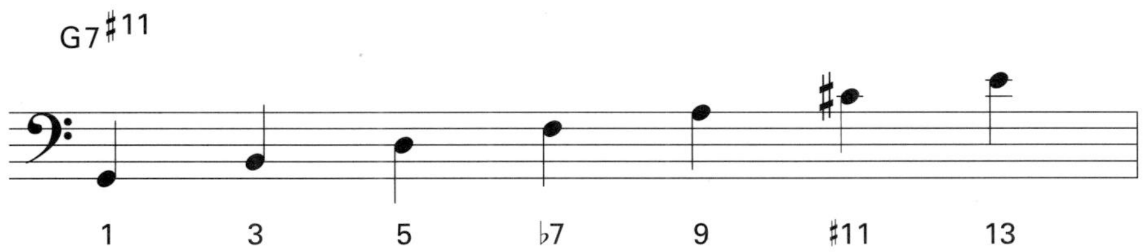

Observe the "hidden" four-note chords in the following three examples. Starting on the 3rd we find a major seventh chord. Beginning from the 5th we find a minor seventh chord, and from the 7th another major seventh chord.

Beachten Sie bei den drei Beispielen, welche Vierklänge in diesen Akkorden enthalten sind: Bei Mollakkorden ab der Terz ein Durseptakkord, ab der Quinte ein Mollseptakkord, ab der Septime ein weiterer Durseptakkord:

Example: A–7,9,11,13 (Dorian)

Beispiel: A–7,9,11,13 (dorisch)

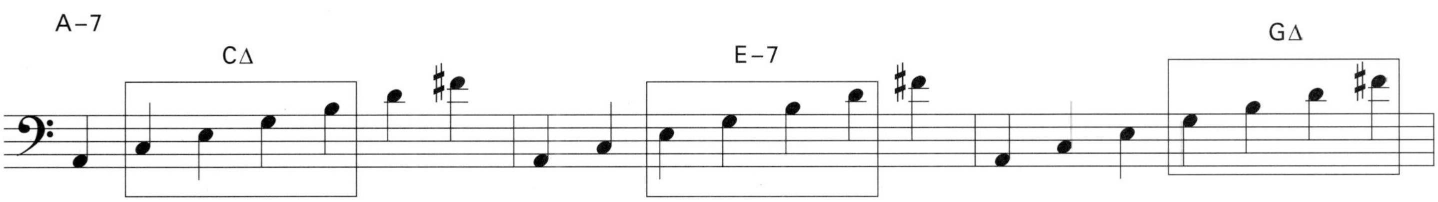

Beginning on the 3rd a major 7, 9, ♯11, 13 chord, one finds a minor seventh chord. From the 5th a major seventh chord, and from the 7th another minor seventh chord.

Ein Durseptakkord mit 9, ♯11 und 13 enthält ab der Terz einen Mollseptakkord, ab der Quinte einen Durseptakkord, ab der Septime einen Mollseptakkord.

Example: FΔ,9,♯11,13:

Beispiel: FΔ,9,♯11,13:

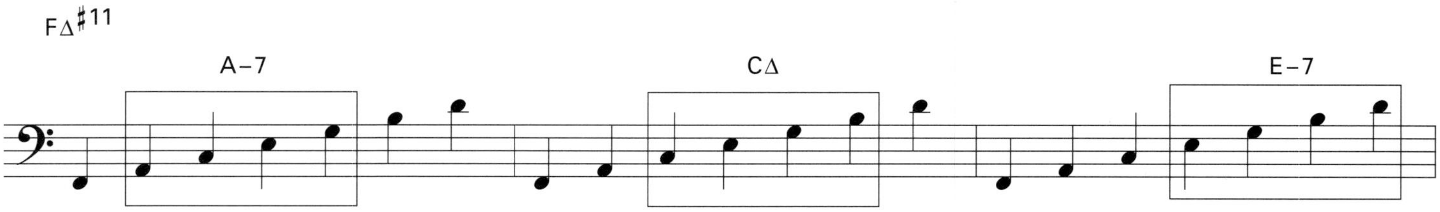

In a V7, 9, ♯11, 13 one finds a half-diminished seventh chord beginning on the third. Starting on the 5th is a minor-major seventh chord, and from the 7th, a major chord with an augmented 5th.

Bei einem Dominantseptakkord mit 9, ♯11 und 13 sind ab der Terz ein halbverminderter Septakkord, ab der Quinte ein Moll Akkord mit großer Septime und ab der Septime ein Durseptakkord mit übermäßiger Quinte zu finden.

Example: A7,9,♯11,13

Beispiel: A7,9,♯11,13

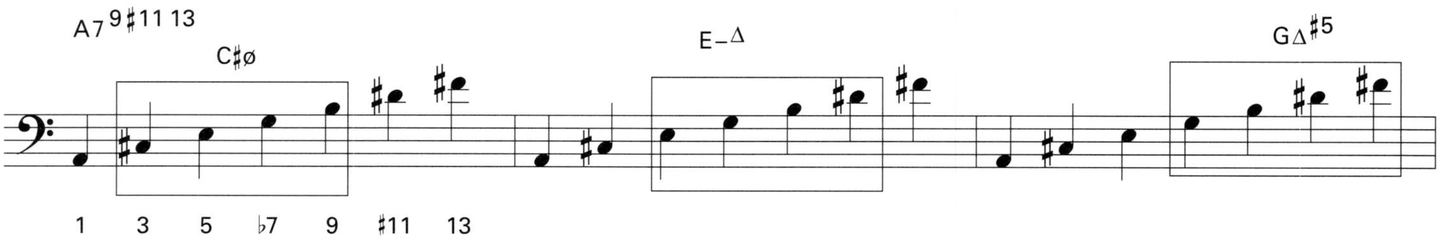

In bebop it is common practice to alter the 5th and 9th of the V7 chord. This increased tension creates a stronger demand for resolution. In regards to the lower register of the bass, it is interesting to see which of these chord alterations sound acceptable. In the following pages you will find examples that you are to play and study very carefully. Play with a very clear intonation. Decide for yourself which sound good and which do not.

Vor allem im Bebop wurden bei den Dominantseptakkorden Quinte und None alteriert, d.h. um einen Halbton nach oben oder unten verändert. Akkorde dieser Art haben eine sehr starke Tendenz zur Auflösung. Sie stehen überwiegend auf der V. Stufe. Im Rahmen einer Baßschule ist es natürlich interessant, zu prüfen, welche Akkorde mit den möglichen Erweiterungen im tiefen Baßregister noch akzeptabel klingen. Einige Beispiele finden Sie auf den folgenden Seiten. Intonieren Sie sehr sorgfältig und entscheiden Sie, was Ihnen gut und was Ihnen weniger gut gefällt.

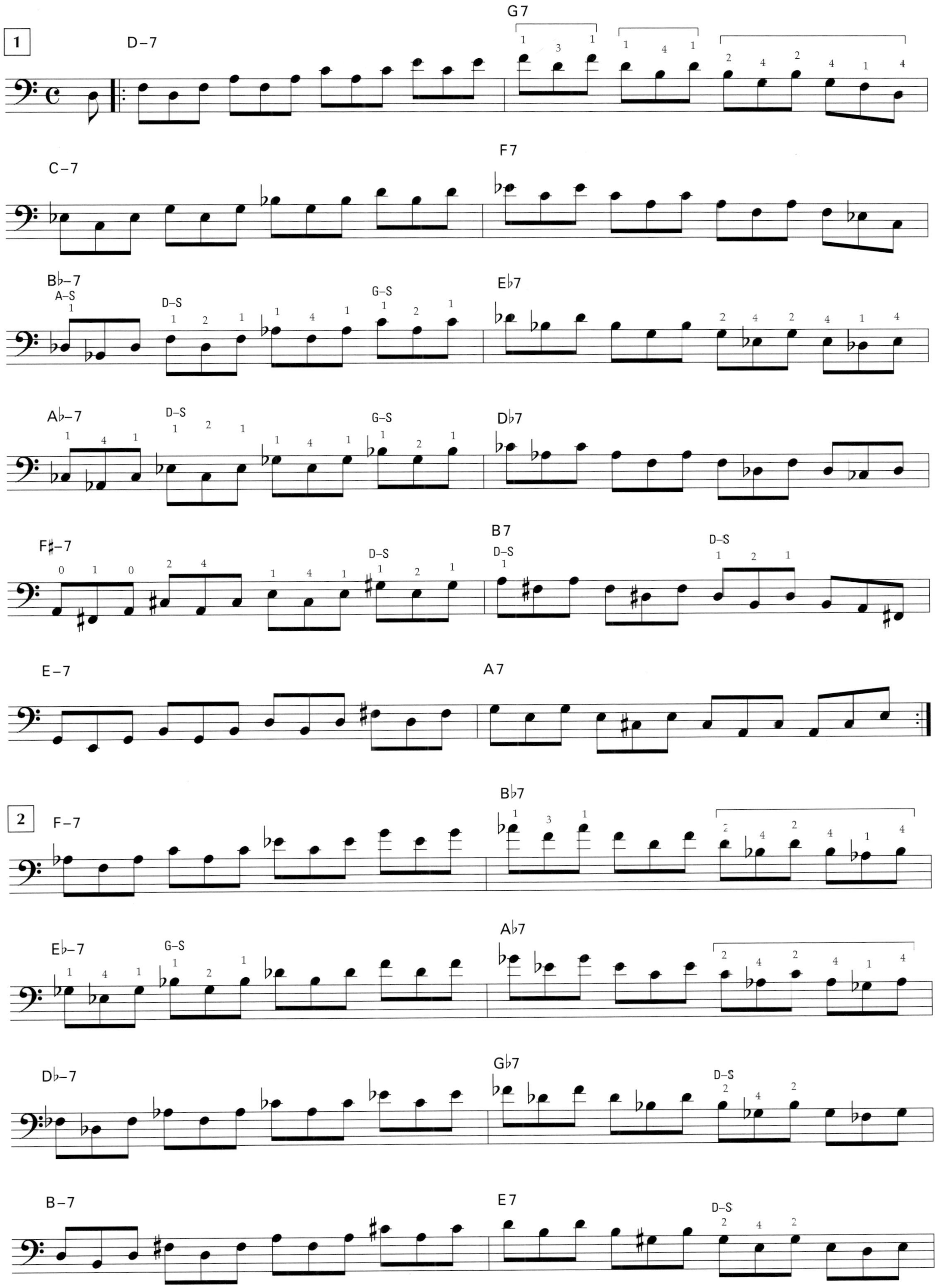
1
D–7
G7
C–7
F7
B♭–7
A–S
D–S
G–S
E♭7
A♭–7
D–S
G–S
D♭7
F♯–7
D–S
B7
D–S
D–S
E–7
A7
2
F–7
B♭7
E♭–7
G–S
A♭7
D♭–7
G♭7
D–S
B–7
E7
D–S

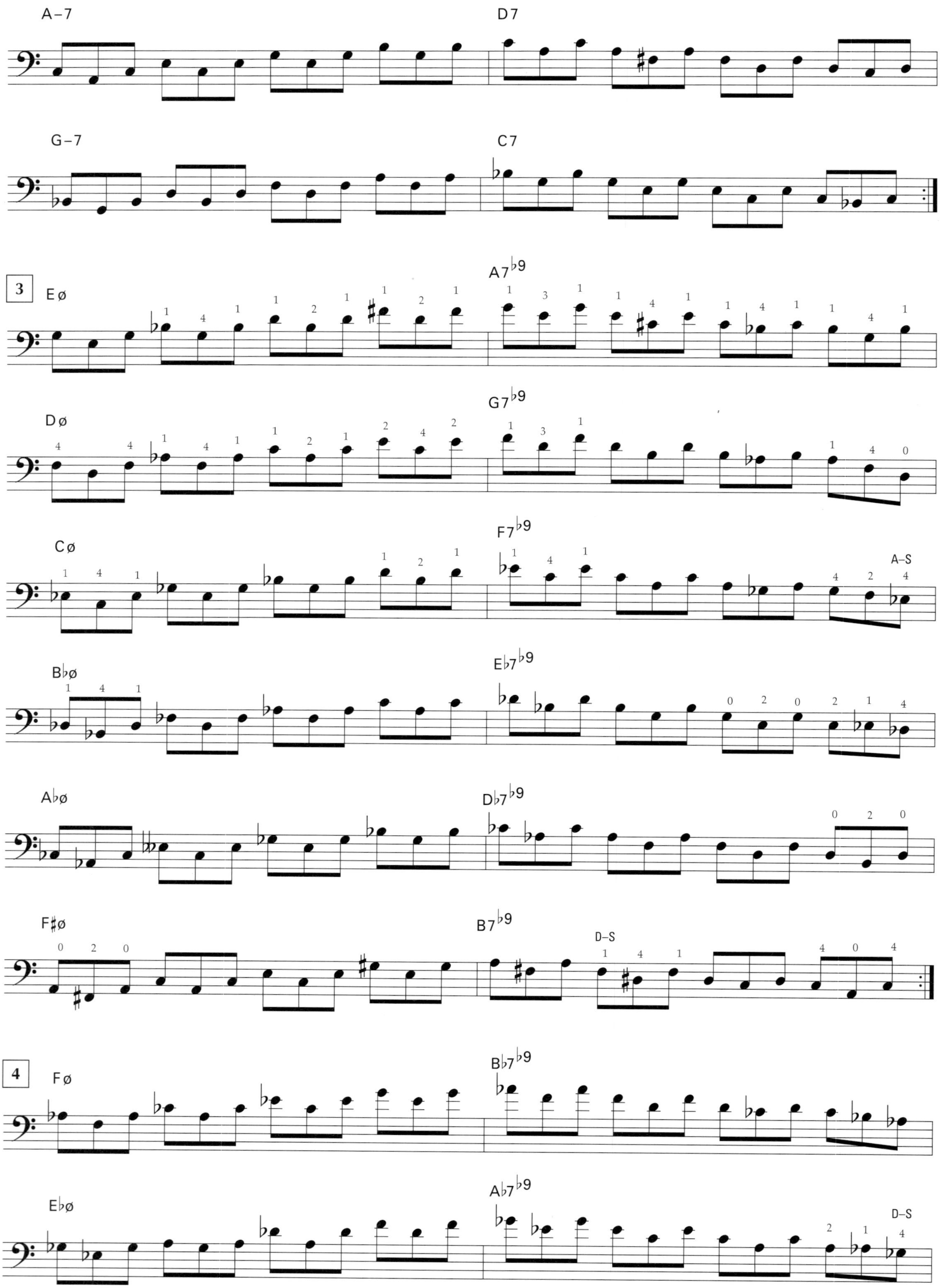
A–7
D7
G–7
C7
3
Eø
A7♭9
Dø
G7♭9
Cø
F7♭9
A–S
B♭ø
E♭7♭9
A♭ø
D♭7♭9
F♯ø
B7♭9
D–S
4
Fø
B♭7♭9
E♭ø
A♭7♭9
D–S

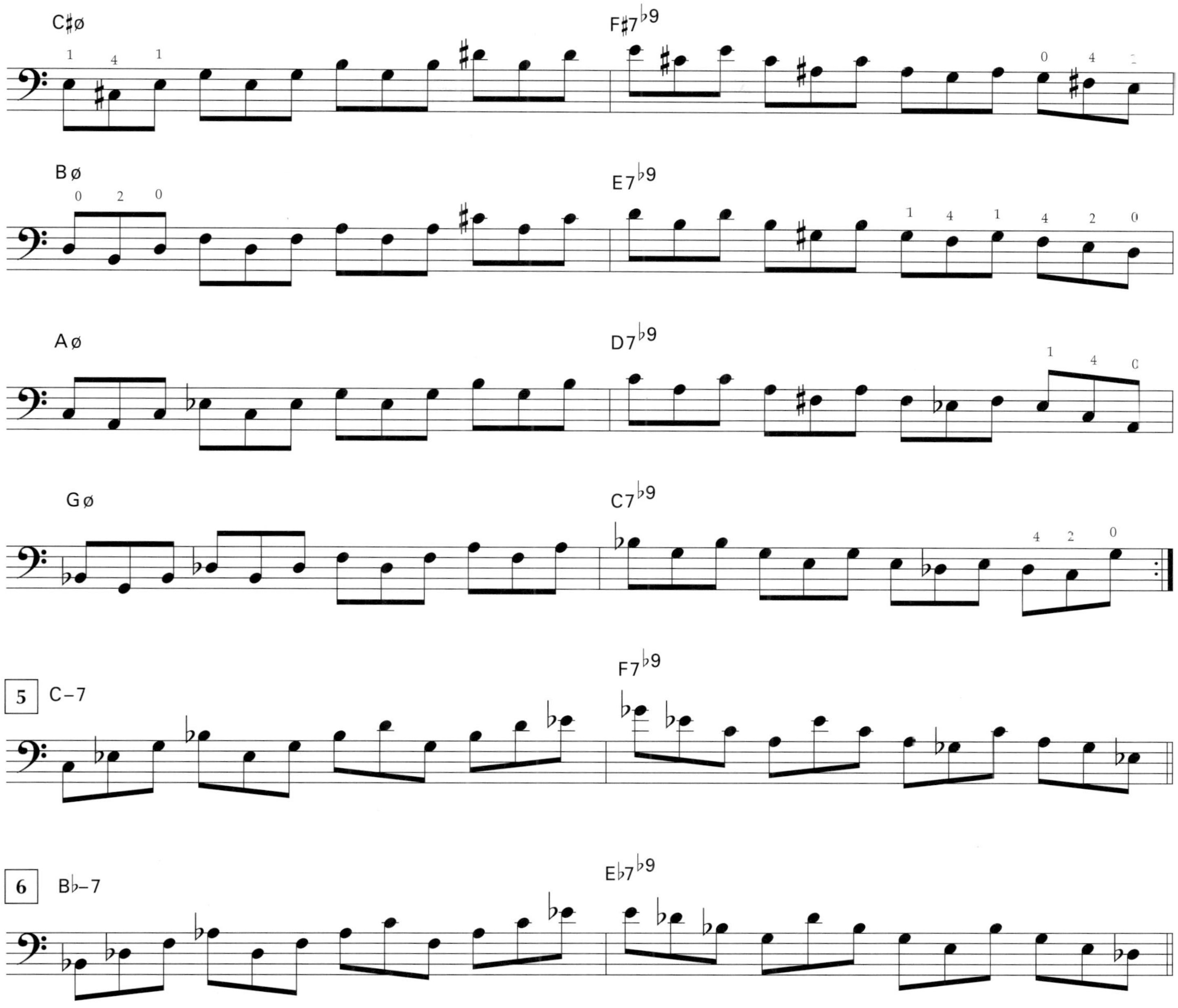

The above exercises are difficult in regards to position shift and intonation. For further study you are to write your own exercises using the progressions from different jazz pieces like *All The Things You Are, There Will Never Be Another You, Just Friends, Days Of Wine And Roses,* etc.

Die vorhergehenden Übungen sind sicherlich im Hinblick auf Lagenwechsel und Intonation schwierig. Schreiben Sie deshalb darüber hinaus Ihre eigenen Etüden über die Akkordverbindungen verschiedener Jazzkompositionen wie z.B. *All The Things You Are, There Will Never Be Another You, Just Friends, Days Of Wine And Roses* etc.

12. Digital Patterns For Chords

Chord tones can also be notated with numbers.

1 = root, 3 = third, 5 = fifth, 7 = seventh, 9 = ninth, 11 = eleventh, and 13 = thirteenth.

Minor and diminished intervals are notated with a "♭" (e.g. ♭3 = a minor 3rd). The augmented intervals are notated with a "♯" (♯11 = augmented eleventh).

12. Digital Patterns für Akkorde

Auch Akkorde kann man in Zahlen notieren:

1 = Grundton, 3 = Terz, 5 = Quinte, 7 = Septime, 9 = None, 11 = Undezime, 13 = Tredezime.

Kleinen und verminderten Intervallen wird ein "♭" vorangestellt (z.B. ♭3 = kleine Terz), übermäßigen Intervallen ein "♯" (z.B. ♯11 = übermäßige Undezime).

Example: Seventh chords

Beispiel: Septakkorde

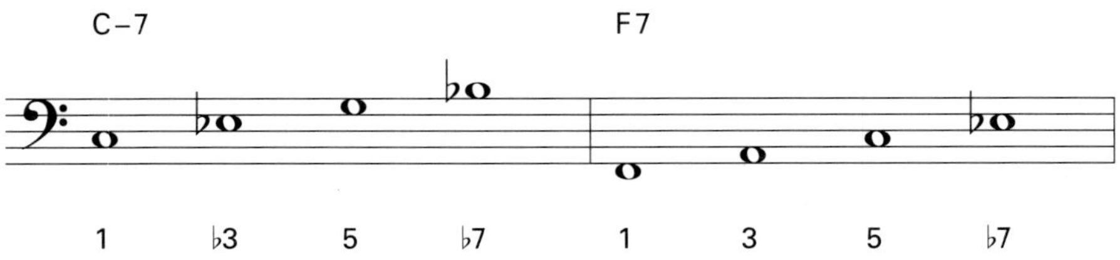

The numbers 1 ♭3 5 ♭7 / 1 3 5 ♭ 7 appearing under the chords C–7 / F7 are played in the following manner.

Die Folge 1 ♭3 5 ♭7 / 1 3 5 ♭ 7 über die Akkorde C–7 / F7 wird so gespielt:

Example:

Beispiel:

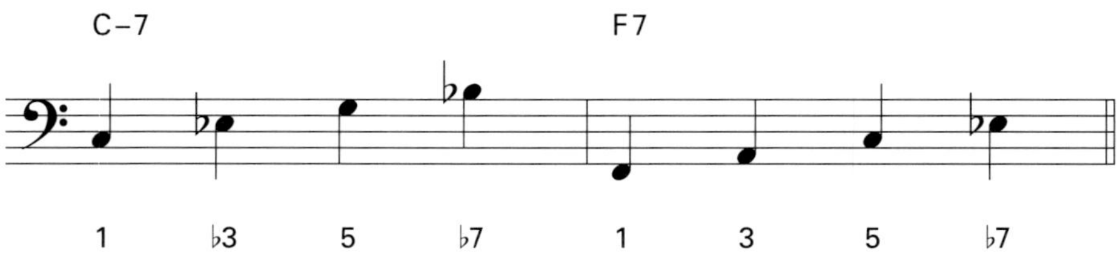

Descending, the same chords played ♭7 5 ♭3 1 / ♭7 5 3 1.

Abwärts ergibt sich über dieselben Akkorde diese Folge: ♭7 5 ♭3 1 / ♭7 5 3 1.

Example:

Beispiel:

On the next two pages only the roots of the chords are notated. You can choose to play the following:

1. Major seventh chords
2. Minor seventh chords
3. Minor-major seventh
4. Dominant seventh chords
5. Half-diminished chords
6. Diminished seventh chords
7. sus 4 seventh chords

using the following patterns:

1 3 5 7	3 5 7 1	5 7 1 3	7 1 3 5
7 5 3 1	5 3 1 7	3 1 5 7	1 7 5 3

Begin practicing the progressions with quarter notes at a very slow tempo to help you get used to the sound and develop your "inner" ear. When you can "hear" the chords before you play them, your intonation will improve. As you progress, play them in faster tempos. Continue then using eighth-notes instead of quarters.

Bei den Akkordfortschreitungen auf den beiden folgenden Seiten sind nur die Grundtöne notiert Darüber können Sie

1. Durseptakkorde (major 7)
2. Mollseptakkorde mit kleiner Septime
3. Mollseptakkorde mit großer Septime
4. Dominantseptakkorde
5. halbverminderte Akkorde
6. verminderte Septakkorde
7. sus 4 Septakkorde

nach folgendem Schema üben:

1 3 5 7	3 5 7 1	5 7 1 3	7 1 3 5
7 5 3 1	5 3 1 7	3 1 5 7	1 7 5 3

Üben Sie alle Akkordbrechungen zuerst in sehr langsamen Vierteln, um sich an den Klang zu gewöhnen und so das "innere Ohr" zu entwickeln. Wenn Sie die Akkorde zuerst innerlich hören, bevor Sie sie spielen, fällt Ihnen die Intonation sehr viel leichter! Anschließend üben Sie die Akkorde in schnelleren Vierteln und dann in Achteln.

a

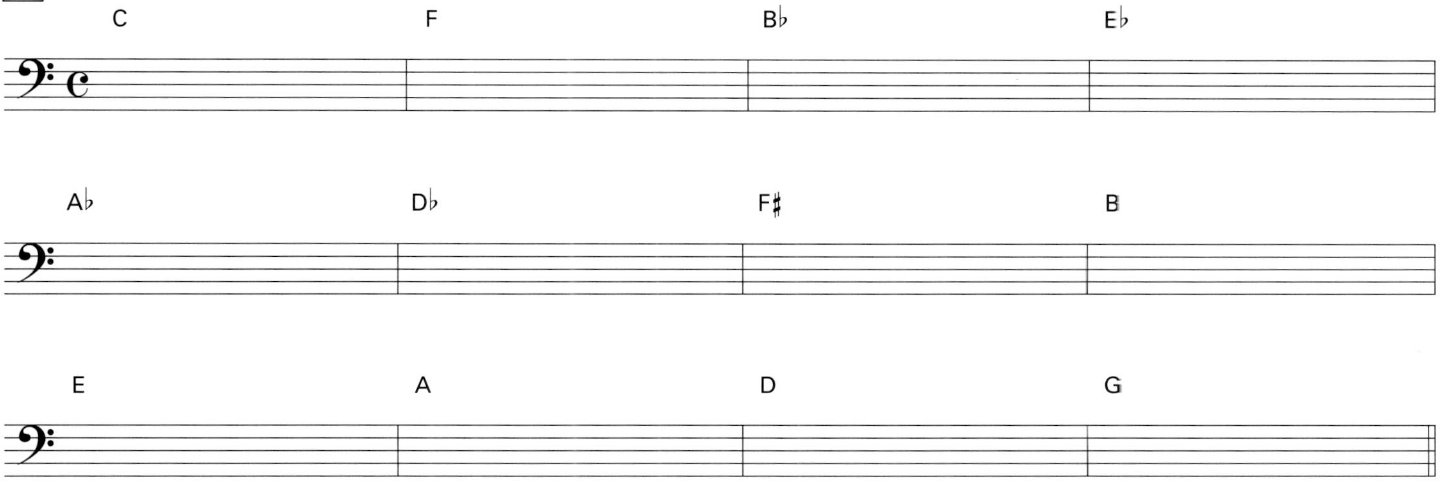

b

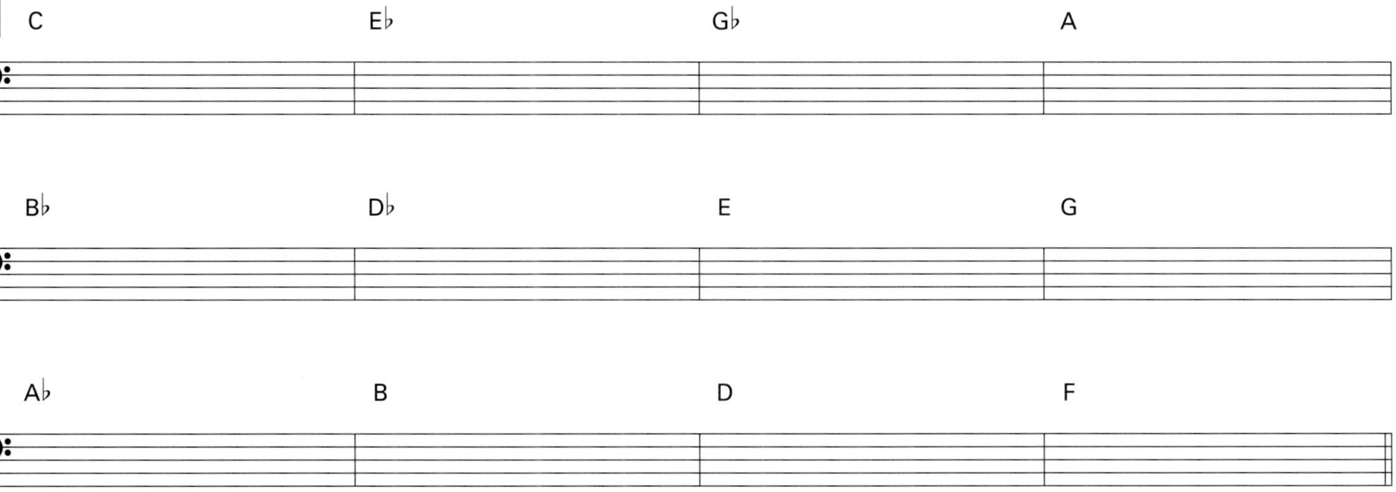

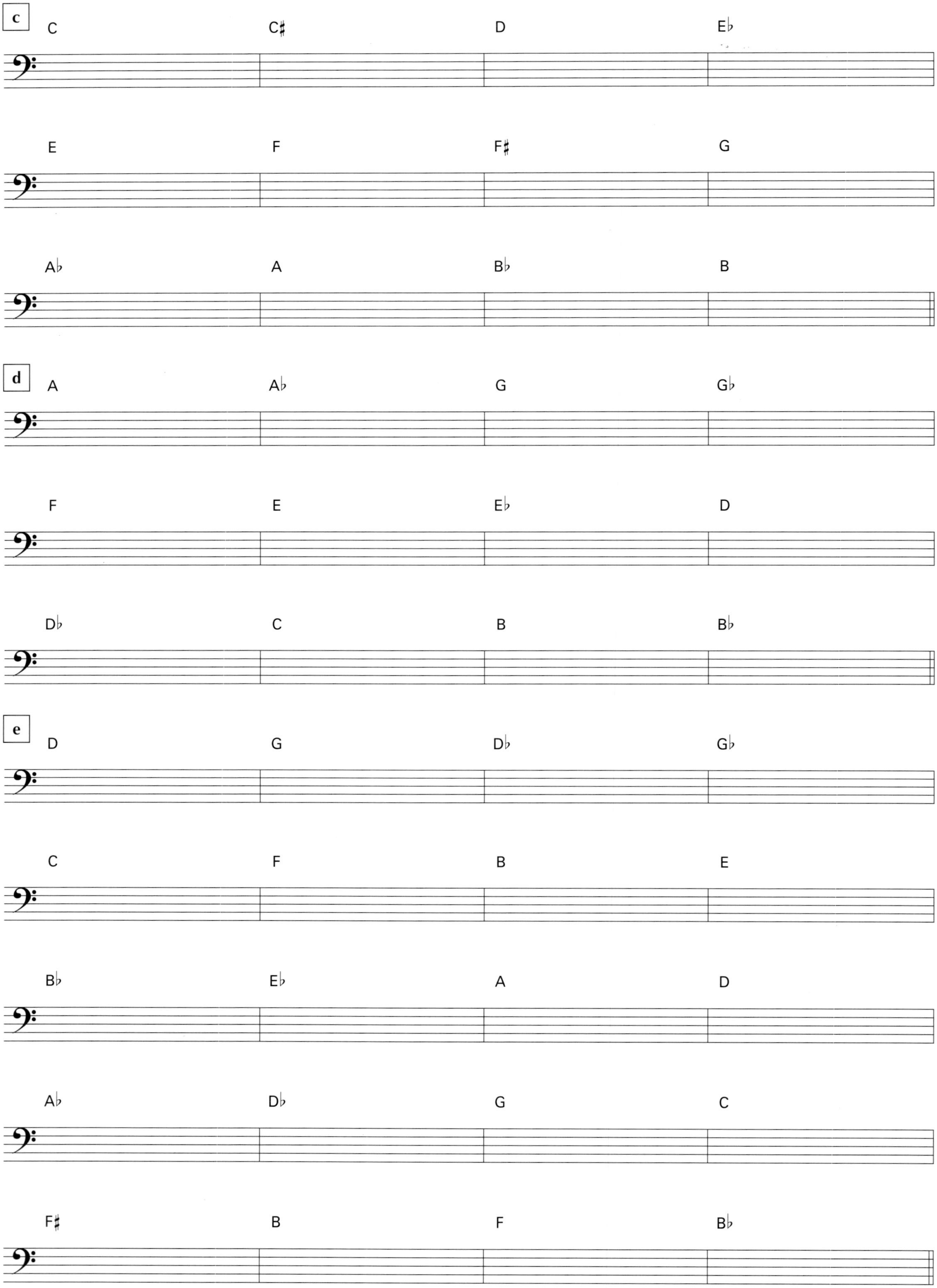
c
C C♯ D E♭
E F F♯ G
A♭ A B♭ B
d
A A♭ G G♭
F E E♭ D
D♭ C B B♭
e
D G D♭ G♭
C F B E
B♭ E♭ A D
A♭ D♭ G C
F♯ B F B♭

12.1 Arpeggios For Half-Measure II V Progression

The following progressions include all twelve II V possibilities. They are grouped in sets to enable you to use the following digital patterns.

II V progressions:

12.1 Arpeggios über halbtaktige II V Verbindungen

Die folgenden Akkordverbindungen enthalten alle 12 möglichen II V Verbindungen. Darüber können Sie alle folgenden Digital-Patterns spielen, die ich in "Sets" organisiert habe.

Akkordschema:

1

2

Set A

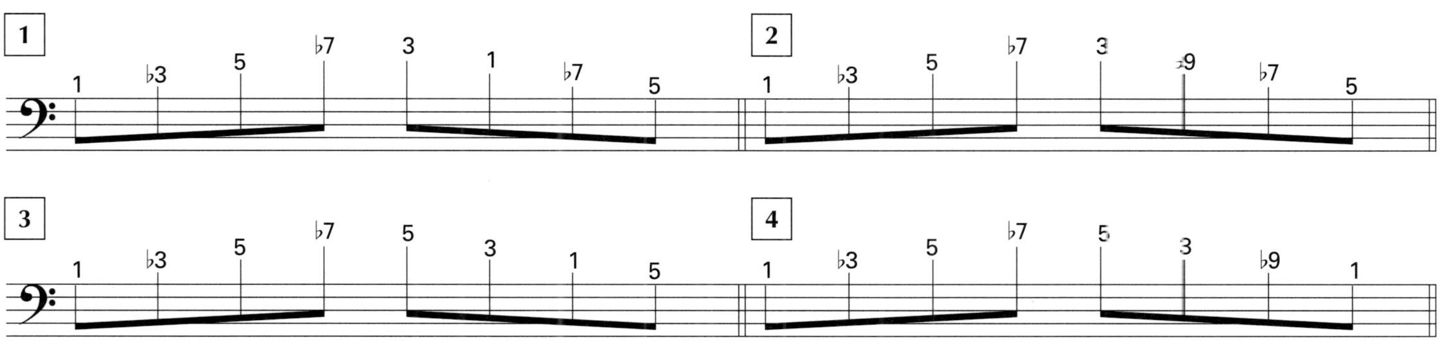

In standard notation pattern 1 from set A looks like this:

Das Pattern 1 aus Set A sieht notiert so aus:

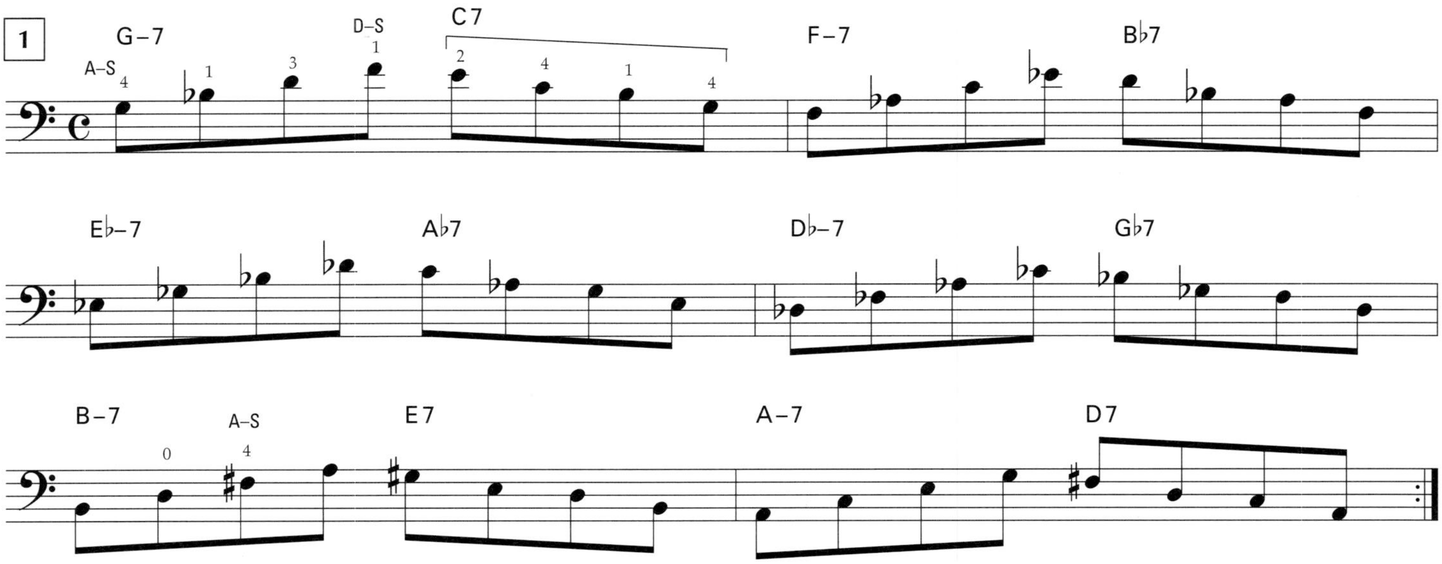

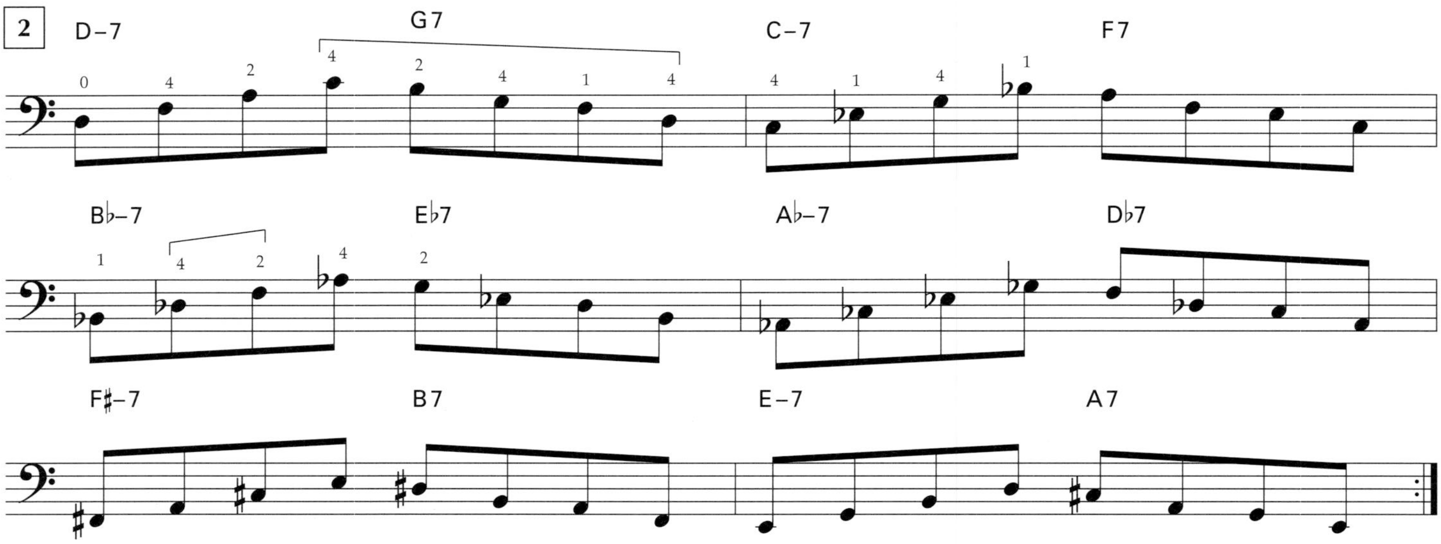

When the first pattern from Set "A" is used in a minor key for IIø V7, it will take the following form.

Wenn Sie das erste Pattern aus Set A auf eine II V Verbindung in Moll übertragen, sieht das so aus:

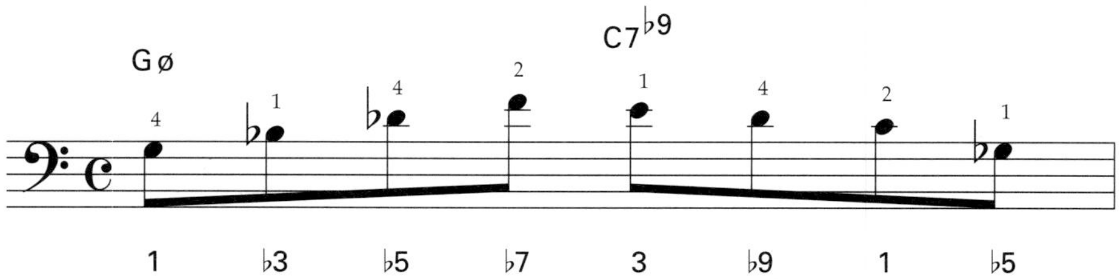

Pay attention to the good voice-leading from the first to second chord. The change of chord is heard clearly when the ♭7 resolves to 3.

Variations of these patterns offer a first step toward improvisation:

a) rhythmic
b) digital

Beachten Sie dabei die gut klingende Stimmführung vom ersten zum zweiten Akkord, die ♭7 wird zur 3 geführt. Der Akkordwechsel ist so sehr deutlich zu hören.

Für einen ersten Schritt in Richtung Improvisation bieten sich Variationen dieser Patterns an:

a) rhythmisch
b) digital

Most of the material is maintained.

Dabei wird das vorhandene Material überwiegend beibehalten.

Example: Rhythmic variation

Beispiel: Rhythmische Variation:

Combinations other than root (1), third (3), fifth (5), and seventh (7) are also possible.

Statt der Reihenfolge Grundton (1), Terz (3), Quinte (5), Septime (7) sind auch andere Kombinationen möglich.

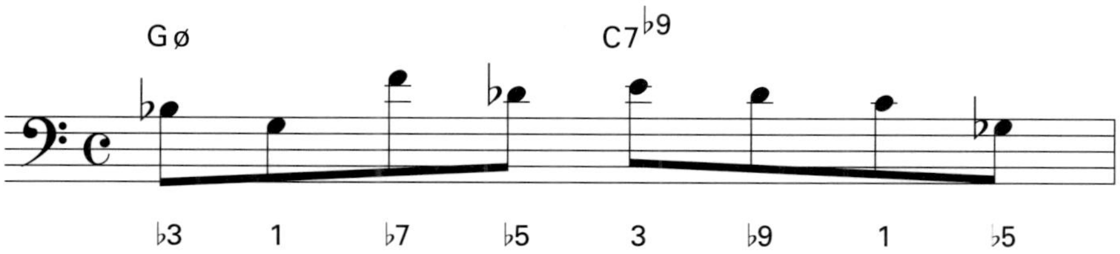

Invent more variations for yourself!

Erfinden Sie weitere Variationen!

Set B

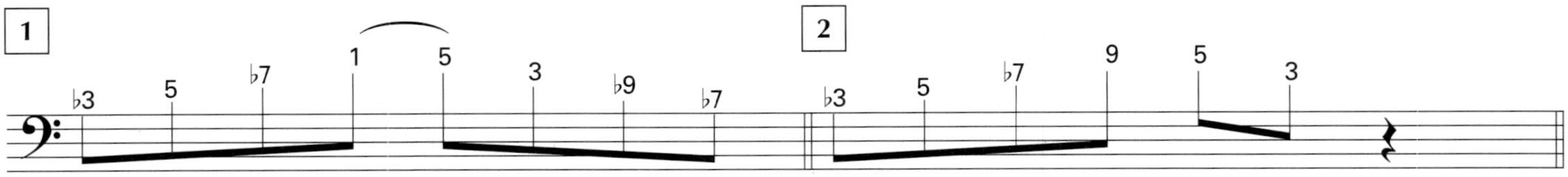

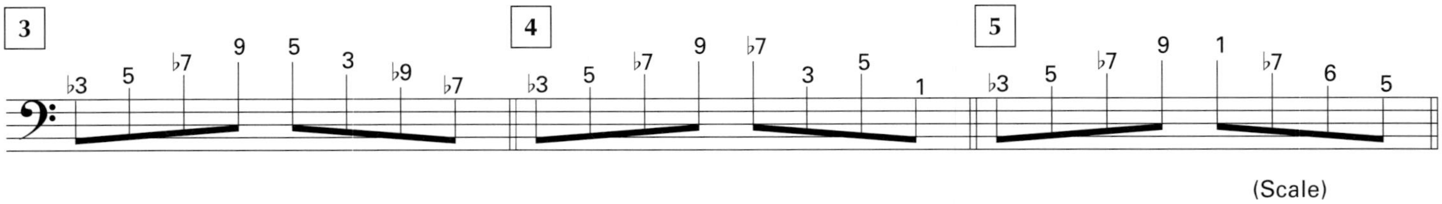

The following examples show the use of the digital patterns from "Set B" for different progressions. Transfer patterns from the examples that correctly fit the given chords in the "open" measures.

Es folgen Beispiele für die Übertragung der digitalen Patterns von Set B auf verschiedene Akkordverbindungen. Übertragen Sie die Patterns aus den verschiedenen Beispielen in die freigelassenen Takte, passend zu den Akkorden.

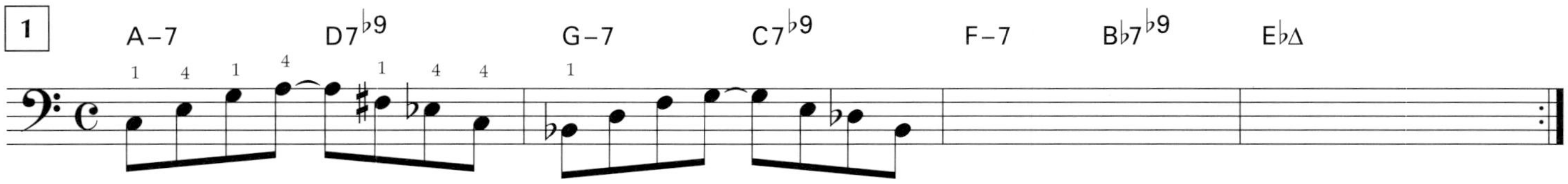

Variation on "2"

Variation von Nr. 2

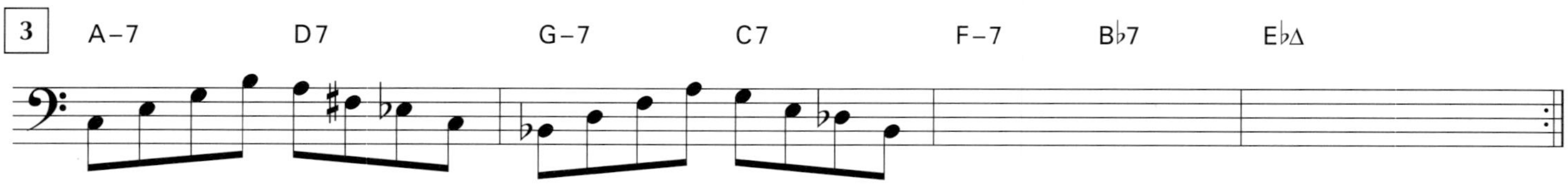

Set C

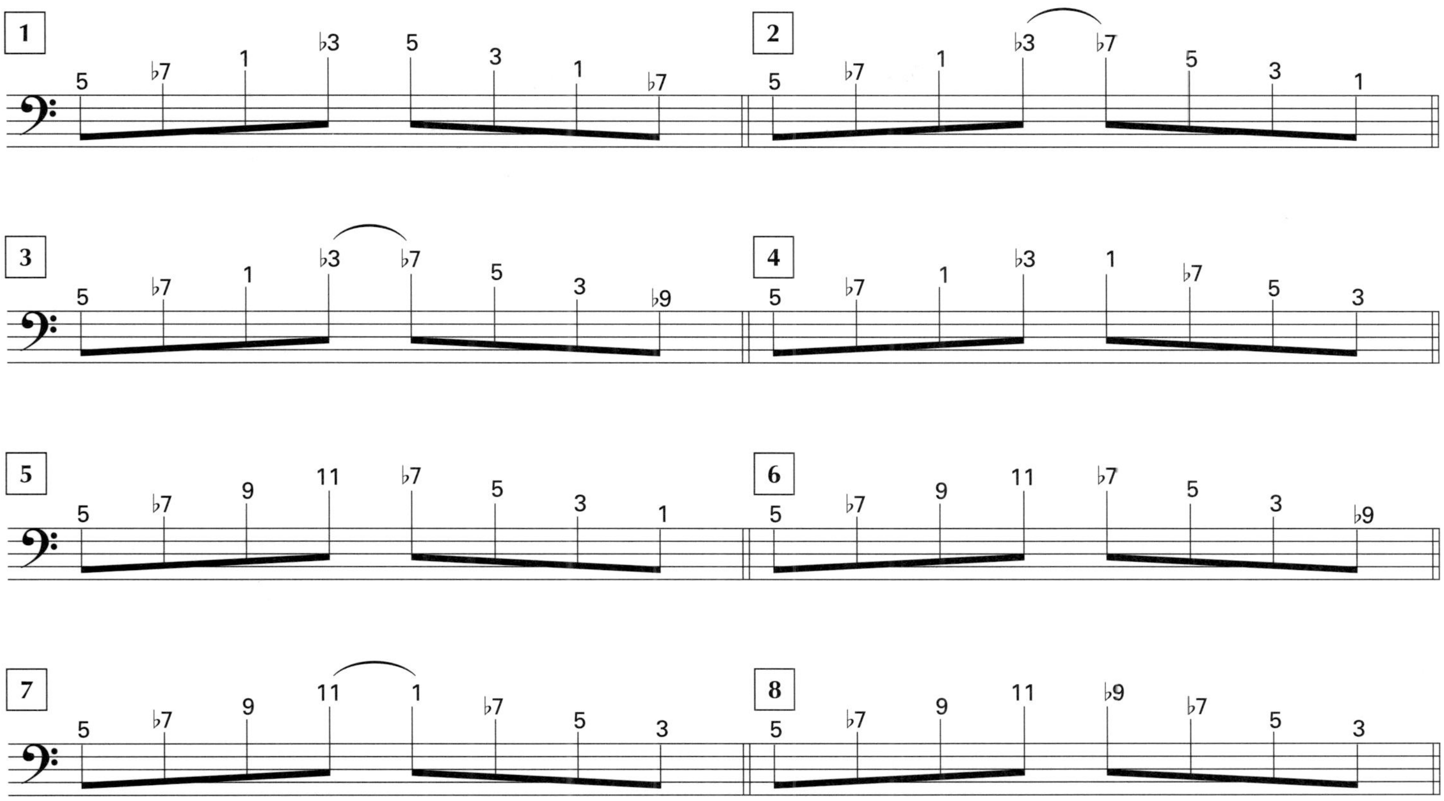

Examples: Set C

Beispiele für Set C

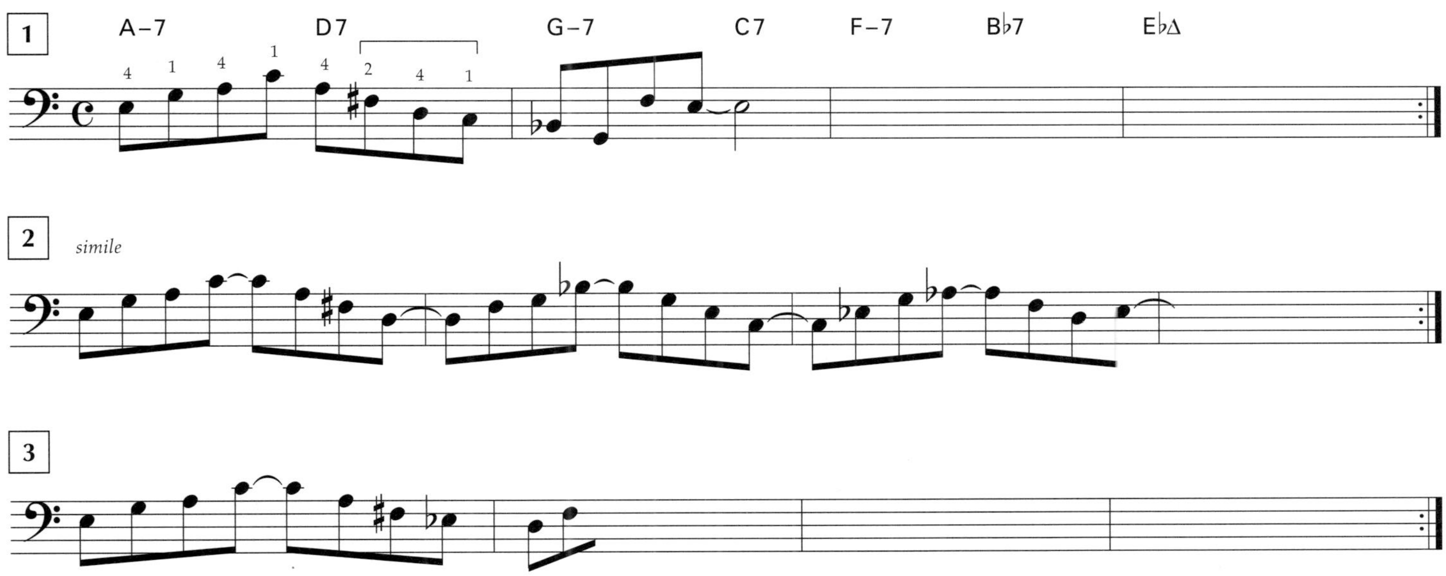

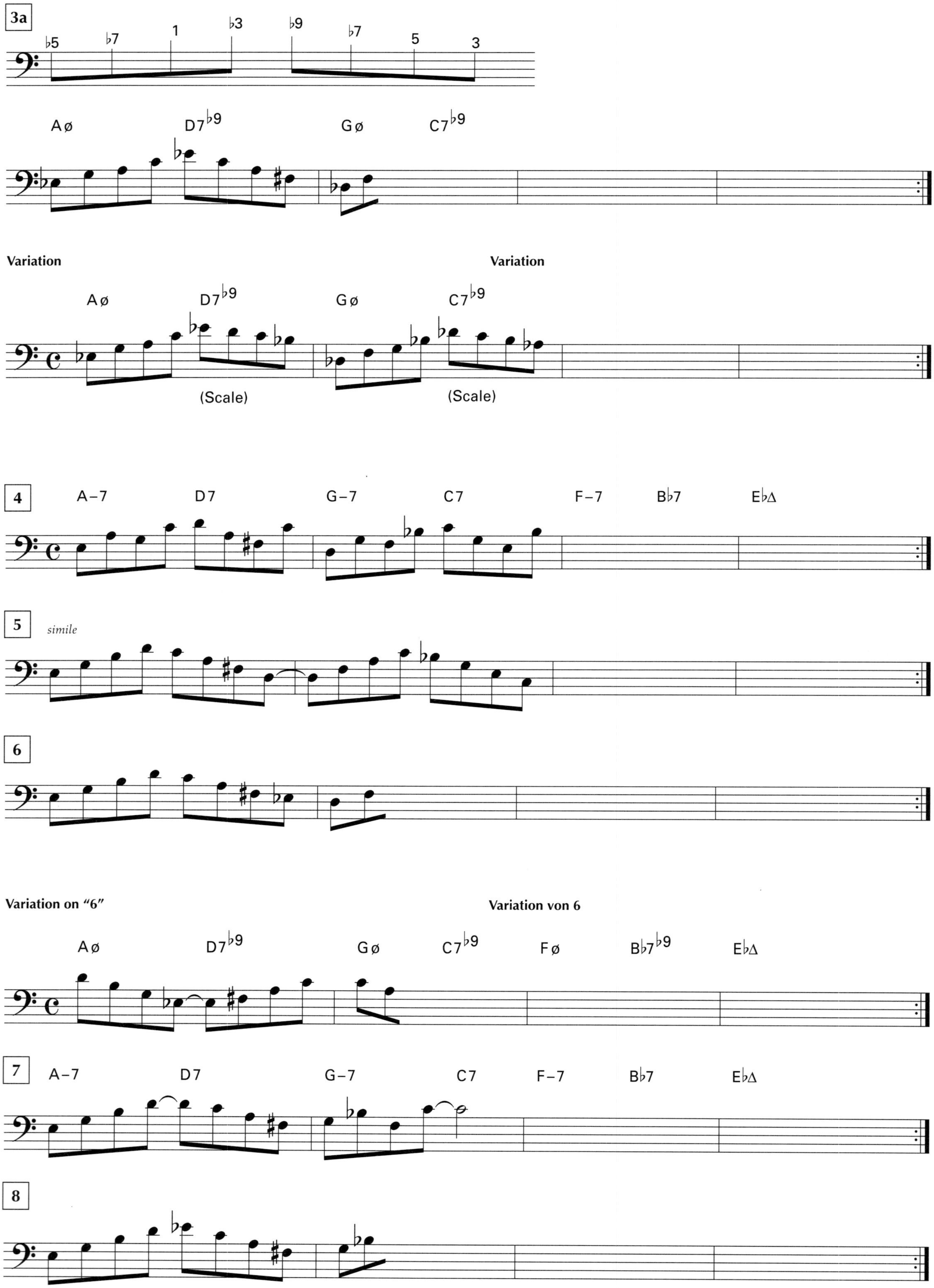
3a
♭5 ♭7 1 ♭3 ♭9 ♭7 5 3
Aø D7♭9 Gø C7♭9
Variation
Variation
Aø D7♭9 Gø C7♭9
(Scale)
(Scale)
4
A–7 D7 G–7 C7 F–7 B♭7 E♭Δ
5
simile
6
Variation on "6"
Variation von 6
Aø D7♭9 Gø C7♭9 Fø B♭7♭9 E♭Δ
7
A–7 D7 G–7 C7 F–7 B♭7 E♭Δ
8

Set D

1 2

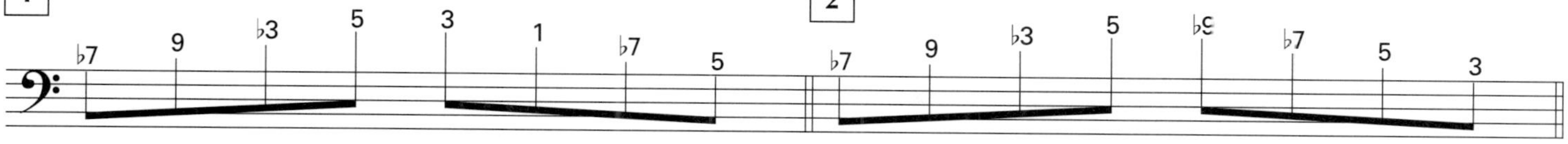

Examples: Set D **Beispiele für Set D**

1

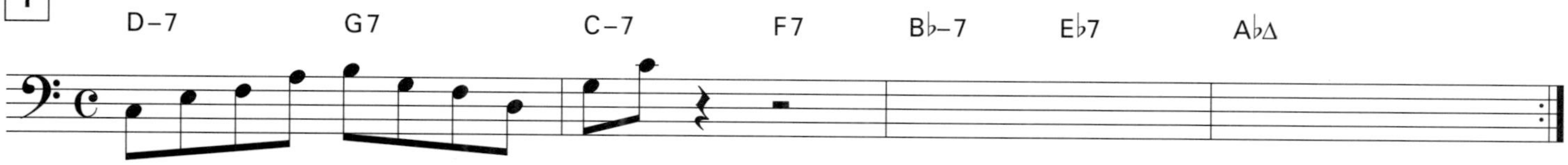

2

Set E

1 2 3

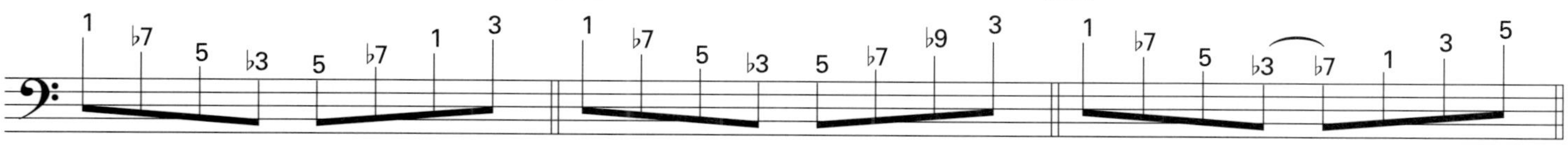

Examples: Set E **Beispiele für Set E**

1

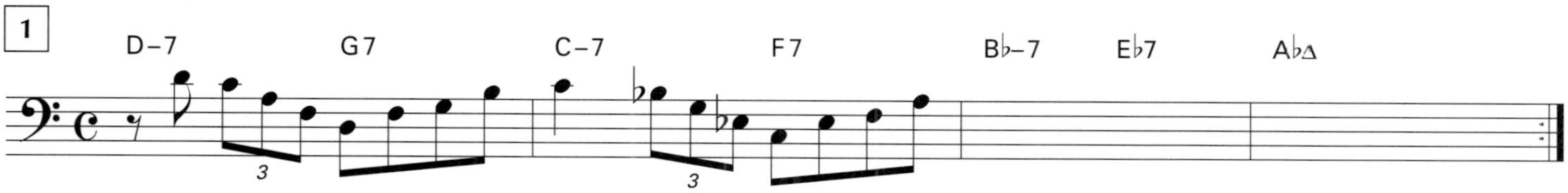

First Variation **1. Variation**

Second Variation **2. Variation**

Set E: Variation using ♭5

Set E: Variation mit ♭5

Set F

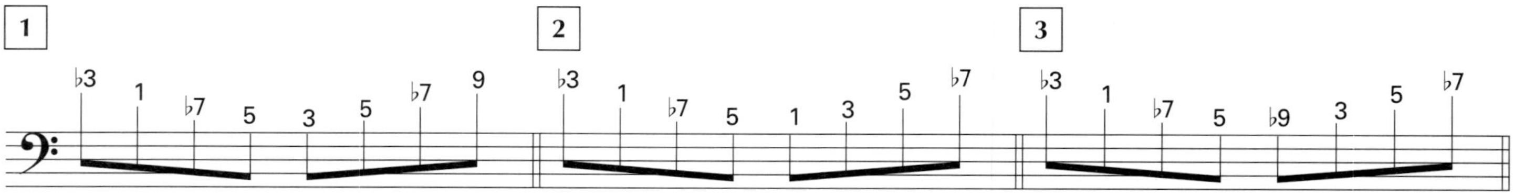

Examples: Set F

Beispiele: Set F

Variation

Variation

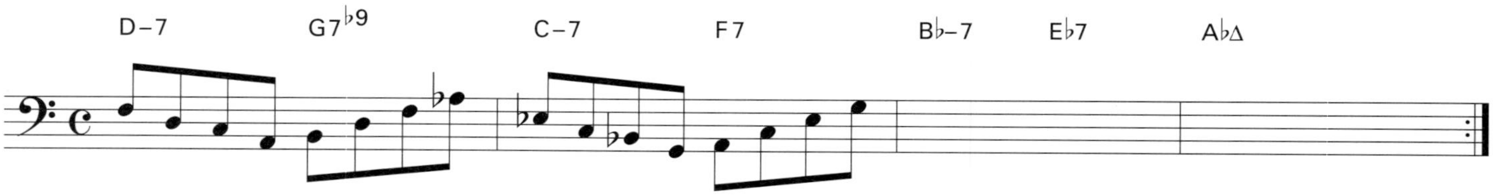

Variation using 9, ♭5

Variation mit 9, ♭5

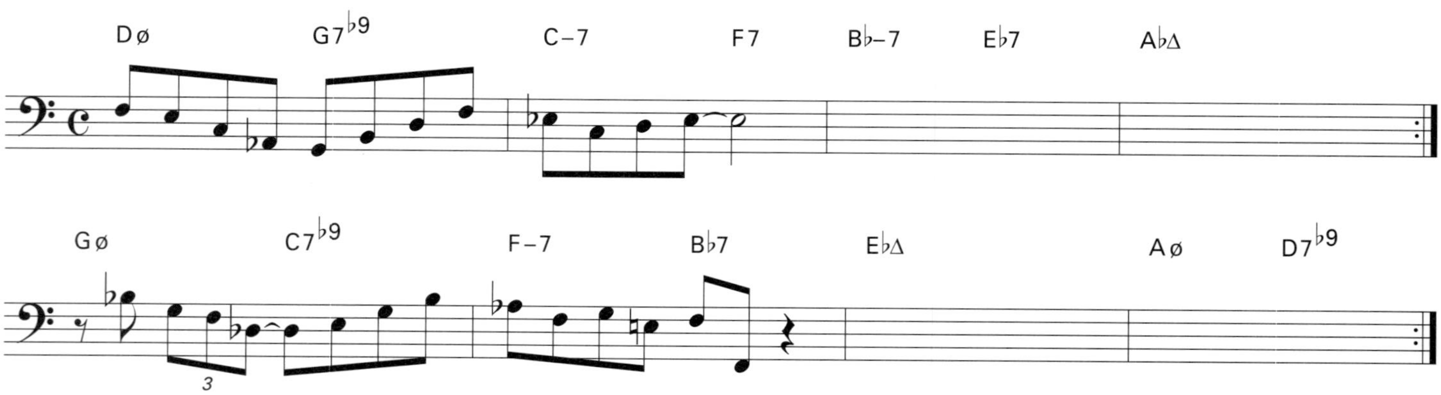

Set G

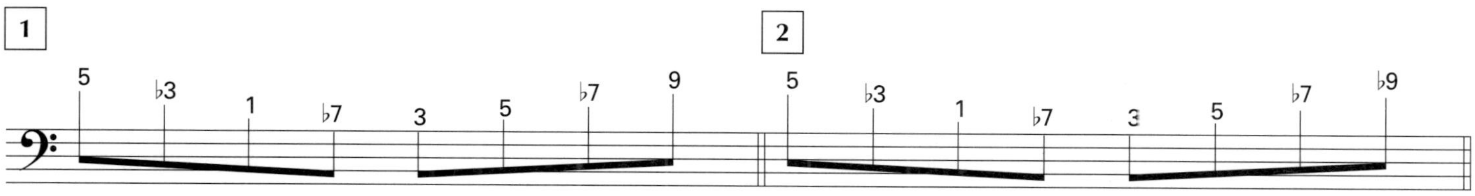

Example: Set G

Beispiel: Set G

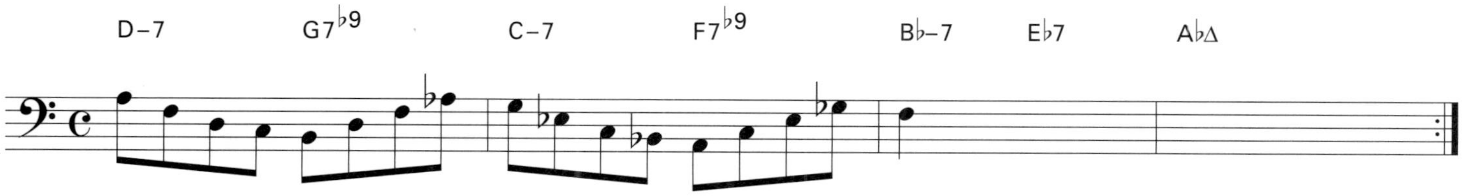

Set H

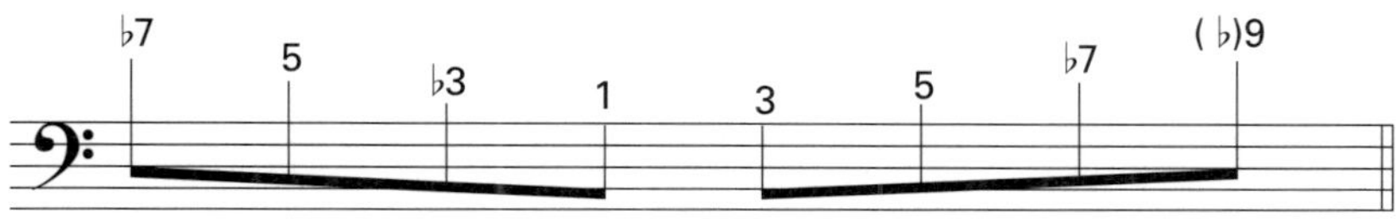

Example: Set H

Beispiel: Set H

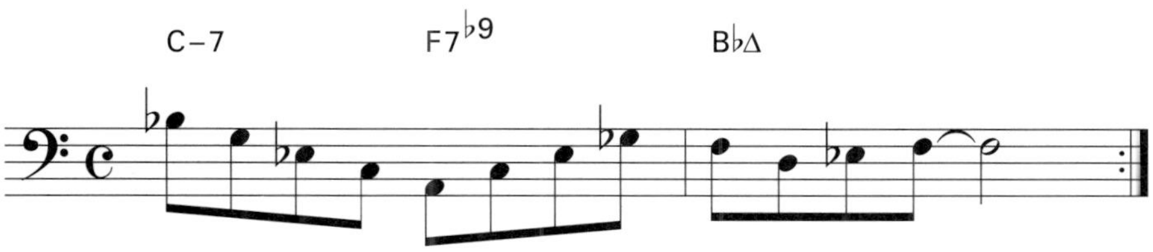

Variation

Variation

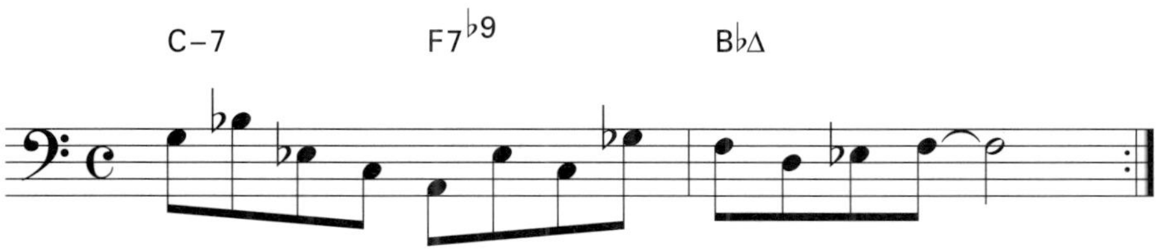

Sounds like bebop, right?

Klingt wie Bebop, oder?

Set I

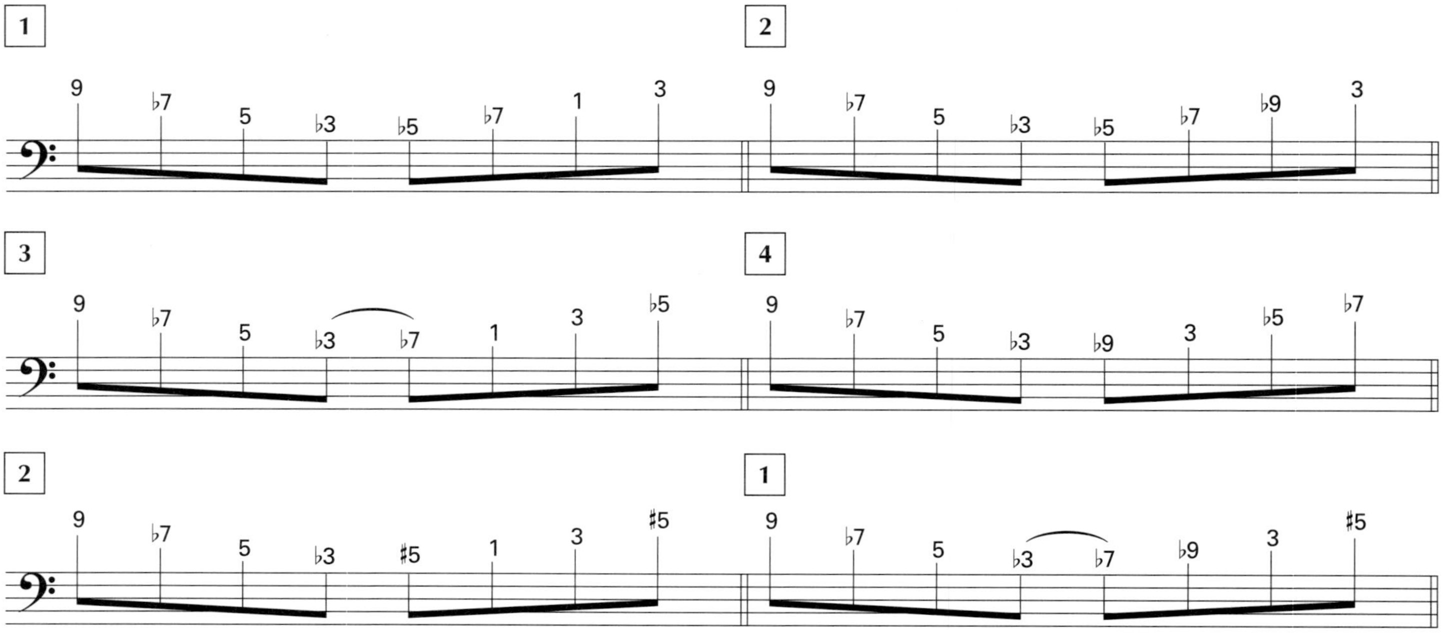

Examples: Set I **Beispiele: Set I**

Variation **Variation**

5

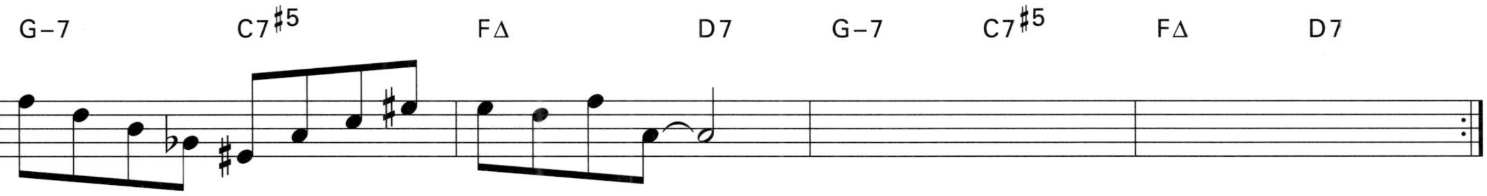

6

Set K

1 **2** **3**

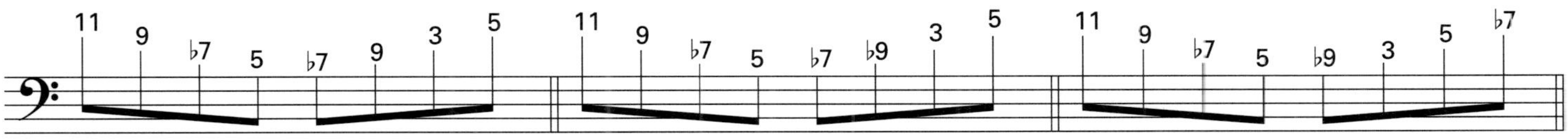

Examples: Set K **Beispiele: Set K**

1

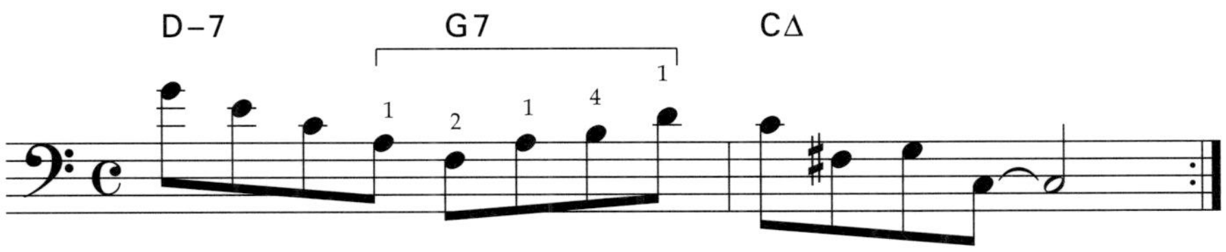

2

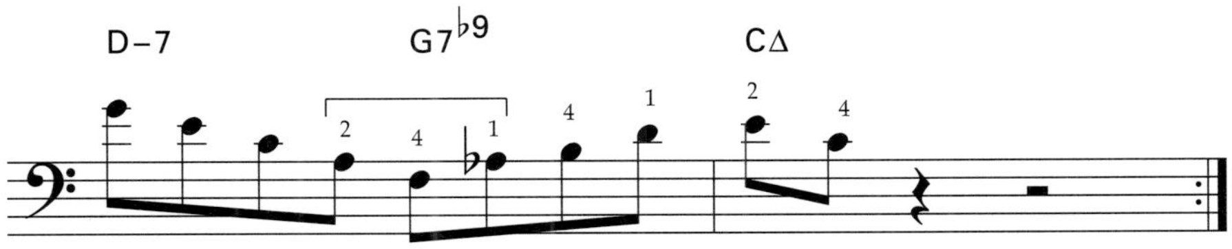

3

Variation **Variation**

The next step is to practice the digital patterns using progressions from different jazz compositions. The following tunes are especially good for this:

- *In Your Own Sweet Way*
- *Confirmation*
- *Joy Spring*
- *Good Bait*
- *When Lights Are Low*
- *Lullaby Of Birdland*
- *Autumn In New York*
- *Moment's Notice (!)*
- *The Masquerade Is Over*
- *The End Of A love Affair*
- *How High The Moon*
- *Whisper Not*

Find more songs that have progressions constructed of half-measure chords (two chords per measure).

Compose your own studies, exercises, and phrases on half-measure progressions. Perhaps some of the progressions from this material will appeal to you and will become a permanent part of your improvisation vocabulary.

Der nächste Schritt liegt nun darin, diese etüdenhaften Übungen der Digital-Patterns über die Harmoniefolgen von Jazzkompositionen zu üben. Folgende Stücke sind dazu sehr gut geeignet:

- *In Your Own Sweet Way*
- *Confirmation*
- *Joy Spring*
- *Good Bait*
- *When Lights Are Low*
- *Lullaby Of Birdland*
- *Autumn In New York*
- *Moment's Notice (!)*
- *The Masquerade Is Over*
- *The End Of A love Affair*
- *How High The Moon*
- *Whisper Not*

Suchen Sie in einem Songbook nach Stücken mit halbtaktigen Akkordverbindungen.

Komponieren Sie Ihre eigenen Etüden, Übungen und Phrasen. Vielleicht gefallen Ihnen einige aus der Fülle des Materials so gut, daß sie zum festen Bestandteil Ihrer Improvisationen werden.

13. Studies And Etudes

The next few pages provide some examples to illustrate the concepts discussed in this chapter.

13. Akkordstudien und Etüden

Auf den folgenden fünf Seiten habe ich einige Studien und Etüden für Sie zusammengestellt, die die bisher besprochenen Konzepte in einen musikalischen Zusammenhang stellen.

Study: *Sunny*

Studie über *Sunny*

even eighths

Study: *Footprints*

Studie über *Footprints*

Study: *I Hear A Rhapsody*

Studie über *I Hear A Rhapsody*

Study: *Solar*

Studie über *Solar*

Study: *Confirmation*

Studie über *Confirmation*

14. Upper Structures

"Upper structures" refers to the triad that is formed by the upper extension of the chord. By using the many alterations of the V7 chord we can divide the chord into two parts, upper and lower. The lower part will denote the type and function of the chord, and the upper part will form triads which for the bass player are rather simple to use for improvisation.

Here is an example G7, 9,♯11,13 notated for piano

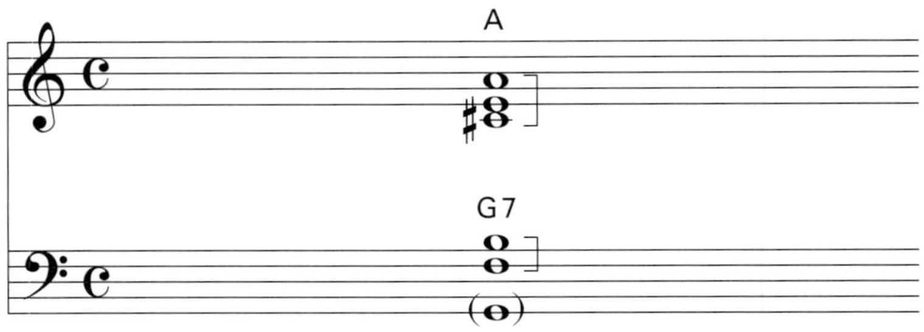

The upper part of the chord forms an A major triad built on the II of the root of the chord. (G)

G7 with the upper structure A is often notated as...

$$\frac{A}{G7}$$

instead of the extensive chord symbol G7,9,♯11,13.

Further major triad possibilities:

$\frac{\flat III}{V7}$	e.g.	$\frac{B\flat}{G7}$	=	G7,♯9
$\frac{\flat V}{V7}$	e.g.	$\frac{G\flat}{C7}$	=	C7,♭9,♯11
$\frac{\flat VI}{V7}$	e.g.	$\frac{A\flat}{C7}$	=	C7alt
$\frac{VI}{V7}$	e.g.	$\frac{B}{D7}$	=	D7,♭9

Upper structure minor chords are also possible.

$\frac{I-}{V7}$	e.g.	$\frac{C-}{C7}$	=	C7,♯9
$\frac{\flat II-}{V7}$	e.g.	$\frac{G\flat-}{F7}$	=	F7,♭9,♭13
$\frac{\flat III-}{V7}$	e.g.	$\frac{C-}{A7}$	=	A7,♯9,♯11
$\frac{\sharp IV-}{V7}$	e.g.	$\frac{F\sharp-}{C7}$	=	C7,♭9,♯11

Also play the following progressions on piano to become familiar with the sound.

14. "Upper Structures"

Mit dem Begriff "Upper Structure" (dt. Oberstruktur (Dreiklänge)) sind Akkorderweiterungen in den "oberen Etagen" eines Akkordes gemeint. Bei Dominantseptakkorden mit vielen Alterationen lassen sich die Akkorde in einen unteren und in einen oberen Bereich einteilen. Unten werden die Töne notiert, die Geschlecht und Funktion anzeigen, wie z.B. Terz und Septime, im oberen Bereich Dreiklänge. Und die sind bei der Improvisation auf dem Baß verhältnismäßig einfach zu spielen.

Zuerst das Notationsbeispiel von G7, 9,♯11,13 auf dem Piano:

Die obere Fraktion hat die Struktur eines Dur Dreiklangs auf der II. Stufe, bezogen auf den Grundton des Akkordes, – hier ein A Dur Dreiklang.

G7 mit Upper Structure A, notiert

$$\frac{A}{G7}$$

wäre eine andere Benennung für das Akkordsymbol G7,9,♯11,13.

Weitere Durdreiklänge sind möglich:

$\frac{\flat III}{V7}$	z.B.	$\frac{B\flat}{G7}$	=	G7,♯9
$\frac{\flat V}{V7}$	z.B.	$\frac{G\flat}{C7}$	=	C7,♭9,♯11
$\frac{\flat VI}{V7}$	z.B.	$\frac{A\flat}{C7}$	=	C7 alt
$\frac{VI}{V7}$	z.B.	$\frac{B}{D7}$	=	D7,♭9

Auch Upper Structure Molldreiklänge sind möglich:

$\frac{I-}{V7}$	z.B.	$\frac{C-}{C7}$	=	C7,♯9
$\frac{\flat II-}{V7}$	z.B.	$\frac{G\flat-}{F7}$	=	F7,♭9,♭13
$\frac{\flat III-}{V7}$	z.B.	$\frac{C-}{A7}$	=	A7,♯9,♯11
$\frac{\sharp IV-}{V7}$	z.B.	$\frac{F\sharp-}{C7}$	=	C7,♭9,♯11

Spielen Sie diese und die folgenden Akkordverbindungen auch auf einem Klavier (Keyboard), um sich an den Klang zu gewöhnen.

Here are some examples of upper structures used in the II V progression.

Hier einige Beispiele von "upper structures" bei der Improvisation über II V Verbindungen:

a
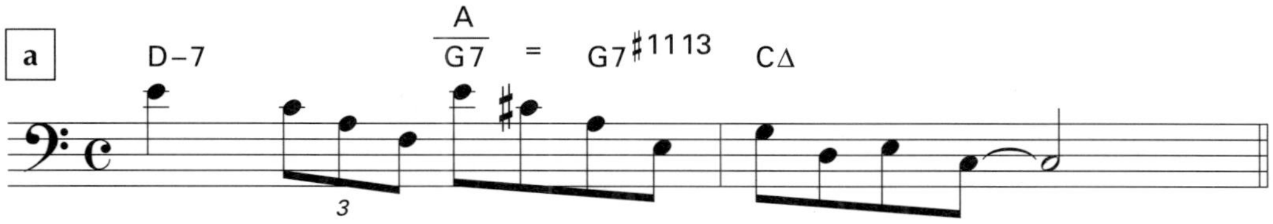

b
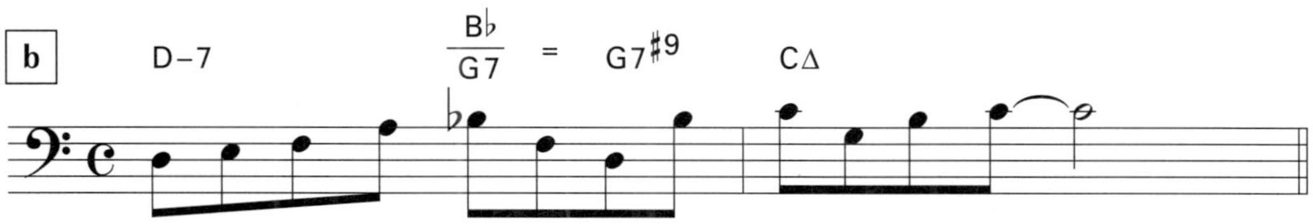

c
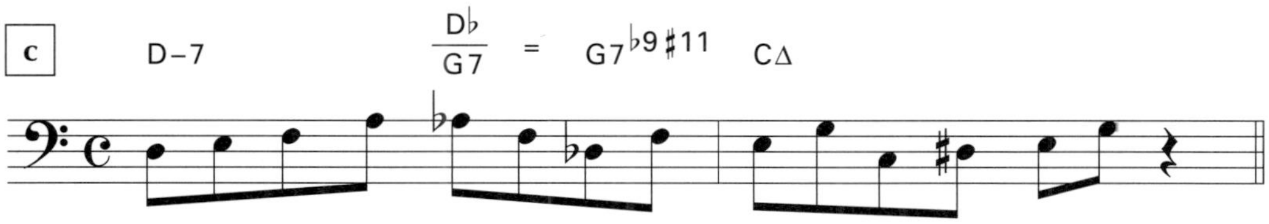

d
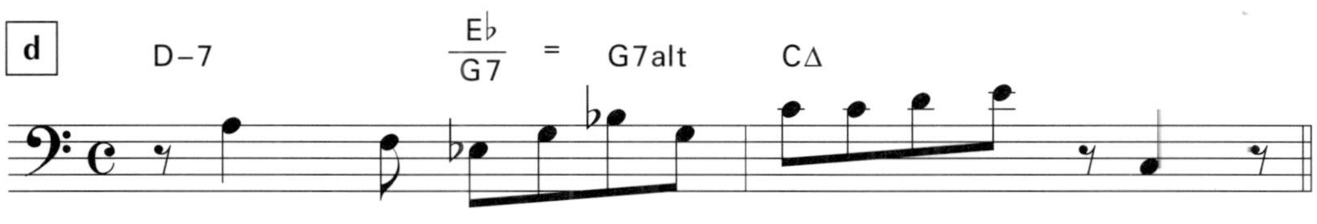

e
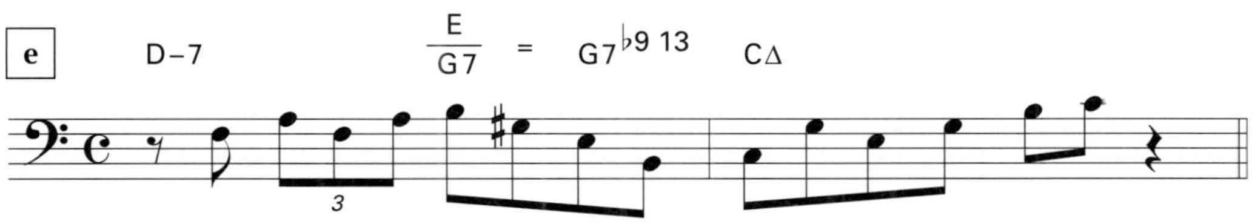

f
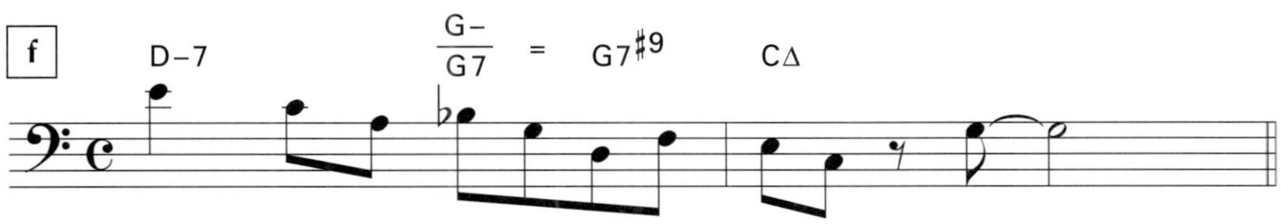

g
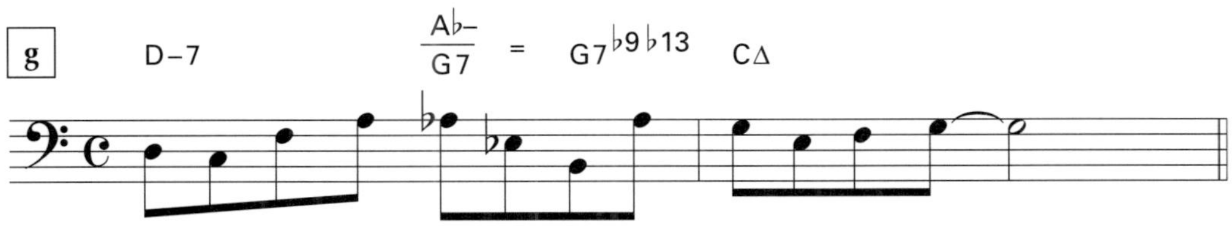

h

i

VII PHRASING AND ARTICULATION

The exact notation of complex music such as jazz, will always be a problem. It is common practice in jazz notation to all but ignore phrasing and articulation. The use of all possible markings would surely overload the notation with so much information that the music would be very difficult to read.

"Phrasing" is understood as the rhythmic, and "articulation" as the melodic expression of the written notation.

VII PHRASIERUNG UND ARTIKULATION

Notation von lebendiger Musik, wie dem Jazz, wird immer problematisch sein. Phrasierung und Artikulation werden bei der herkömmlichen Jazz-Notation kaum berücksichtigt, sie würden sicherlich auch das Notenbild mit Information überladen und damit das Notenlesen erschweren.

Unter "Phrasierung" ist die rhythmische, unter "Artikulation" die melodische Gestaltung der Noten zu verstehen.

1. Phrasing

Jazz and rock music each follow their own rules regarding the way consecutive eighth and sixteenth notes are performed. We distinguish between the even "straight-eight" (binary) phrasing in rock music and the uneven "swing" (ternary) phrasing in jazz.

- Straight eighth-notes are exactly notated and played even.
- Swing eighth-notes are played so that the eighth notes on the downbeats are played as written. The off-beat eighth-notes are played as if they were the third eighth of a triplet.

1. Phrasierung

Für das Spielen von Jazz- und Rockmusik haben sich eigene Gesetzmäßigkeiten herausgebildet, besonders bei Phrasen, die aus mehreren aufeinanderfolgenden Achteln oder Sechzehnteln bestehen. Man unterscheidet zwischen "binärer" Phrasierung – vor allem im Rock und lateinamerikanischer Musik – und "ternärer" Phrasierung im Jazz.

- Binäre Achtel (Sechzehntel) werden gleichmäßig gespielt, also genau wie notiert.
- Ternäre Achtel werden wie folgt ausgeführt:
  die auf das Metrum fallenden Achtel werden so gespielt, wie sie notiert sind;
  die zwischen das Metrum fallenden Achtel werden als dritte Achteltriole gespielt.

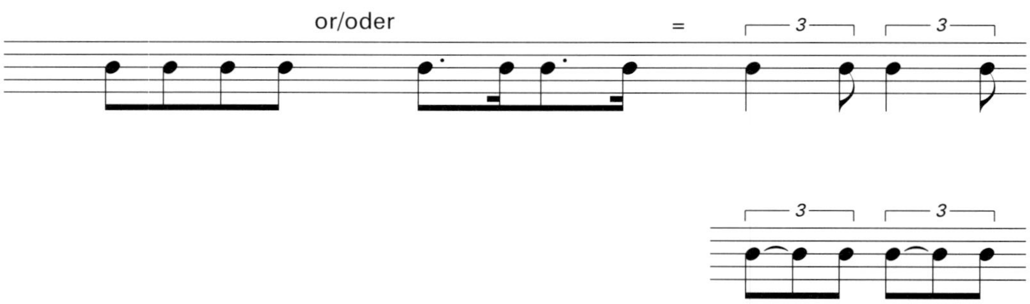

Tempo plays a large role in phrasing. As the tempo increases, the swing eighth-note phrasing becomes ever closer to the straight eighth-note phrasing.

Dabei spielt das Tempo allerdings eine große Rolle. Bei langsamen Tempi trifft das oben Gesagte voll zu, bei mittleren bis schnellen Tempi gleicht sich die ternäre Phrasierung immer mehr der binären an.

2. Articulation

Although two notes that may look alike on paper can be interpreted quite differently, there are certain articulations that remain the same for both swing and straight phrasings.

- = long, equivalent to the syllable "doo".
∧ = short, equivalent to the syllable "dot".
> = the note is accented and held full value.

Sing the following exercises first with the swing phrasing, then straight as notated.

Phrase using the syllables "doo" and "dot".

Exercises:

2. Artikulation

Obwohl einzelne Notenwerte auf dem Papier völlig gleich aussehen, werden sie trotzdem unterschiedlich gespielt. Eine bestimmte Art der Artikulation ist allgemein üblich, unabhängig davon, ob ternär oder binär phrasiert wird.

Die dabei benutzten Symbole bedeuten:

- = lang, entsprechend der gesungenen Silbe "duh".
∧ = kurz, entsprechend der gesungenen Silbe "dot".
> = diese Note erhält einen Akzent durch stärkere Betonung, wird aber genau entsprechend ihrem Notenwert ausgehalten.

Singen Sie die folgenden Übungen zuerst mit ternärer, dann mit binärer Phrasierung mit den Silben "duh" und "dot". Spielen Sie sie mit derselben Artikulation erst ternär, dann binär phrasiert.

Übungen:

Exercise: slowly

Übung: langsames Tempo

Exercise: medium to fast

Übung: mittleres bis schnelles Tempo

First sing the exercises with the "doo-dot" articulation and then play them on your instrument.

Singen Sie diese Übungen zuerst mit der "duh-dot"-Artikulation und spielen Sie sie dann erst auf Ihrem Instrument.

Exercise:

Übung:

As already stated, in medium up and up-tempos the phrasing becomes more even, but the last eighth note of a phrase is very often played as if it were the third note of a triplet.

Bei ternärer Phrasierung wird das letzte Achtel einer Phrase, wenn es zwischen das Metrum auf "und" fällt (offbeat), oft sehr spät als dritte Achteltriole gespielt – auch bei mittleren bis schnellen Tempi.

Examples:

Beispiele:

(s. page/Seite 28)

This also applies to the following tied eighth-notes and the short articulated off-beat quarter-notes.

Examples:

Good exercises for articulation are bebop tunes like *Straight, No Chaser, Donna Lee,* and *Ornithology.*

Das gilt auch für an die folgende Note angebundene Achtel sowie für kurz artikulierte Viertelnoten auf Offbeats.

Beispiele:

Spielen Sie Bebop Themen wie *Straight, No Chaser, Donna Lee, Ornithology* und andere auf dem Baß. Das sind gute Übungen für die Artikulation.

3. Slurs

Melodies constructed from rows of eighth-notes sound much livelier whenever the second eighth-note of one beat is slurred to the first eighth-note of the following beat. On the bass this is possible only with notes that form the interval of a 2nd.

The note that falls on the beat is plucked with the right hand and the second eighth-note of the beat is sounded two different by "hammering" with the left hand ascending, and by "pulling off" descending. (See pages 28/29)

3. Bindungen

Melodien, die aus aufeinanderfolgenden Achteln bestehen, klingen viel lebendiger, wenn man die zwischen das Metrum fallenden Achtel an die auf das Metrum fallenden Achtel anbindet. Das ist auf dem Kontrabaß allerdings nur bei Noten, die im Intervall einer Sekunde nebeneinanderliegen, möglich.

Die auf "und" fallenden Töne werden mit der rechten Hand gezupft, die auf das Metrum fallenden Achtel werden aufwärts durch "hämmern" der linken Hand zum Klingen gebracht, abwärts durch "abziehen". (Siehe S. 28/29)

Example: *Ornithology* (C. Parker)

Beispiel: *Ornithology* (C. Parker)

Example: *Polka Dots And Moonbeam* (J. van Heusen), medium tempo

Beispiel: *Polka Dots And Moonbeam* (J. van Heusen), mittelschnelles Tempo

"Puzzle"

VIII SCALES

1. General

In the following chapter some of the scales for building phrases, patterns and melodies in jazz improvisation are introduced. A well grounded study of this material is a prerequisite for a good, solid improvisation. From all the numerous scales that exist, I have addressed only those that are especially important for the bassist. These are the modes, some of the minors, pentatonic, eight-note, whole-tone, bebop, and blues scales.

In learning the scales, one must observe their individual characteristics, such as the placement of the whole-steps and half-steps, as well as the relationships that the tones have to one another.

VIII SKALEN

1. Allgemeines

Als Material für die Improvisation im Jazz werden sehr häufig Skalen und daraus gebildete Phrasen, Motive und Melodien verwendet. Eine eingehende Beschäftigung mit diesem Thema ist daher eine der Voraussetzungen für eine gute, fundierte Improvisation. Aus einer Vielzahl von Skalen habe ich die herausgegriffen, die ich für einen Bassisten als besonders wichtig ansehe: die Kirchentonleitern, die verschiedenen Mollskalen, einige pentatonische Skalen, Achtton- und Ganztonskalen, die Bebop-Skalen und die Blues-Skalen.

Beim Erlernen und Erkennen von Skalen muß man besonders auf deren typische Merkmale achten: wie ist das Verhältnis der Tonschritte untereinander, wo liegen die Ganztonschritte, wo liegen die Halbtonschritte?

2. The Church Scales / Modes

The so called "Church Scales" or "Modes" are constructed by beginning a new scale on each of the different steps of a major scale. In the following examples all the scales are from F major, but transposition to any key is possible. ("A Mixolydian" for instance, is a scale that begins with the note "A" but has the key signature of "D major")

2. Die Kirchentonleitern / Modi

Die sog. Kirchentonleitern erhält man dadurch, daß man Tonleitern jeweils auf den verschiedenen Stufen einer Durtonleiter beginnt. Im folgenden Beispiel sind alle Skalen auf F Dur bezogen – selbstverständlich ist das auch mit allen anderen möglich. "A Mixolydisch" z.B. ist eine Skala, die mit dem Ton "A" beginnt, aber die Vorzeichen von D Dur besitzt.

Ionian — **1. Stufe: Ionisch**

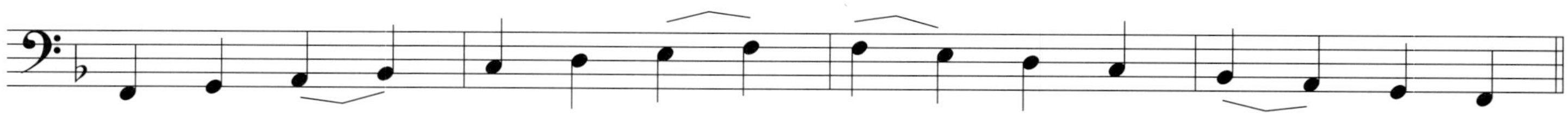

Dorian — **2. Stufe: Dorisch**

Phrygian — **3. Stufe: Phrygisch**

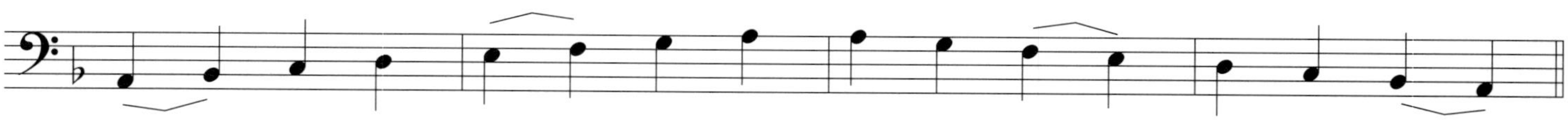

Lydian — **4. Stufe: Lydisch**

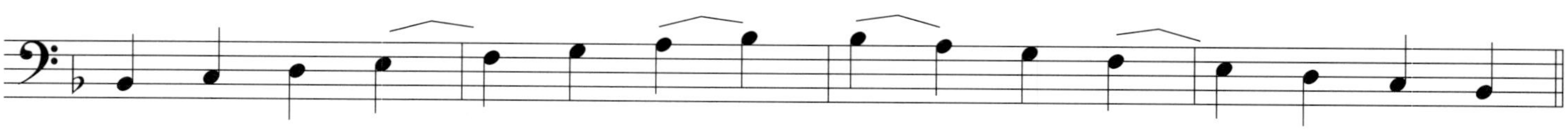

Mixolydian

5. Stufe: Mixolydisch

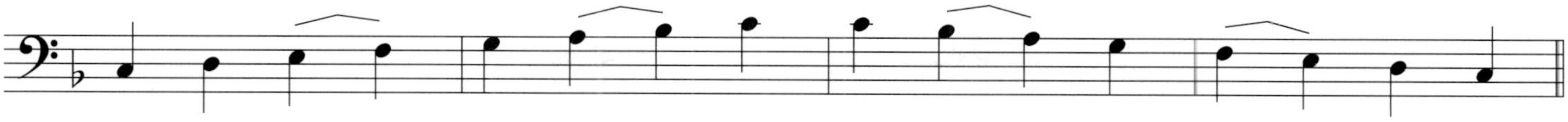

Aeolian

6. Stufe: Äolisch

Locrian

7. Stufe: Lokrisch

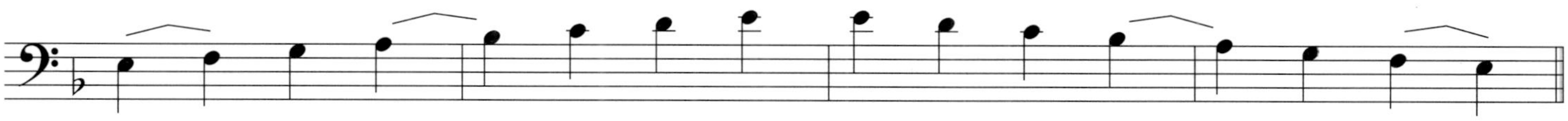

Each of the scales shown above is built from two tonal groups called "Tetrachords" which one can play with a typical fingering pattern. (see page 152.) Observe the half-tone steps marked by ⌒.

Jede der vorstehenden Skalen besteht aus zwei Viertongruppen, auch Tetrachorde genannt, die man jeweils mit einem typischen Fingersatz spielen kann. (vgl. auch Seite S. 152). Beachten Sie die Kennzeichnung der Halbtonschritte.

3. Minor Scales

The minor scales are also a source for constructing new scales in the same way as we did with the major scales. Especially interesting are the scales constructed from the different steps of the melodic minor.

Practice all minor scales ascending and descending from each individual scale step. (See page 174ff)

3. Molltonleitern

Auch aus den Molltonleitern lassen sich stufenweise neue Skalen entwickeln, wie ich es schon für die Durtonleiter vorgeführt habe. Besonders interessant sind Skalen, die aus der melodischen Molltonleiter abgeleitet sind.

Üben Sie also auch die Molltonleitern von jeder Stufe auf- und abwärts. (Siehe auch Seite 174ff.)

Pure

Rein

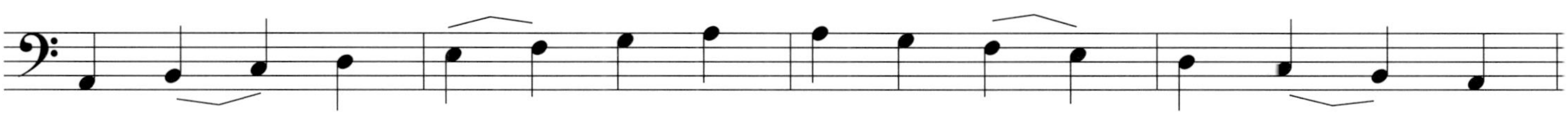

Harmonic

Harmonisch

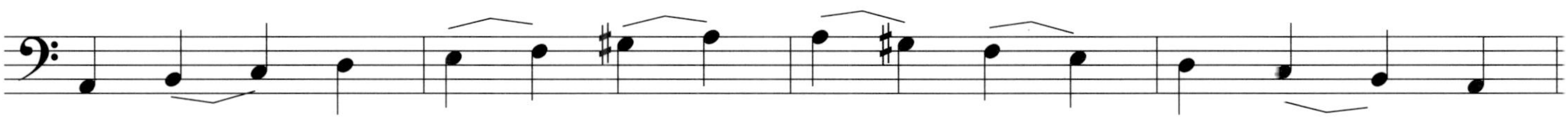

Melodic (In jazz it is the same ascending and descending)

Melodisch (in der Jazzmusik auf- und abwärts gleich)

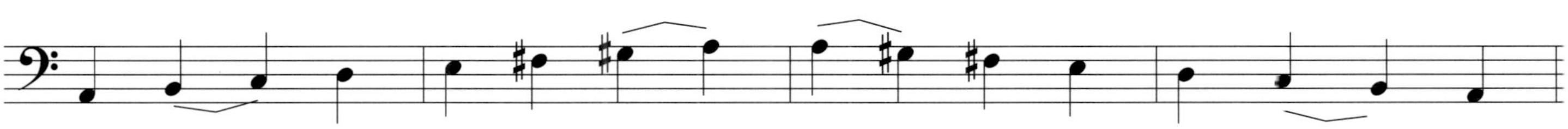

4. Typical Fingerings

4. Typische Fingersätze

For some people, memorizing the left-hand fingerings can be a real help in learning the scales. A good fingering for a *major scale* using two strings is:

1 4, 2 4, 1 4, 2 4

Manche Leute lernen Skalen besser, wenn sie sich die typischen Bewegungsabläufe der linken Hand, d.h. die Fingersätze einprägen. Ein guter Fingersatz für eine *Durtonleiter* ist (auf zwei Saiten verteilt):

1 4, 2 4, 1 4, 2 4

Example: F major

Beispiel: F Dur

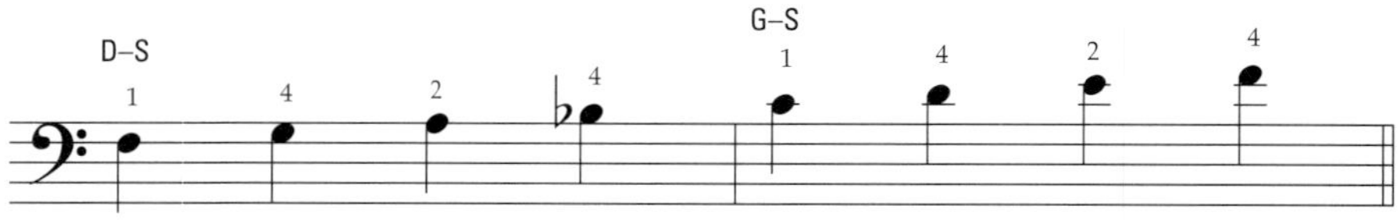

PLEASE NOTE:
Major and minor scales as well as their derived scales consist of two disjunct tetrachords (succession of four tones).

This fingering is also easy to play in other positions for other major scales. Transpose them to:

E, E♭, G♭, G, A♭ major, beginning on the D string
B♭, B, C, D♭, D major, beginning on the A string

ANMERKUNG:
Alle Dur- und Mollskalen sowie die daraus abgeleiteten Modi bestehen aus zwei Viertongruppen (Tetrachorde).

Dieser Fingersatz läßt sich leicht in andere Lagen, und damit in andere Tonarten, übertragen z.B. nach:

E, E♭, G♭, G, A♭ Dur, beginnend auf der D-Saite
B♭, B, C, D♭, D Dur, beginnend auf der A-Seite

Example: C major using the same fingering.

Beispiel: C Dur (mit dem gleichen Griff-Pattern)

The fingering for the A major scale beginning on the D string would be:

1 4, 2 4, 1 4, 2 3.

With this you can now use all 12 of the *major scales*.

The *Mixolydian scale* has the following fingering:

1 4, 2 4, cross strings, 1 4, 1 4.

Bei A Dur, beginnend auf der D-Saite, ist der Fingersatz

1 4, 2 4, 1 4, 2 3.

Damit stehen Ihnen alle 12 *Durtonleitern* zur Verfügung.

Die *mixolydische Tonleiter* hat das Griff-Pattern:

1 4, 2 4, Saitenwechsel, 1 4, 1 4.

Example: F Mixolydian

Beispiel: F mixolydisch

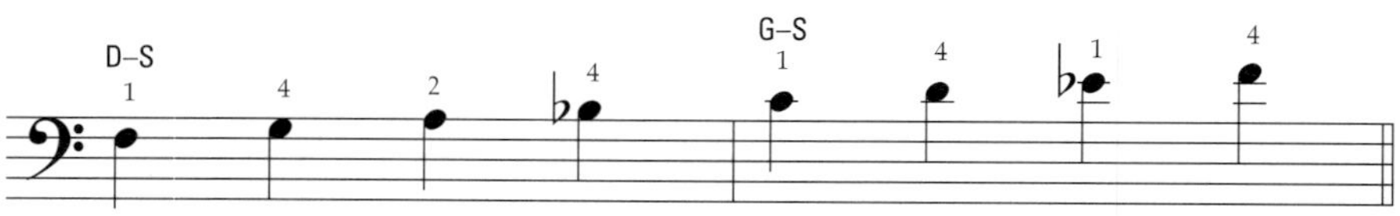

For the *Phrygian scale* one uses the following pattern.

1 2, 1 4, cross strings, 1 2, 1 4.

You may use "2 4" instead of "1 2"

Die *phrygische Tonleiter* kann man mit dem Griff-Pattern

1 2, 1 4, Saitenwechsel, 1 2, 1 4

spielen. Statt jeweils "1 2" ist auch "2 4" möglich.

Example: E Phrygian

Beispiel: E phrygisch

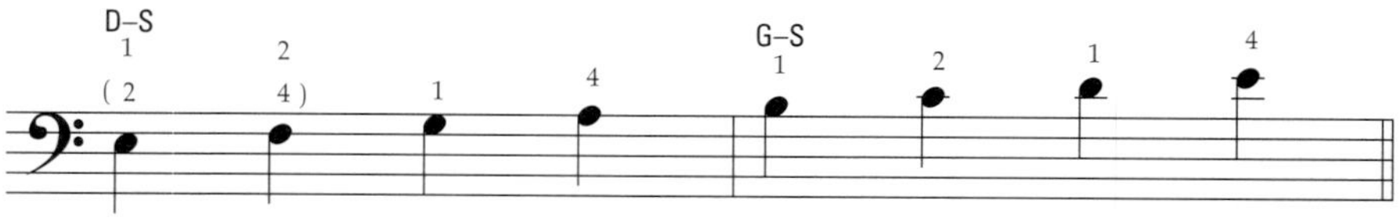

More characteristic fingerings:
Melodic minor: 1 4, 1 4, 1 4, 2 4.

Weitere typische Fingersätze:
Melodisch Moll: 1 4, 1 4, 1 4, 2 4.

Example: F melodic minor

Beispiel: F melodisch Moll

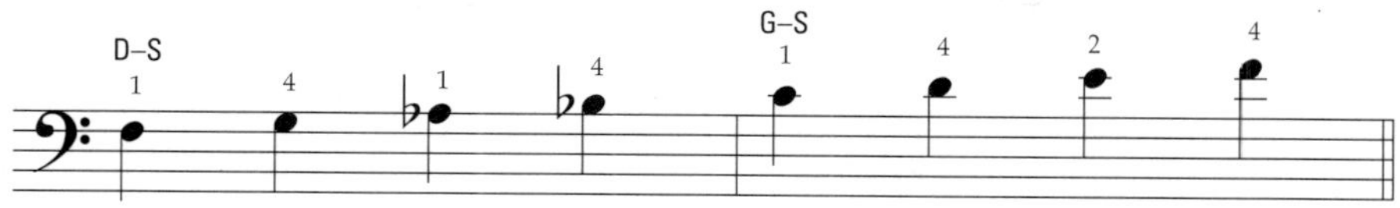

Dorian: 1 4, 1 4, 1 4, 1 4.

Dorisch Moll: 1 4, 1 4, 1 4, 1 4.

Example: E♭ Dorian:

Beispiel: E♭ dorisch:

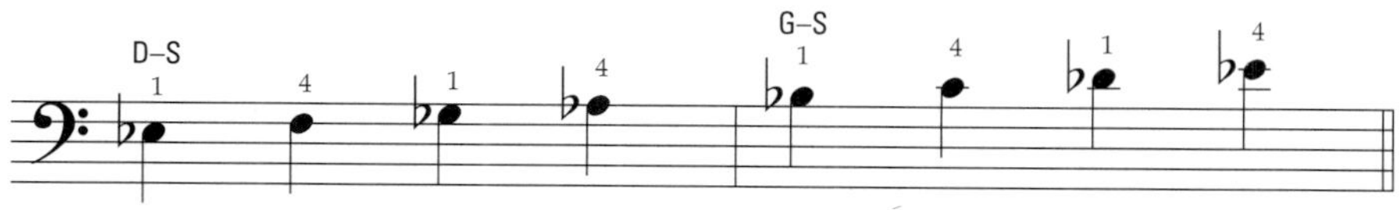

Following these principles, notate your own fingerings for other scales.

Notieren Sie selbst nach diesem Prinzip Fingersätze für eine Reihe von anderen Skalen.

5. Rhythm Patterns For Scales

Scales can be transferred to rhythm patterns. This has two advantages. First you should be motivated to invent, practice, and memorize your own rhythm patterns for all possible scales, and the pages of this book will not be full of unnecessary material. Think of these exercises as being the beginning steps toward improvisation.

5. Rhythmus-Patterns für Skalen

Rhythmische Patterns können mit Skalen aufgefüllt werden. Das hat zwei entscheidende Vorteile: Zum einen werden die Seiten dieses Buches nicht unnötig mit Material gefüllt, zum zweiten sollen Sie angeregt werden, alle möglichen Skalen über verschiedene Rhythmus-Patterns selbständig und auswendig zu spielen. Betrachten Sie die Übungen als erste Schritte in Richtung Improvisation.

Examples:

Beispiele:

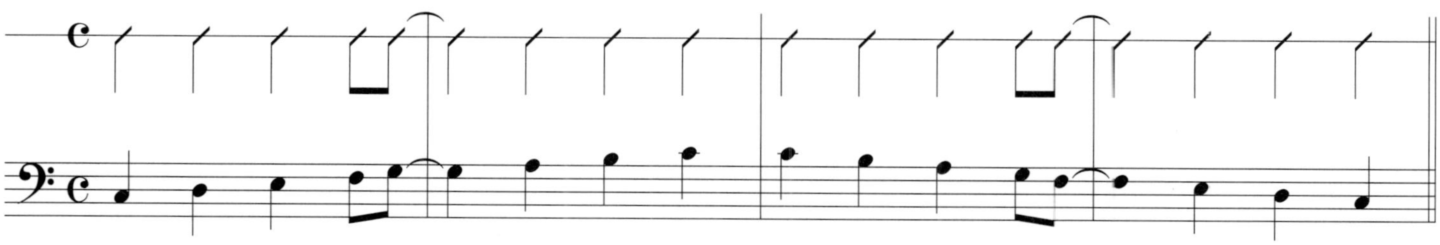

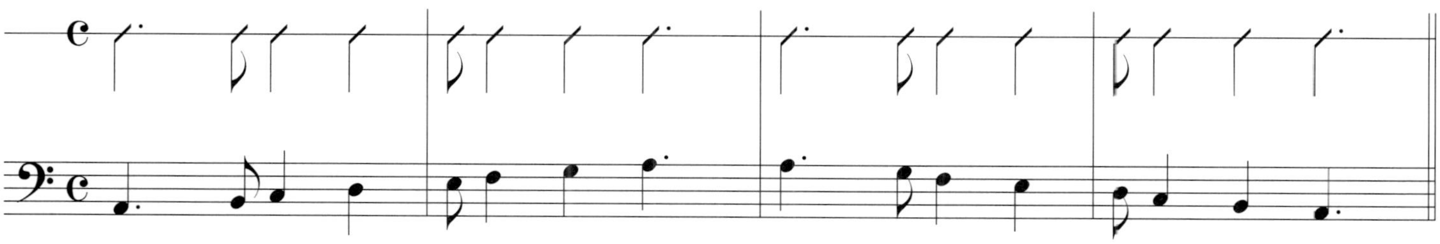

Your practice routine could look something like this:

- Choose a scale
- Choose or create a rhythm pattern
- Choose a tempo (metronome click on beats 2 and 4)
- Define fingerings
- Practice the scale in different keys.

Ihre Überoutine könnte dabei so aussehen:

- Skala auswählen
- Rhythmus-Pattern festlegen
- Tempo wählen (Metronom auf 2 und 4)
- Fingersatz klären
- Skalen in verschiedenen Tonarten spielen.

Here are more rhythm patterns. On the following page I have provided you with examples by filling out the patterns with scales.

Hier sind mehrere Rhythmus-Patterns. Auf der nächsten Seite habe ich sie (unter der gleichen Nummer) mit verschiedenen Skalen "aufgefüllt".

1

2

3

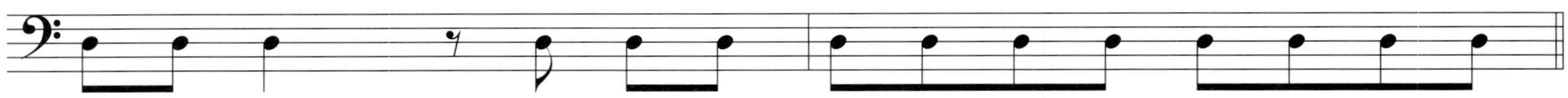

4

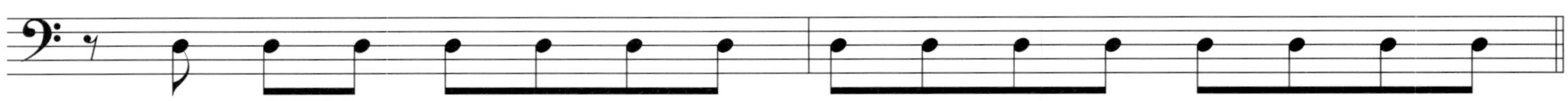

5

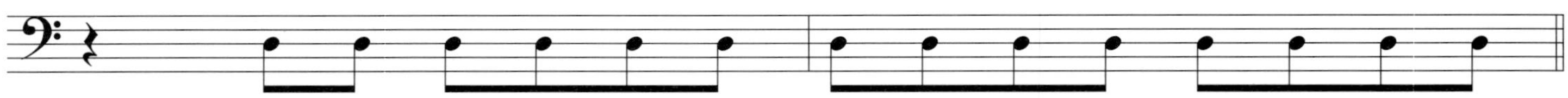

6

7

8

9

10

1 B♭7 **Scale: B♭ Mixolydian** — **B♭ mixolydisch**

2 G–Δ **Scale: G Melodic minor** — **G melodisch Moll**

3 Aø **Scale: A Locrian ♮2** — **A lokrisch ♮2**

4 CΔ♯11 **Scale: C Lydian** — **C lydisch**

5 DΔ♯5 **Scale: D Lydian augmented** — **D lydisch ♯5 (III. Stufe von B melodisch Moll)**

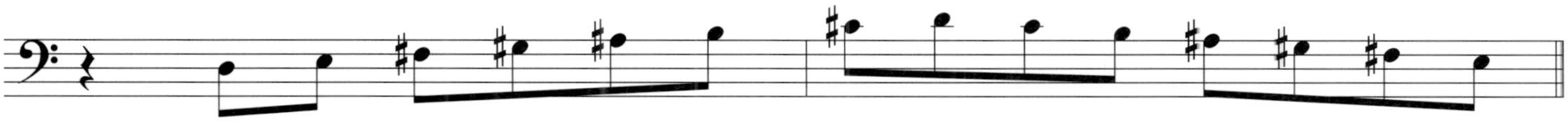

6 GΔ **Scale: G Ionian (major)** — **G ionisch (Dur)**

7 F♯–7 **Scale: F♯ Dorian** — **F♯ dorisch**

8 B♭7♯11 **Scale: B♭ Lydian ♭7** — **B♭ lydisch ♭7**

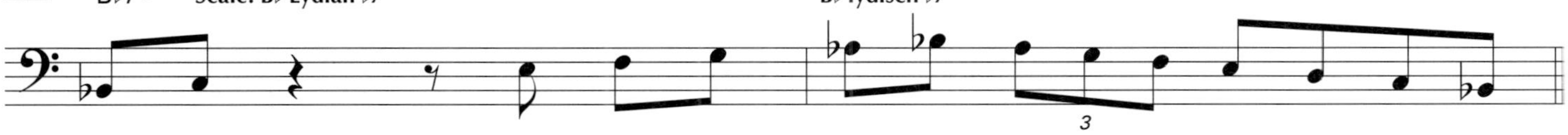

9 E–7 **Scale: E Phrygian** — **E phrygisch**

10 Cø **Scale: C Locrian** — **C lokrisch**

Combine these exercises with those in Chapter VII. 3, page 143 (Slurs).

Spielen Sie diese Übungen auch im Zusammenhang mit Kapitel VII. 3, Seite 143 (Bindungen).

When improvising a chord progression, it is important to know which scale fits to which chord. For more information on this subject I suggest "Jazz Improvisation" by David Baker.

I would like to also point out the following.

In my view, the study of scales is not a subject unto itself, but something to help one create a good, melodious improvisation. Care must be taken to avoid always beginning a scale with the tonic, or always beginning the scale on the first beat of the measure. Try to think in long melodic curves, not just from one chord to the next, nor from one scale to the next.

Keep in mind that the harmonic function of the II V I progression is not a progression from Dorian, Mixolydian, and Ionian (looking at it modally), but a harmonic movement within a single major scale.

Bei der Improvisation über Akkorde ist es wichtig zu wissen, welche Skala zu welchem Akkord paßt. Für weitere Informationen dazu empfehle ich das Buch "Jazz Improvisation" von David Baker.

Aus meiner Sicht möchte ich dazu folgendes bemerken:

Skalen sind nichts weiter als Hilfsmittel für eine gute, melodische Improvisation. Sie sind nie Selbstzweck. Bemühen Sie sich zu vermeiden, Skalen immer mit dem Grundton oder auf der 1 eines Taktes zu beginnen. Denken sie von vornherein in längeren melodischen Bögen, nicht nur von einem Akkord zum nächsten und von einer Skala zur nächsten.

Bedenken Sie, daß funktionsharmonisch eine II V I Verbindung nicht eine Abfolge von dorisch, mixolydisch und ionisch ist (das wäre die modale Auffassung), sondern einfach eine harmonische Bewegung innerhalb einer einzigen Durtonleiter.

6. Pentatonic Scales

The pentatonic scales are comprised of five tones. The harmonic ambiguity and their variation possibilities make the pentatonic scales extremely useful in jazz improvisation.

It is commonly accepted that the pentatonic scales are the major pentatonic (mode 1 of the below example in F major), the minor pentatonic (mode 5, starting on D). Strictly speaking however, a pentatonic scale is any scale comprised of 5 notes within the octave.

Dozens of such scales can be found in Nicholas Slonimsky's "Thesaurus of Scales and Melodic Patterns". Even more interesting for our purposes, is the book from Adelhard Roidinger, "Jazz Improvisation & Pentatonic", in which he offers the performer a great many variations for improvisation by using pentatonic scales.

The following should be sufficient to help you develop the "modes" from the major and minor mentatonic scales, and to explore their many possibilities.

6. Pentatonische Skalen

Diese Skalen bestehen aus fünf Tönen. Sie sind mit ihren vielfältigen Möglichkeiten und Mehrdeutigkeiten in der Jazz Improvisation sehr gebräuchlich.

Meist versteht man unter "pentatonischen Skalen"" nur die beiden als Modus 1 und 5 im Notenbeispiel gezeigten Tonleitern als Dur-Pentatonik (Nr. 1, hier in F) und Moll-Pentatonik (Nr. 5, hier in D). Genaugenommen ist aber jede Skala mit fünf Tönen innerhalb einer Oktave eine pentatonische Skala.

Im "Thesaurus of Scales and Melodic Patterns" von Nicholas Slonimsky werden einige Dutzend solcher Skalen aufgezählt. Noch interessanter für unsere Zwecke ist aber das Buch von Adelhard Roidinger, "Jazz Improvisation & Pentatonic", in dem die Tonleitern aus der Skalenlehre in pentatonische Tonleitern überführt werden. Dabei entstehen zahlreiche Mehrdeutigkeiten, die man sich in der Improvisation zunutze machen kann.

Hier soll es reichen, die "Modi" aus der Dur- und Moll-Pentatonik zu entwickeln und auf ihre Möglichkeiten hin "abzuklopfen".

Mode 1 (major pentatonic) — **1. Modus (Dur-Pentatonik)**

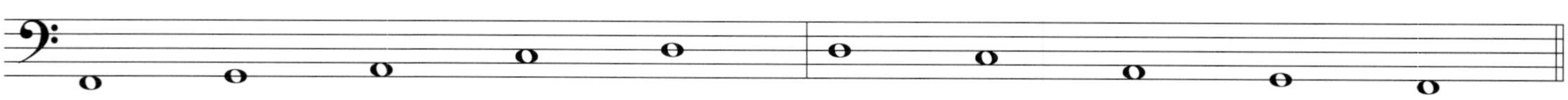

Mode 2 — **2. Modus**

Mode 3

3. Modus

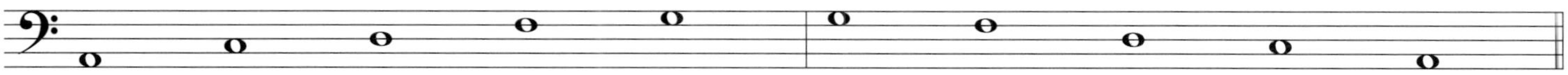

Mode 4

4. Modus

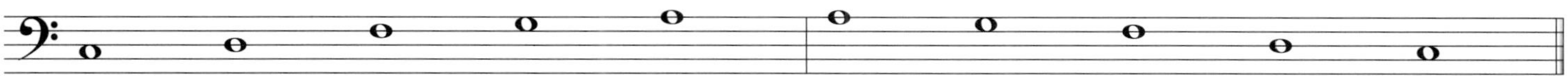

Mode 5 (minor pentatonic)

5. Modus (Moll-Pentatonik)

Exercises:

Übungen:

1

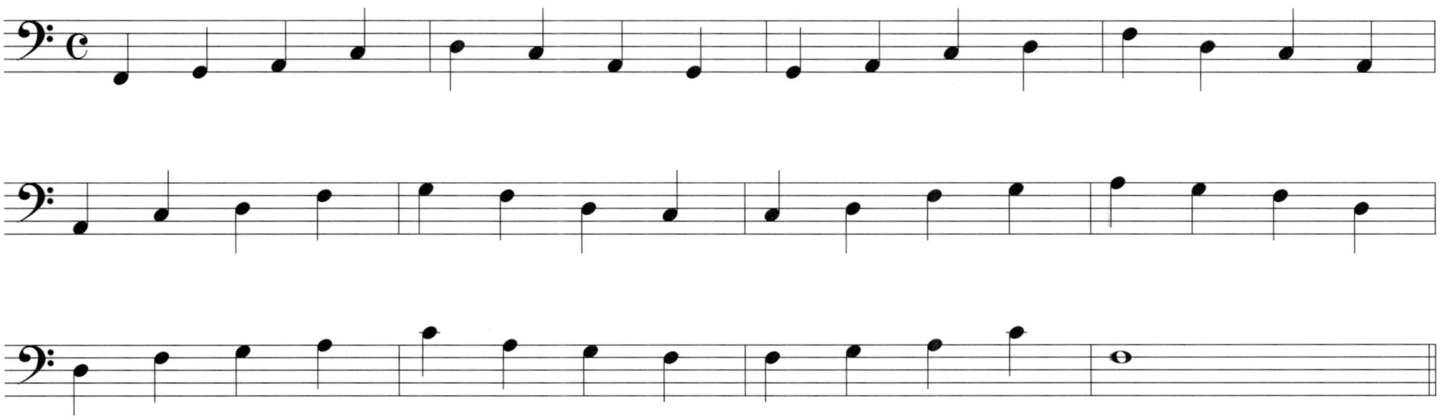

2

3

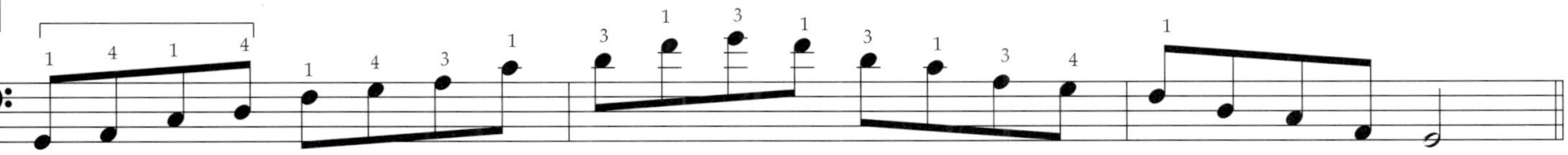

4

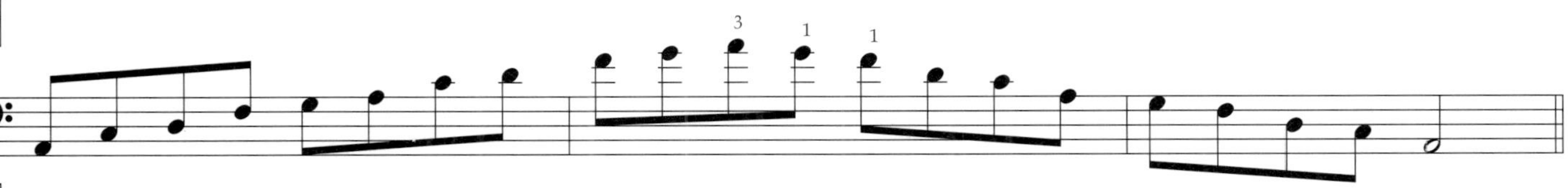

5

6

7. Rhythm Patterns For The Pentatonic Scales

7. Rhythmus-Patterns für pentatonische Skalen

1

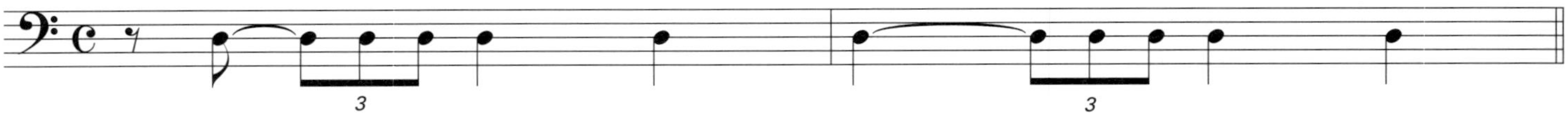

2

3

4

5

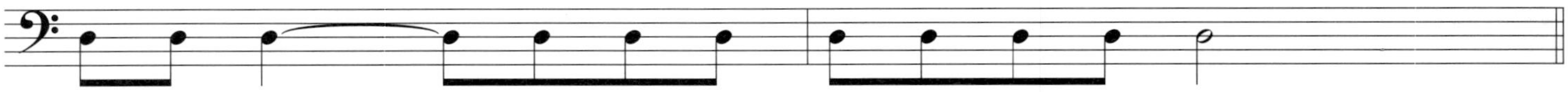

6

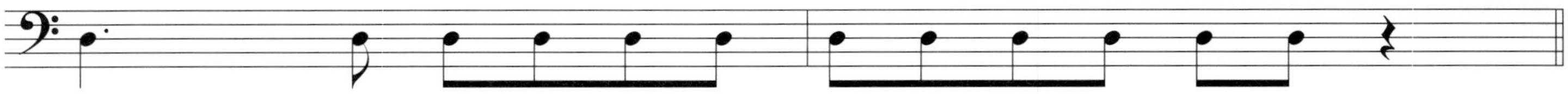

7

8

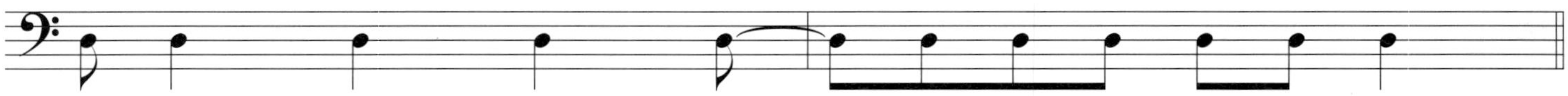

9

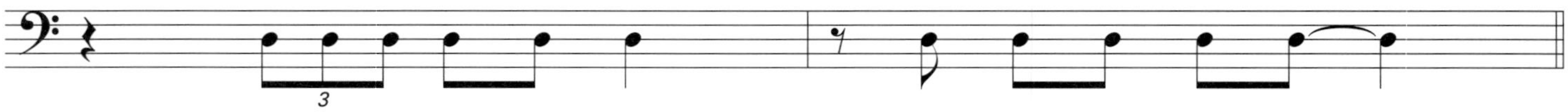

10

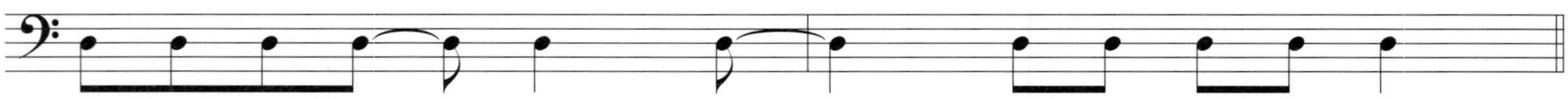

Examples of how the above rhythm patterns can be used for the pentatonic scales.

Beispiele, wie man die vorangehenden Rhythmus-Patterns mit pentatonischen Skalen auffüllen kann.

1

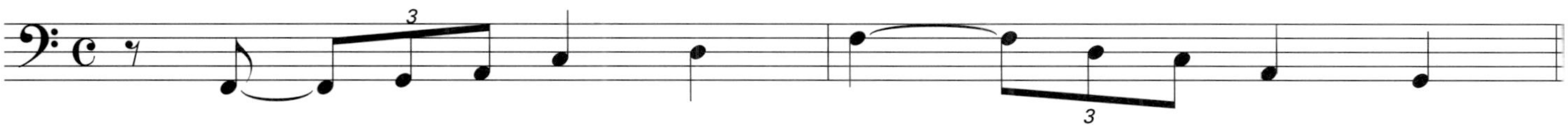

2

3

4

5

6

7

8

9

10

8. Use Of The Pentatonic Scales

The following examples are based on the F major pentatonic respectively the D minor pentatonic scale.

The scale fits:
FΔ, D–7, G7sus4, B♭6^{9}, E♭Δ$^{\sharp 11}$, B7alt, A7$^{\flat 9 \sharp 9 \sharp 5}$,
C7sus4 or D♭7alt (very daring!).

Before you begin to play these examples on the bass, you should first try out the different harmonic possibilities on a piano or keyboard to develop the inner ear.

8. Anwendungen pentatonischer Skalen

Die folgenden Beispiele basieren auf der F Dur-Pentatonik, bzw. deren 5. Modus, der D Moll-Pentatonik. Man kann sie z.B. über folgende Akkorde spielen:
FΔ, D–7, G7sus 4, B♭6^{9}, E♭Δ$^{\sharp 11}$, B7alt, A7$^{\flat 9 \sharp 9 \sharp 5}$,
C7sus4, F7 oder D♭7alt (sehr gewagt!).

Bevor Sie diese Vorschläge auf dem Baß spielen, sollten Sie auch hier das innere Ohr für die verschiedenen Anwendungen entwickeln, indem Sie am Klavier (Keyboard) zuerst einmal alle Möglichkeiten ausprobieren.

Examples:

Beispiele:

1

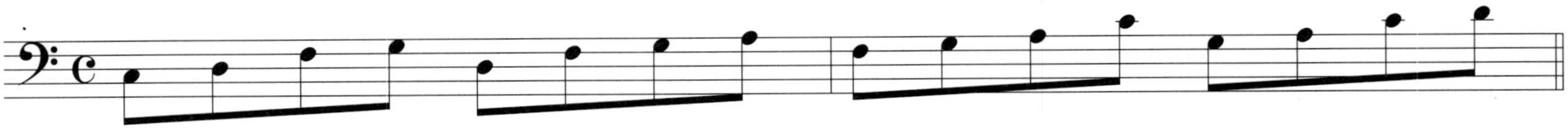

2

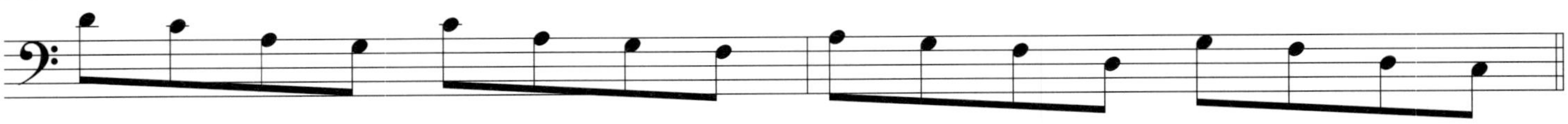

3

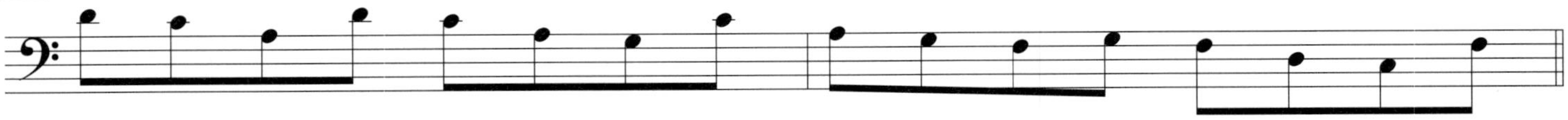

4

5

The pentatonic scale can also be used for the II V progression with a dominant pedal. (Refer to page 65)

Auch über II V Verbindungen mit Dominantpedal kann man pentatonische Skalen spielen (siehe S. 65).

Example: Medium up-tempo

Beispiel: Medium up-tempo

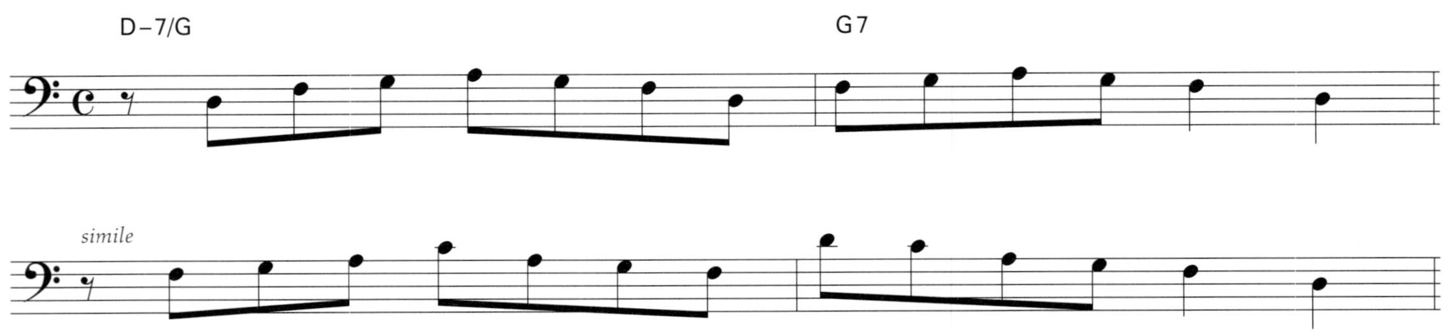

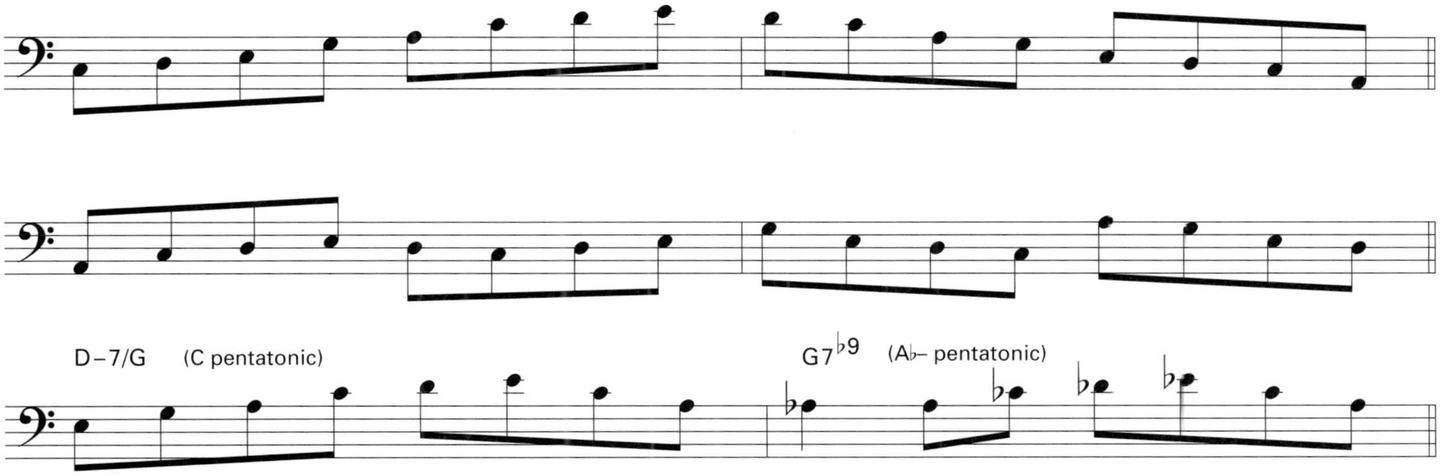

Suggested Practice For The Beginner

Whether or not one uses the pentatonic scales in his/her improvising is a question of one's style and personal musical taste. In a bebop oriented improvisation, it's probably better for one to use a chord-based method. On the other hand, with modal pieces, one can easily use pentatonic scales, as in Herbie Hancock's composition *Maiden Voyage*. You will find this piece along with others on the "Volume 11" of the Jamey Aebersold "Play-Along" CD series.

Prepare your practice session using the following steps:

- Obtain the music, including the chord progression.
- Find the pentatonic scales to fit the chords. For instance, use the A minor pentatonic for A–/D (also written as D7sus4), the C minor pentatonic for C–/F, etc.
- Transpose the pentatonic scales to the rhythm patterns from page 158. It is easier to begin by first notating the patterns. Write your own exercises.
- Play the patterns with the "play-along" recording
- Repeat the routine using other pieces like *Watermelon Man, Cantaloupe Island, Blue Bossa, Song For My Father, Sister Sadie,* or similar easy pieces from the common jazz repertoire.

Further information for the use of pentatonic scales can be found in "Inside Improvisation, Vol. 2 Pentatonics" by Jerry Bergonzi (book with play-along CD) and "Pentatonic Scales For Improvisation" by Ramon Ricker.

Übeanregung für Einsteiger

Ob und wann man pentatonische Skalen innerhalb der Improvisation spielt, ist eine Frage der Stilistik und des persönlichen Geschmacks. Bei einer am Bebop orientierten Improvisation benutzt man vielleicht besser eine akkordbezogene Methode. Dagegen kann man bei modalen Stücken pentatonische Skalen gut einsetzen, so z.B. bei der Herbie Hancock Komposition *Maiden Voyage*. Sie finden dieses Stück u.a. auf der Play-Along CD der Jamey Aebersold Reihe, Vol. 11.

Bereiten Sie eine Übesession folgendermaßen vor:

- Sie besorgen sich die Noten inkl. der Akkordverbindungen.
- Sie finden die zu den Akkorden passenden pentatonischen Skalen, z.B. bei A–/D (manchmal auch als D7sus4 notiert) die A Moll-Pentatonik bei C–/F die C Moll-Pentatonik etc.
- Übertragen Sie diese pentatonischen Skalen auf ein Rhythm-Pattern von Seite 158. Zu Beginn ist es hilfreich, die Patterns zu notieren. Schreiben Sie Ihre eigene Etüde.
- Spielen Sie die Patterns zur Mitspiel-CD.
- Übertragen Sie die Überoutine auch auf andere Stücke wie z.B. *Watermelon Man, Cantaloupe Island, Blue Bossa, Song For My Father, Sister Sadie* oder ähnliche, einfache Stücke aus dem allgemeinen Jazzrepertoire.

Weitere Hinweise für die Anwendung von pentatonischen Skalen finden Sie in "Inside Improvisation, Vol. 2 Pentatonik" von Jerry Bergonzi (Buch mit Play-Along CD) und in "Pentatonic Scales For Improvisation" von Ramon Ricker.

9. The Blues Scale

9. Die Blues-Skala

First came the "Blues", and then much later the blues scale as a melodic abstraction. For this reason different opinions exist as to which notes truly belong to the blues scale. The scale I have given, excluding the notes in parentheses, is the one most often used.

The characteristics are

- the minor third
- the diminished fifth
- the minor seventh

In some sources, the notes I have given in parentheses are also included in the blues scale. "First came the blues, then the academicians..."

One can use the blues scale for every dominant seventh (V7) chord. (For example C7 in F major.) One can even use the scale for an entire twelve-bar blues progression to create the dissonance that is typical of the blues style.

This device loses it's effectiveness with overuse. It is therefore better to include other phrases as well, e.g. from the minor pentatonic, or the Mixolydian scale in your solo.

Zuerst gab es den Blues, und viel später erst die Blues-Skala als melodische Abstraktion. Aus diesem Grunde gibt es verschiedene Ansichten, welche Töne zur Blues-Skala gehören. Am häufigsten habe ich die o.a. Skala ohne die eingeklammerten Töne gehört.

Ihre wesentlichen Merkmale sind

- die kleine Terz
- die verminderte Quinte
- die kleine Septime

In manchen Büchern werden auch die eingeklammerten Noten als zur Blues-Skala gehörig angesehen. "Zuerst war da der Blues, dann irgendwelche Musikgelehrten..."

Man kann die Blues-Skala über jeden Dominantseptakkord (V7) spielen, z.B. C7 in F Dur. Beim zwölftaktigen Blues sogar über das ganze Akkordschema. Dabei entstehen dann die für den Blues so typischen Reibungen.

Aber: auch hier wirkt ein "zuviel" langweilig, daher ist es besser, im Chorus verschiedene Phrasen z.B. aus der Moll-Pentatonik oder der mixolydischen Skala zu mischen.

Example: Typical blues phrases in F major

Beispiel: Typische Blues-Phrasen (in F)

10. Eight-Tone Scales

These scales are derived from either whole-step/half-step, or half-step/whole-step patterns. The whole-step/half-step being used for diminished chords, and the half-step/whole-step for altered V7 chords.

10.1 Diminished Scale

Similar as with diminished chords, the symmetry of the diminished scales result in only three different scales. Depending on which note of the scale one begins, each scale can be used with four different chords.

10. Achttonskalen

Diese Skalen sind abwechselnd entweder aus Halb- und Ganztonschritten oder aus Ganz- und Halbtonschritten zusammengesetzt. Achttonskalen aus Ganz- und Halbtonschritten werden bei verminderten Akkorden verwendet, die aus Halb- und Ganztonschritten bei alterierten Dominantseptakkorden der V. Stufe.

10.1 Verminderte Achttonskala

Ähnlich wie bei den verminderten Akkorden gibt es aufgrund ihrer Symmetrie jeweils nur drei verschiedene Arten von Achttonskalen. Eine Skala paßt zu vier verschiedenen Akkorden, je nachdem, auf welchem Ton man beginnt.

Example: Whole-step / Half-step Scale

Beispiel: Ganzton-Halbton Skala

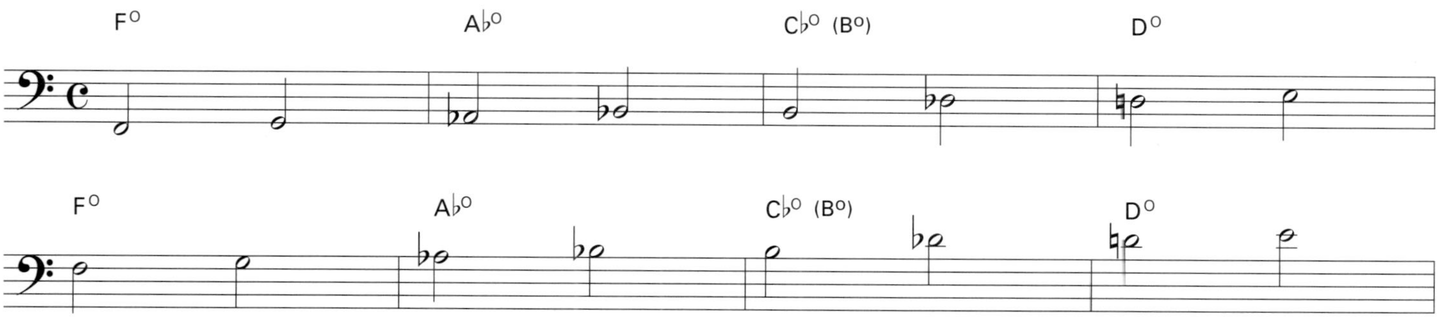

Typical fingering:
- ascending: 1 4, 1 4 (lower minor tetrachord), 1 4, 1 4 (upper minor tetrachord)
- descending: 4, 4 1, 4 1, 4 1, 4 1.

Typischer Fingersatz :
- aufwärts: 1 4, 1 4 (Moll-Tetrachord), 1 4, 1 4 (weiterer Moll-Tetrachord)
- abwärts: 4, 4 1, 4 1, 4 1, 4 1.

These chord-scales begin with a whole step and fit with the diminished chords notated in the chord symbols. Practice these slowly with the bow in order to become familiar with the sound.

Diese Achttonskalen beginnen mit einem Ganztonschritt. Sie passen zu den darüberstehenden verminderten Akkorden. Üben Sie sie langsam, am besten mit dem Bogen, damit Sie sich an den Klang gewöhnen.

10.2 Dominant Eight-Tone Scale

The fingerings given are commonly used.

Example: Half-step / Whole-step scale

10.2 Dominant Achttonskala

Beachten Sie auch hier die typischen Fingersätze.

Beispiel: Halbton-Ganzton Skala

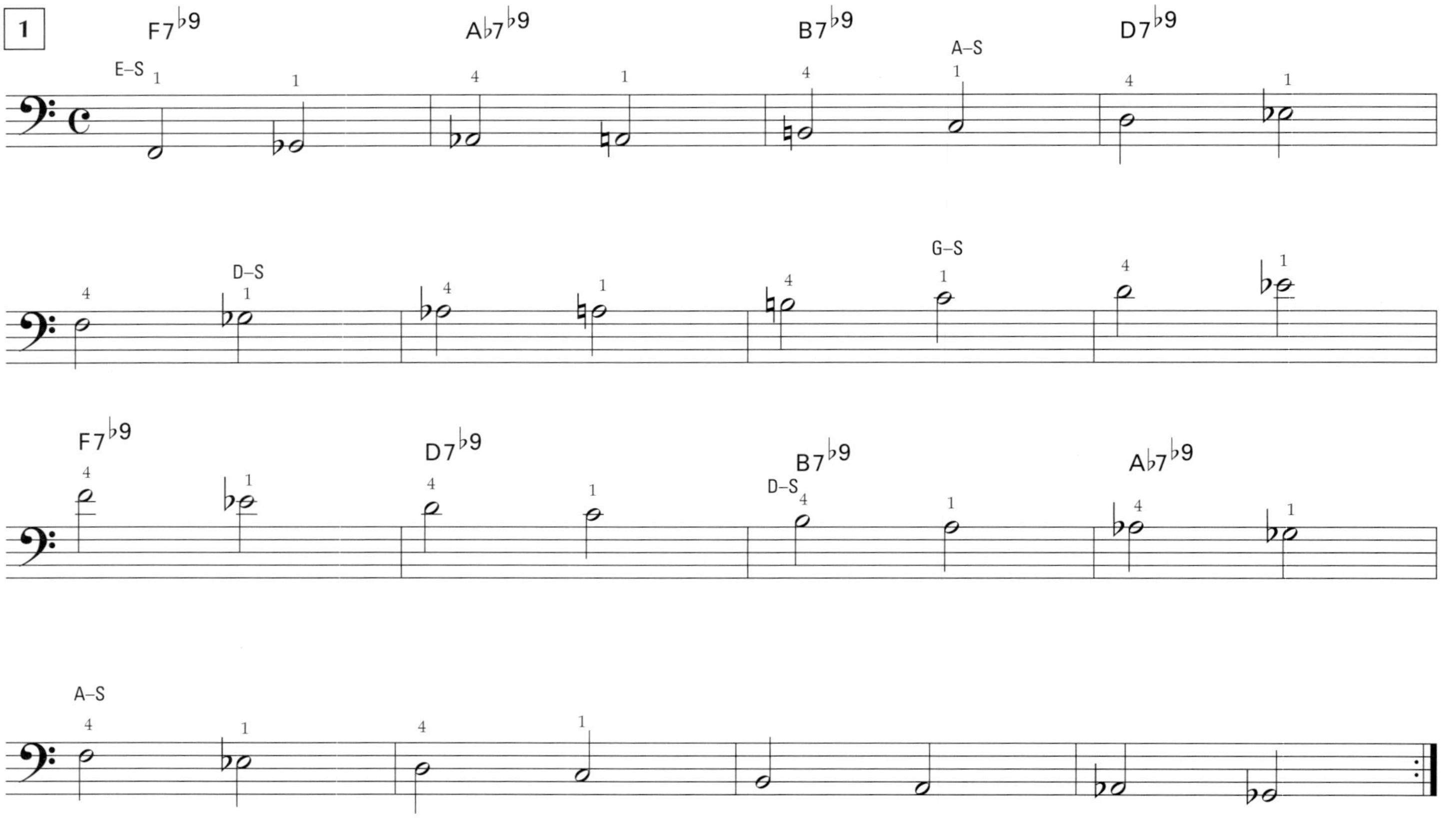

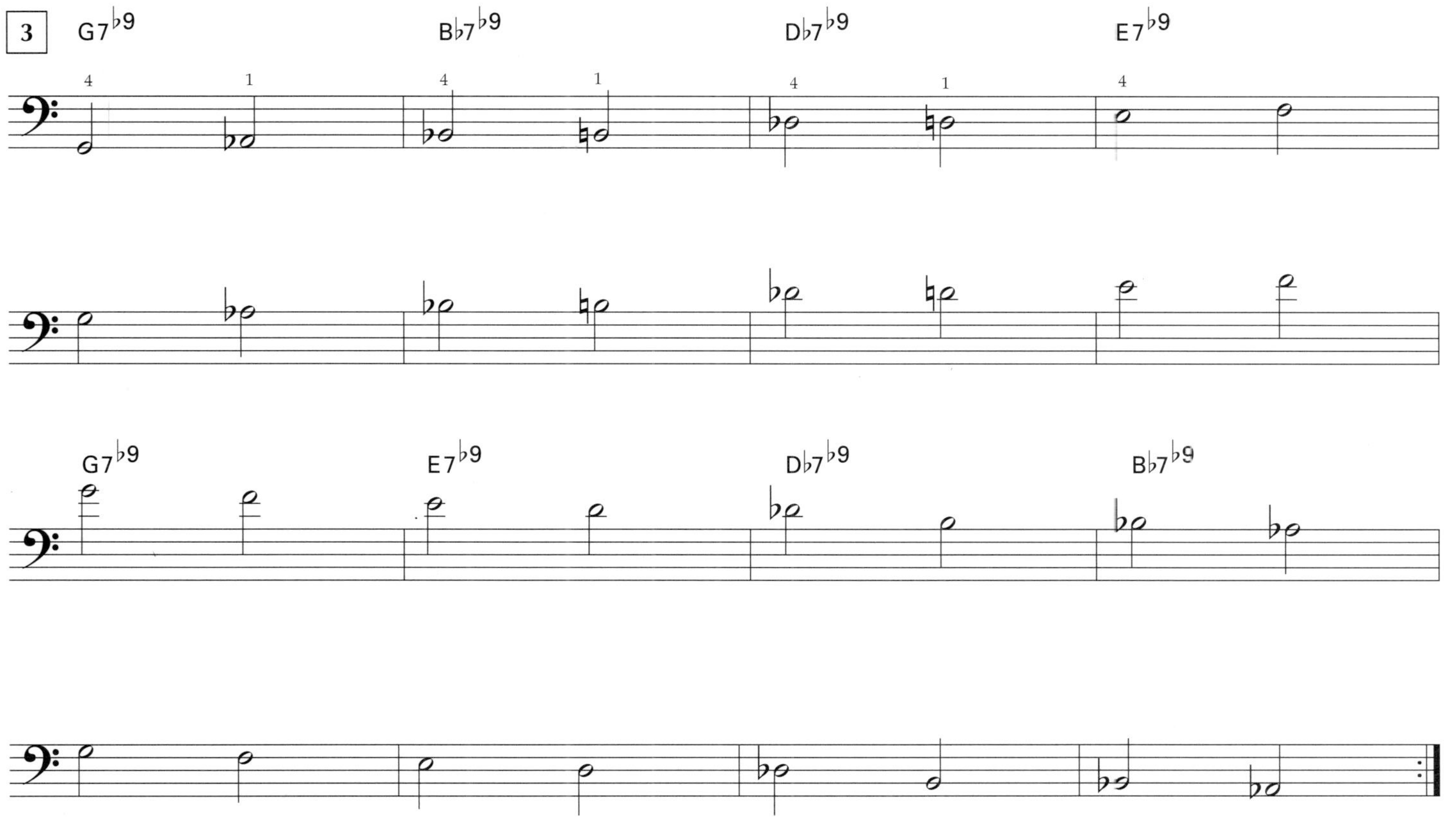

10.3 Uses Of The Dominant Eight-Tone Scales

The eight-tone scale is used mostly with the "altered V7" chord. (G7♭9, G7♯9, G7 13, etc.) The scale consists of two ascending minor tetrachords, one beginning from the tonic, and another beginning from the diminished fifth.

Beginning on G, the eight-tone scale descending would sound so;

10.3 Anwendung von Achttonskalen

Am häufigsten werden Achttonskalen im Zusammenhang mit der alterierten V. Stufe (z.B. G7♭9, G7♯9, G7 13 o.ä.) verwendet. Eine abwärts gespielte Achttonskala über Akkorde dieser Art setzt sich aus zwei Tetrachorden zusammen: einem abwärts gespielten Moll-Tetrachord ab Grundton und einem abwärts gespielten Moll-Tetrachord ab verminderter Quinte. Die ab G abwärts gespielte Achttonskala klingt dann so:

Minor tetrachord from G (1)
Minor tetrachord from D♭ (♭5)

Moll-Tetrachord ab Grundton (G)
Moll-Tetrachord ab ♭5 (D♭)

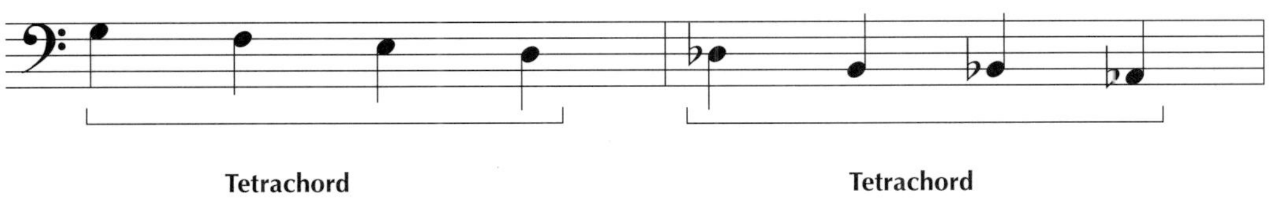

Practice the following dominant eight-tone scales using the rhythm patterns.

Üben Sie nun die Achttonskalen über die folgenden Rhythmus-Patterns.

These three rhythm patterns using the eight-tone scale built on C (half-step/whole-step) sounds:

Diese drei Rhythmus-Patterns mit der Achttonskala auf C (Halbton-Ganzton) klingen dann so:

10.4 Examples Using The Dominant Eight-Tone Scale

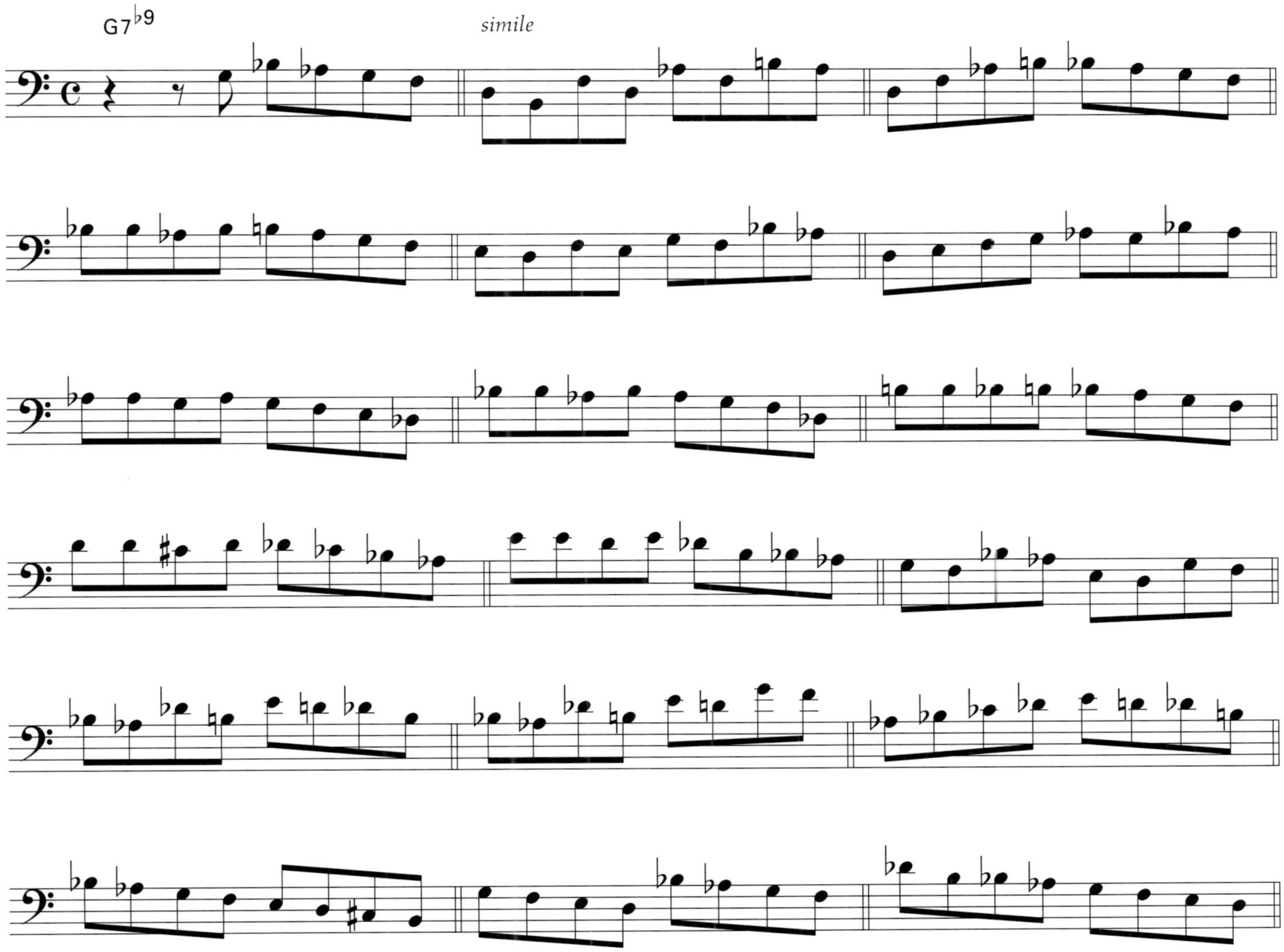

As already said, there are only three transpositions of eight-tone scales.

The above examples can be played not only with a G7♭9 but also with the B♭7♭9, D♭7♭9 or E7♭9 chords.

When listening to recordings, pay close attention to where these scales are used. Write them down and memorize them. Use them to invent your own phrases.

10.4 Beispiele für die Anwendung von Achttonskalen

Wie schon erwähnt, gibt es nur drei Transpositionen der Achttonleitern. Diese Beispiele oben, bei denen aus einer davon Phrasen gebildet worden sind, kann man demnach nicht nur über G7♭9 spielen, sondern ebenso über B♭7♭9, D♭7♭9 oder E7♭9.

Achten Sie beim Anhören von Aufnahmen darauf, wer wann und wo Achttonskalen spielt. Merken Sie sie sich, schreiben Sie sie auf und lernen Sie sie auswendig. Erfinden Sie eigene Phrasen mit Achttonskalen.

11. Bebop Scales

11.1 General

The term "Bebop Scale" first came into use in the 70's. By this time the peak of the bebop style had already passed. Bebop improvisation was also generally less scalar and more chord-based. Still these scales are useful for building phrases and melodies.

11. Bebop-Skalen

11.1 Allgemeines

Der Begriff "Bebop-Skala" tauchte zum ersten Mal in den siebziger Jahren in der Improvisationslehre auf. Da war sicherlich die Blütezeit des Bebop längst vorbei. Im allgemeinen wurde im Bebop auch mehr mit Akkordmaterial improvisiert und weniger mit Skalen. Trotzdem: Diese Skala eignet sich gut, um daraus Phrasen und Melodien zu bilden.

11.2 The Bebop Dominant Scale

11.2 Die Bebop-Dominantskala

These scales fit with B♭7 and F–7 as well as complete II V progression.

- they are played mostly descending
- a half-step exists between seventh and tonic

Play the bebop dominant scale from

- the tonic
- minor seventh
- fifth
- third

Diese Skala paßt zu B♭7 und zu F–7, also zu einer kompletten II V Verbindung. Ihre typischen Merkmale sind:

- sie wird meistens abwärts gespielt
- Grundton und kleine Septime werden durch einen Halbtonschritt miteinander verbunden

Spielen Sie die Bebop-Dominantskala ab

- Grundton
- kleiner Septime
- Quinte
- Terz

Example: Bebop dominant scale with a II V progression

Beispiel: Bebop-Dominantskala über einer II V Verbindung

Play the bebop dominant scale in C using the following rhythm patterns.

Spielen Sie die Bebop-Dominantskala in C über die folgenden Rhythmus-Patterns.

Exercise:

Übung:

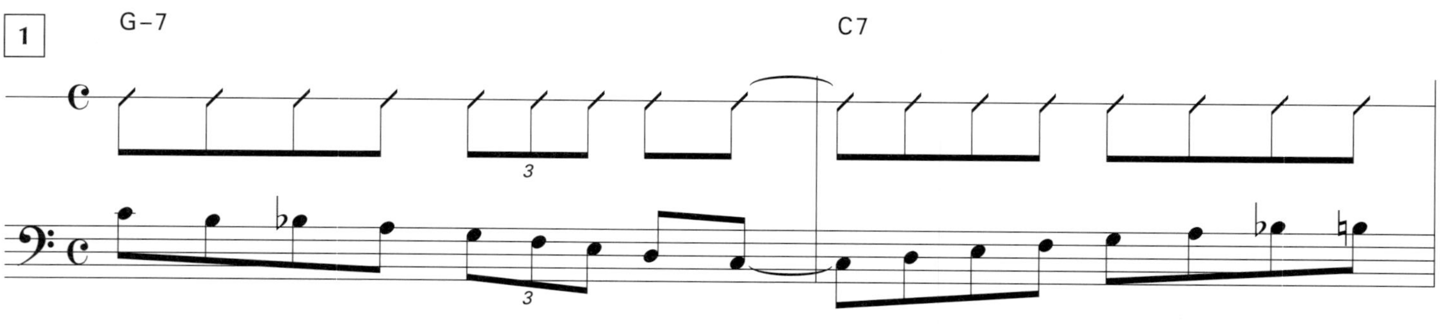

2

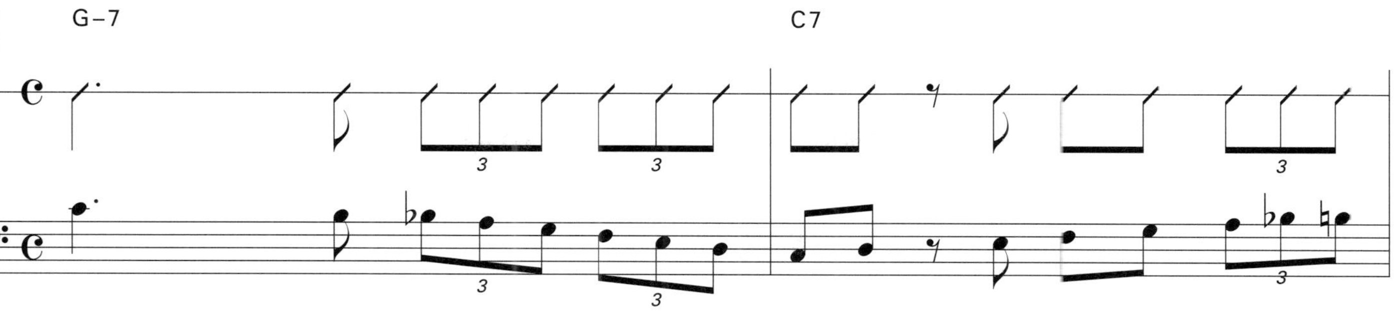

3

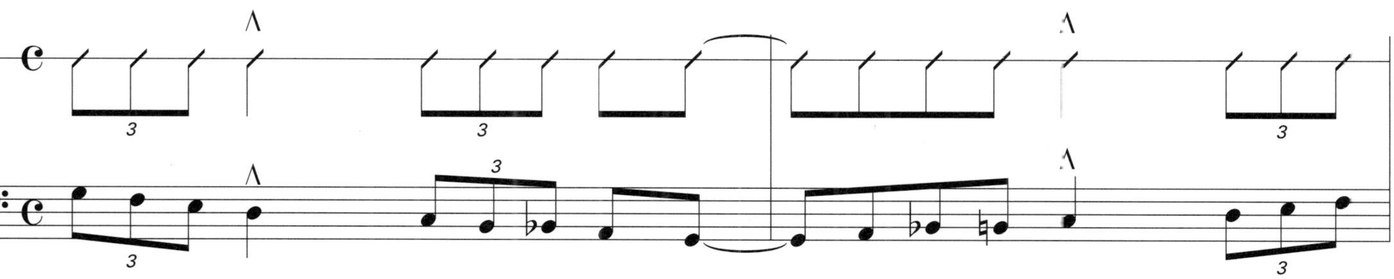

4

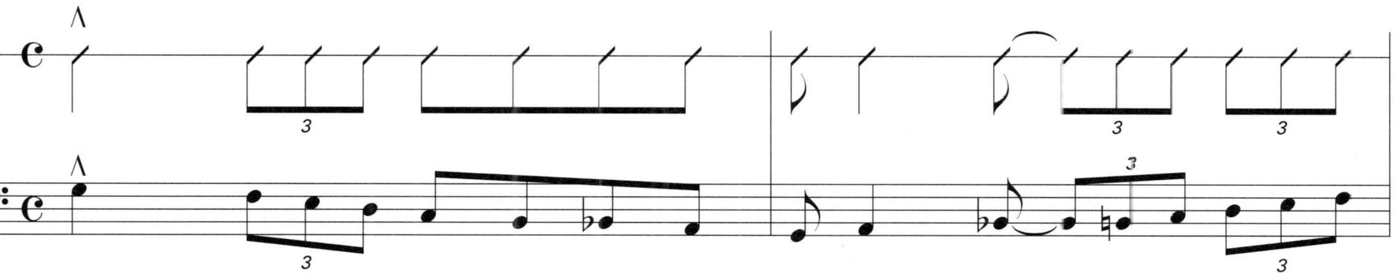

Study for II V progression using the bebop dominant scale. Find appropriate phrases for the last four measures.

Studie über II V Verbindungen unter Verwendung der Bebop-Dominantskala. Finden Sie für die letzten vier Takte eigene entsprechende Phrasen.

Study:

Übung:

Bebop dominant scales used with 1-measure II V progressions.

Bebop-Dominantskalen über eintaktige II V Verbindungen.

Study:

Übung:

11.3 The Bebop Major Scale

The following scale fits with B♭Δ.

The typical characteristics of the bebop major scale are:

- they are played mostly descending.
- a half-step exists between steps 6 and 5.

Play the bebop major scale from the

- tonic
- sixth
- fifth
- third (always figured from the root of the corresponding major chord)

Examples:

Exercise: Rhythm patterns (CΔ)

1

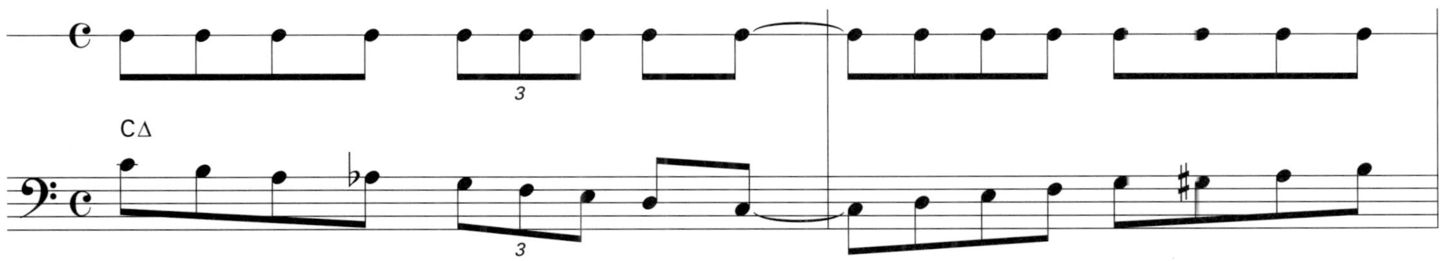

2

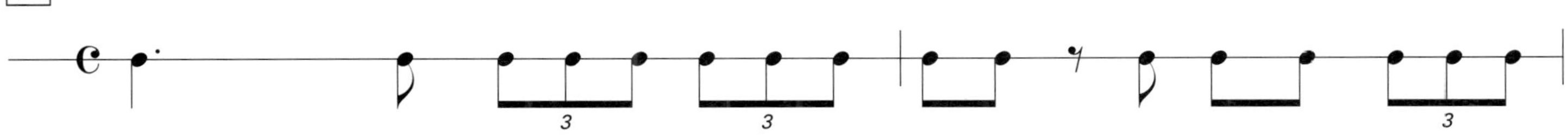

3

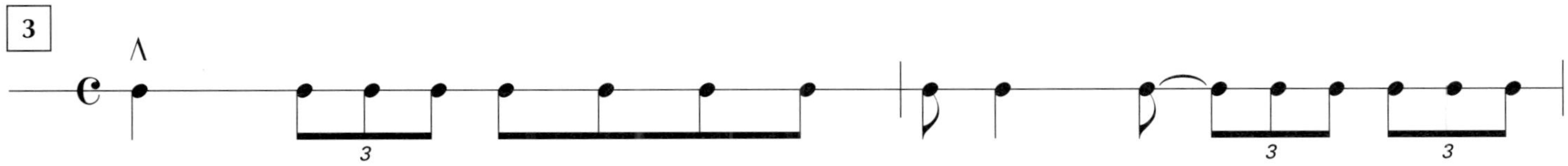

11.3 Die Bebop-Durskala

Die folgende Skala paßt zu B♭Δ.

Ihre typischen Merkmale sind:

- sie wird meistens abwärts gespielt.
- Halbtonschritt zwischen Sexte und Quinte.

Spielen Sie die Bebop-Durskala ab:

- Grundton
- Sexte
- Quinte
- Terz (immer bezogen auf den Grundton des jeweiligen Durakkordes)

Beispiele:

Übung: Rhythmus-Patterns (CΔ)

Play the bebop major scale using the above three rhythm patterns beginning with the tonic.

Spielen Sie die Bebop-Durskala über die drei obenstehenden Rhythmus-Patterns beginnend mit diesen Grundtönen:

1	C	E♭	F♯	A
	C♯	E	G	B♭
	D	F	A♭	B
2	C	C♯	D	E♭
	E	F	F♯	G
	A♭	A	B♭	B

Here are a few examples for the use of dominant and major bebop scales for the II V I progression. Transpose the four-measure phrases beginning from measure 13 to fit with the chord symbols.

Hier sind einige Beispiele für die Anwendung von Bebop-Skalen (Dominant und Dur) über II V I Verbindungen. Transponieren Sie ab Takt 13 die vorgegebene viertaktige Phrase passend zu den Akkordsymbolen.

NOTE:
The above examples use strictly bebop scales. Of course in good improvisation these scales are mixed with other scales and chords. Listen to the recordings of Charlie Parker, Clifford Brown, or other bebop jazz greats. Try to transcribe a solo. You will definitely learn a great deal by doing so. For more information on bebop scales I recommend David Baker's "Jazz Improvisation".

ANMERKUNG:
Das obenstehende Beispiel verwendet ausschließlich Bebop-Skalen. Bei einer guten Improvisation werden diese Skalen natürlich mit anderen Skalen oder Akkordbrechungen gemischt. Hören Sie sich dazu Bebop-Aufnahmen mit Charlie Parker, Clifford Brown oder anderen Bebop Jazzgrößen an. Versuchen Sie auch einmal ein Solo zu transkribieren. Daraus werden Sie bestimmt sehr viel lernen. Zwecks weiterer Information über die Bebop-Skalen empfehle ich David Bakers "Jazz Improvisation".

12. The Melodic Minor Scale

12. Melodische Molltonleitern

Example: E melodic minor

Beispiel: E melodisch Moll

Example: F melodic minor

Beispiel: F melodisch Moll

Example: F♯ melodic minor

Beispiel: F♯ melodisch Moll

Example: G melodic minor

Beispiel: G melodisch Moll

Example: A♭ melodic minor

Beispiel: A♭ melodisch Moll

The A melodic minor scale has the same fingerings as E melodic minor, except one string higher. That also holds true for

B♭ melodic minor to F melodic minor
B melodic minor to F♯ melodic minor
C melodic minor to G melodic minor
D♭ melodic minor to A♭ melodic minor

Die A melodische Molltonleiter hat den gleichen Fingersatz wie E melodisch Moll, nur eine Saite höher. Dasselbe gilt für das Verhältnis von:

B♭ melodisch Moll zu F melodisch Moll
B melodisch Moll zu F♯ melodisch Moll
C melodisch Moll zu G melodisch Moll
D♭ melodisch Moll zu A♭ melodisch Moll

Example: D melodic minor

Beispiel: D melodisch Moll

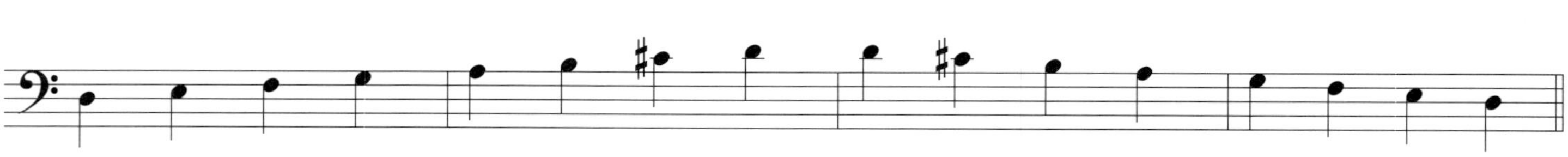

Example: E♭ melodic minor with typical fingerings

Beispiel: E♭ melodisch Moll mit typischem Fingersatz

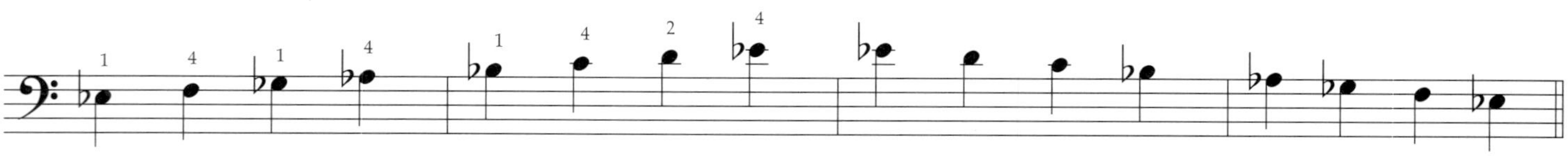

NOTE:
Melodic minor scales in jazz are played the same way both ascending and descending. Their sounds are defined by the minor third, major sixth, and major seventh.

ANMERKUNG:
Melodische Molltonleitern werden in der Jazzmusik auf- und abwärts gleich gespielt. Ihre Klangfarbe wird durch die kleine Terz, die große Sexte und die große Septime bestimmt.

12.1 Chords And Modes Of The Melodic Minor Scale

The following can be derived from each step of the melodic minor; (the examples given below are derived from the E melodic minor scale.)

1. four-voice chord
2. corresponding modes

12.1 Akkorde und Modi der melodischen Molltonleiter

Auf jeder Stufe von E melodisch Moll sind aus skaleneigenem Material

1. vierstimmige Akkorde,
2. entsprechende Modi gebildet worden.

Example: E melodic minor

Beispiel: E melodisch Moll

Example: F♯ Dorian ♭2

Beispiel: F♯ dorisch ♭2

Example: G Lydian augmented

Beispiel: G lydisch-übermäßig

Example: A Lydian ♭7 (also: Mixolydian ♯11)

Beispiel: A lydisch ♭7 (auch: mixolydisch ♯11)

Example: B Mixolydian ♭6

Beispiel: B mixolydisch ♭6

Example: C♯ Locrian ♮2

Beispiel: C♯ lokrisch ♮2

Example: D♯ Super Locrian

Beispiel: D♯ superlokrisch

The "Super Locrian" scale is often referred to as an "altered" scale. This scale fits with the dominant seventh (V7) chord with any combination of ♭5/♯11, ♯5/♭13, ♭9, or ♯9. This could also be spelled enharmonically as an "E♭ altered" scale over the E♭7♯5♯9 chord.

Die superlokrische Skala wird auch häufig als "alterierte" Skala bezeichnet. Sie paßt zu Dominantseptakkorden (V7), die ♭5/♯11, ♯5/♭13, ♭9 oder ♯9 bzw. Kombinationen daraus enthalten. Enharmonisch verwechselt würde das Beispiel oben also zu einer "E♭ alterierten Skala" über den Akkord (z.B.) E♭7♯5♯9 werden.

Example: E♭ altered

Beispiel: E♭ alteriert

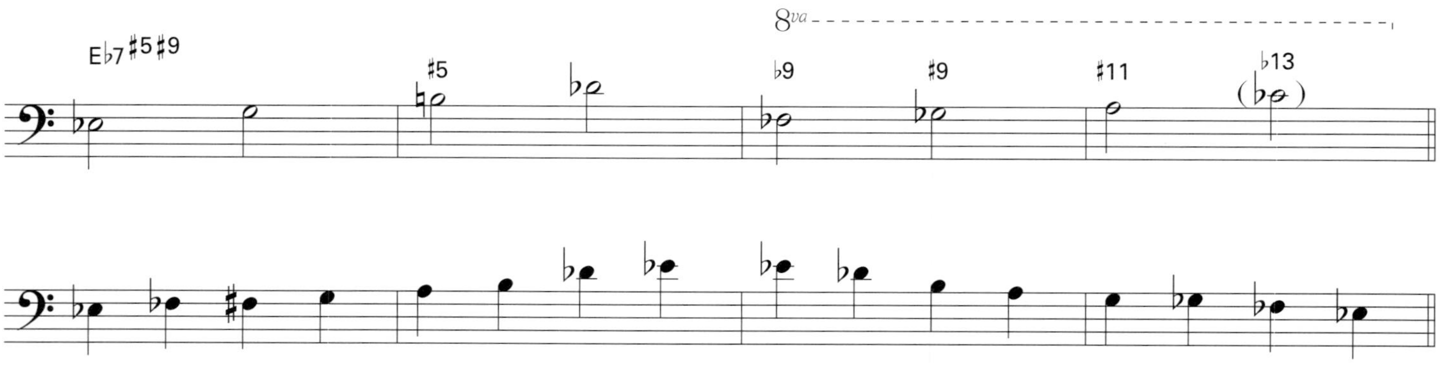

13. Whole-Tone Scales

Whole-tone scales are derived from a row of tones in whole-steps, resulting in there being only two different whole-tone scales with each having six different transpositions.

13. Ganztonleitern

Ganztonleitern bestehen nur aus Ganztonschritten. Daher gibt es nur zwei verschiedene mit je sechs Transpositionen.

The whole-tone scale can be used with the augmented triad (♯5) or the augmented dominant seventh chord. (V7♯5).

Ganztonleitern kann man bei übermäßigen Dreiklängen (♯5) oder bei Dominantseptakkorden mit übermäßiger Quinte spielen (V7♯5).

14. The Chromatic Scale

The chromatic scale is derived from a row of tones in half-steps (minor seconds).

14. Die chromatische Tonleiter

Die chromatische Tonleiter umfaßt alle Halbtonschritte unseres Tonsystems.

15. Harmonic Minor, 5th Mode

The abbreviation for this scale will be "HM5" and would appear as in the following example beginning on G.

Example: G HM5

"HM5" denotes a scale that begins on the 5th step of the harmonic minor scale. G HM5 would be derived from C harmonic minor.

Special characteristics are the

- minor second (the tension ♭9)
- major third
- minor sixth (the tension ♭13)
- minor 7

The half-steps occur between 1-2, 3-4, and 5-6.

The "HM5" scale is used for dominant chords in a minor key.

Example: Measure 12 from *Solar* by Miles Davis

Suggestion for practice:
In compositions with minor cadences like *Blue Bossa, Softly As In The Morning Sunrise, What Is This Thing Called Love,* etc., the HM5 can easily be used for the V7♭9 chord. Of course this also works with one-measure II V progressions in the minor key (IIø V7♭9) such as found in *Confirmation* and *In Your Own Sweet Way*.

15. Harmonisch Moll, 5. Modus

Diese Tonleiter, abgekürzt HM 5, klingt ab G so:

Beispiel: G HM5

Mit HM 5 wird eine Skala bezeichnet, die auf der 5. Stufe einer harmonischen Molltonleiter beginnt. G HM 5 wird demnach von C harmonisch Moll abgeleitet.

Besondere Merkmale sind

- die kleine Sekunde (als Spannungston die ♭9)
- die große Terz
- die kleine Sexte (als Spannungston die ♭13)
- und die kleine Septime.

Die Halbtonschritte befinden sich von 1-2, 3-4, und 5-6.

Angewendet wird die Skala über Akkorde der V. Stufe in Moll.

Beispiel: Takt 12 aus *Solar* von Miles Davis

Übevorschlag:
Bei Kompositionen mit Moll Kadenzen wie *Blue Bossa, Softly As In The Morning Sunrise, What Is This Thing Called Love* u.ä. läßt sich die HM5 gut über den V7♭9 spielen – natürlich auch bei eintaktigen II V Kadenzen in Moll (IIø V7♭9), wie in *Confirmation* oder *In Your Own Sweet Way*.

16 First Steps In Using Scales

16.1 Scales For The II V Progression In Major

I want to stress again that scales are nothing but "abstractions" of melodies. First came the melody and much later the scales. With this in mind, the following exercises are first and foremost nothing more than etudes and technical studies. They are meant as only the first step to the understanding of the theory of chords and chord-scales.

In the following progression, D–7 G7 CΔ, one chord per measure, only the C major scale and the modes of Dorian (step II), Mixolydian (step V), and the Ionian (step I), are to be used.

16 Erste Schritte für die Anwendung von Skalen

16.1 Skalen über II V Verbindungen in Dur

Selbst auf die Gefahr hin, mich zu wiederholen: Skalen sind nichts weiter als Abstraktionen von Melodien. Zuerst gab es Melodien, dann (viel später) die Tonleitern, bzw. Skalen. Unter diesem Aspekt sind die folgenden Übungen zuerst einmal nichts weiter als Etüden und technische Studien. Sie sind der erste Schritt zum Kennenlernen der Akkord/Skalen Theorie.

Bei der folgenden Akkordverbindung D–7 G7 CΔ – jeweils eintaktig – wird als melodisches Material nur die C Dur Tonleiter verwendet, bzw. daraus abgeleitete Kirchentonleitern: dorisch (II. Stufe), mixolydisch (V. Stufe), ionisch (I. Stufe).

Examples:

Beispiele:

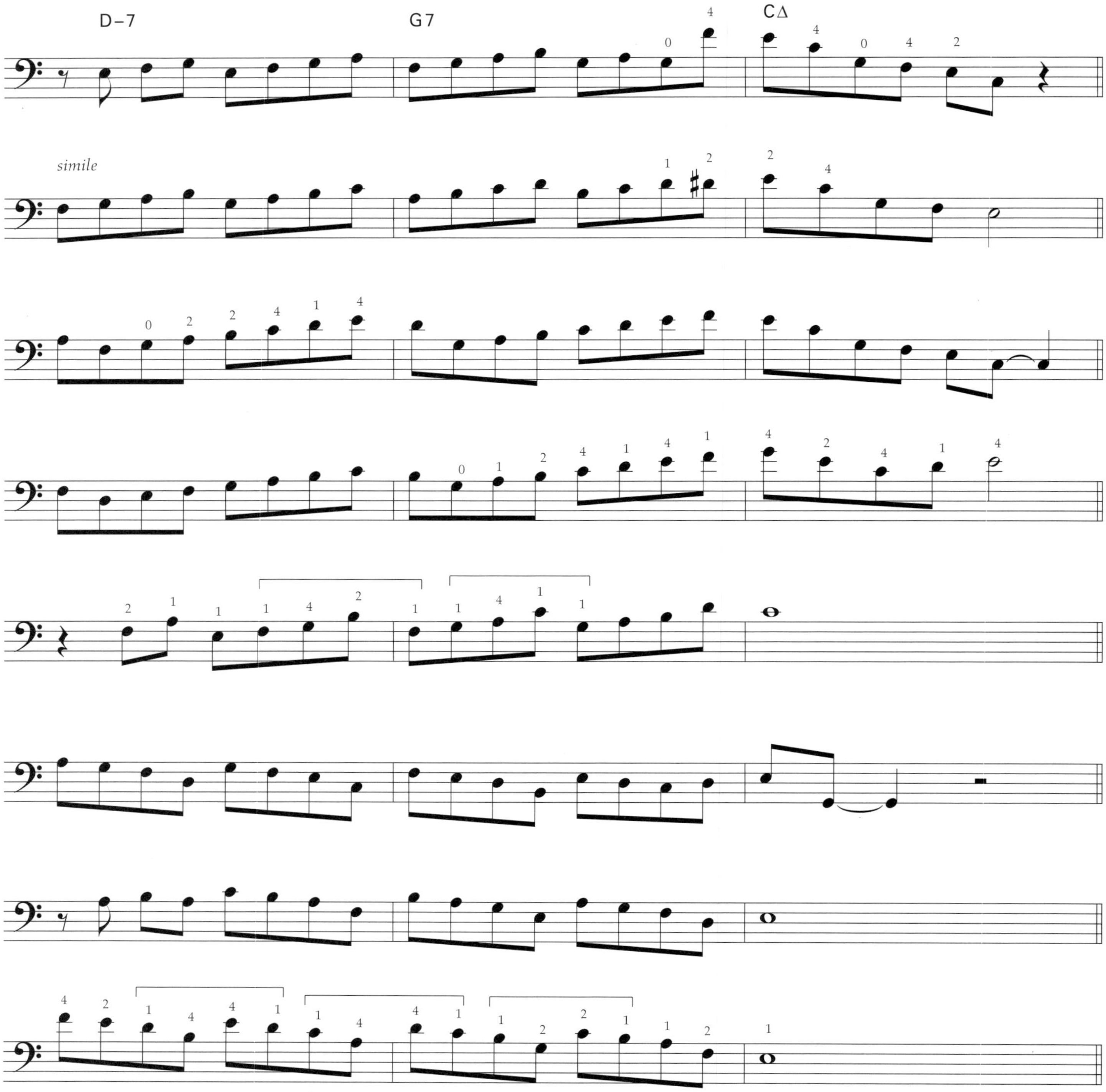
D–7
G7
CΔ
simile

16.2 Scales For The II–7 V7♯9 Progression

In these examples the dominant eight-tone scale (half-step/whole-step) for G7♯9 is used.

16.2 Skalen über II–7 V7♯9

In diesem Beispiel wird die Halbton-Ganztonleiter (Achttonleiter) über G7♯9 verwendet.

SUGGESTION FOR PRACTICE:
Using different, simple pieces from the standard jazz repertoire such as *But Not For Me, Recorda Me,* and *Satin Doll,* play the correct scales first from the tonic which is device that you will later wish to avoid. While improvising bassists very often tend to start the scale from the root. Then begin the scale from the 3rd, and finally from the 7th. In this way you will learn to hear the appropriate scales for each chord even before you begin playing them.

Suggested reading: "Scales For Improvisation" by Dan Haerle.

ÜBEVORSCHLAG:
Spielen Sie zu verschiedenen einfachen Stücken aus dem Jazzrepertoire wie *But Not For Me, Recorda Me, Satin Doll* die jeweils passenden Skalen zuerst ab Grundton (später nie mehr, Bassisten neigen dazu, bei der Improvisation mit Skalen immer vom Grundton aus anzufangen), dann ab Terz und schließlich ab Septime. So lernen Sie Schritt für Schritt, die zu den Akkorden passenden Skalen zu hören, schon bevor Sie sie spielen.

Literaturvorschlag: "Scales For Improvisation" von Dan Haerle.

16.3 Scales For The II V Progression in Minor

16.3 Skalen über II V Verbindungen in Moll

What I said in Chapter VIII.5 (page 156) applies here also. No one uses only scales for an improvisation. That would be boring. It is necessary to combine different methods in order to create an interesting solo.

SUGGESTION FOR PRACTICE:
Practice compositions with II V progressions in minor using different scales (altered, HM5, and diminished) on the dominant while keeping in mind the choosen chord alterations.

Examples: *Blue Bossa, Autumn Leaves, Woody 'n You, What Is This Thing Called Love.*

Beachten Sie auch die Anmerkungen zu Kapitel VIII. 5 (S. 156) – was ich da erwähnt habe, gilt auch hier. Niemand spielt in seinen Soli nur allein Skalen. Das ist langweilig. Deshalb sollten verschiedene Methoden miteinander verknüpft werden, um so ein spannendes Solo zu spielen

ÜBEVORSCHLAG:
Üben Sie bei Kompositionen mit Moll II V Verbindungen wie z.B. *Blue Bossa, Autumn Leaves, Woody 'n You, What Is This Thing Called Love,* bei den Akkorden der V. Stufe verschiedene Skalen: Alterierte Skala, HM5 und Achtton Dominant. Berücksichtigen Sie dabei die gewählte Alteration des Akkordes.

17. Study For II V Progressions

Memorize the phrase found in the first four measures and transpose it for the empty measures.

17. Studie über II V Verbindungen

Lernen Sie die Phrase der ersten vier Takte auswendig und übertragen Sie sie in die leerstehenden Takte.

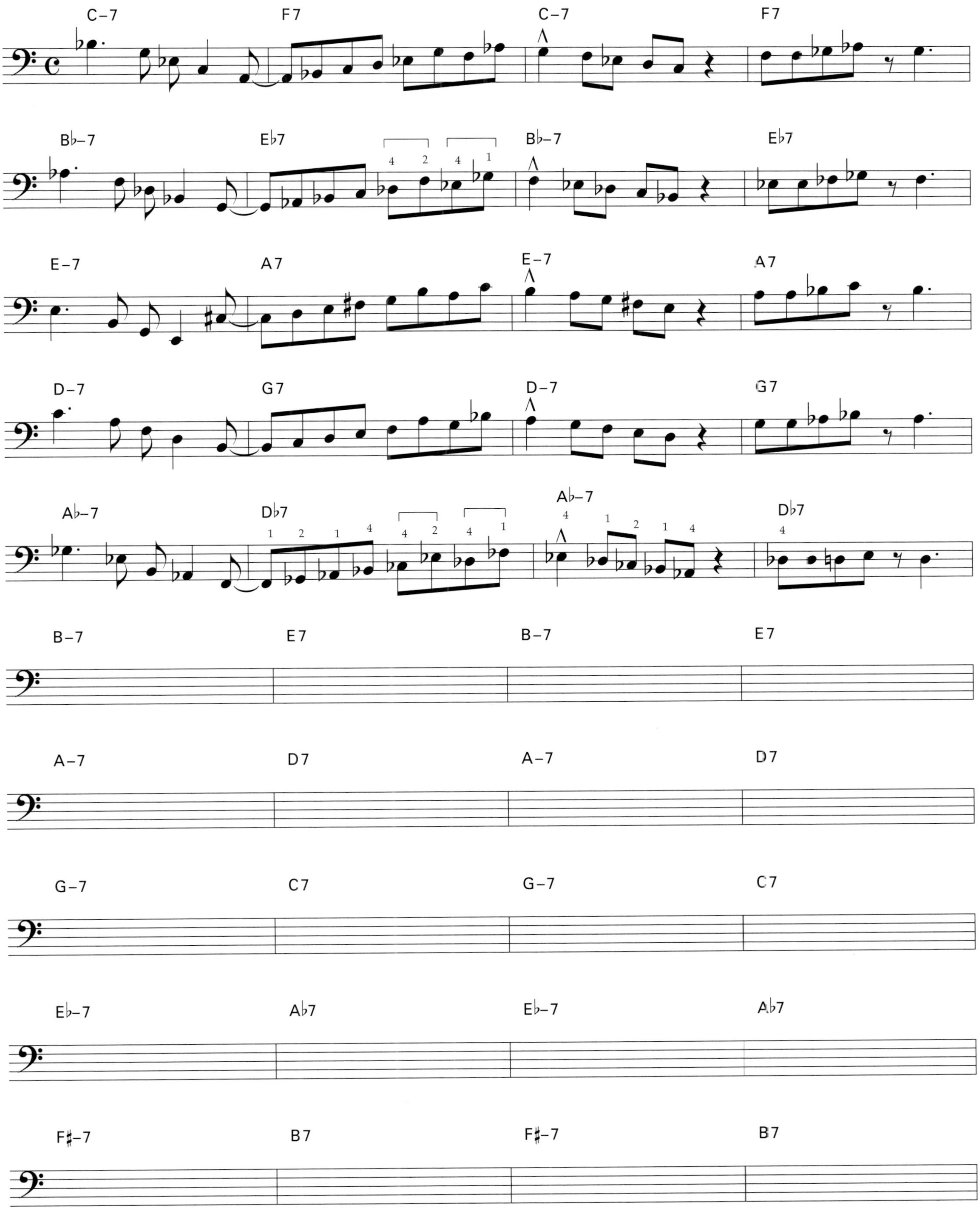

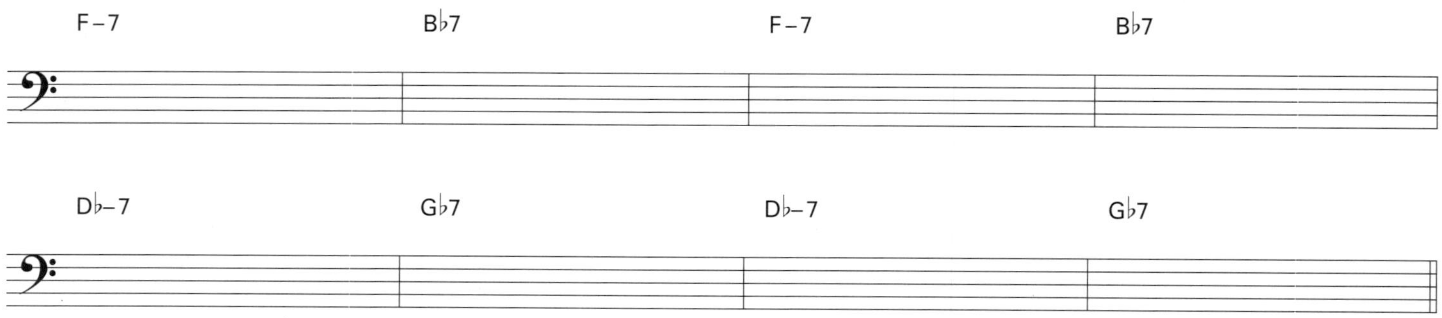

Suggestions for practice:
Jamey Aebersold "Play-Along" series, Vol. 3, has many II V progressions to use for scale practice.

Übevorschlag:
Vol. 3 der Jamey Aebersold Play-Along Serie enthält jede Menge II V Verbindungen, zu denen man sehr gut Skalen üben kann.

18. Study For Half-Measure II V Progressions

18. Studie über halbtaktige II V Verbindungen

This study is particularly good for developing your inner ear. Transpose the given pattern to the chord symbols in the empty measures.

Auch diese Studie soll dazu beitragen, daß Sie Ihr "inneres Ohr" entwickeln. Spielen Sie das gleiche Pattern auch über die Takte, bei denen nur das Akkordsymbol notiert ist.

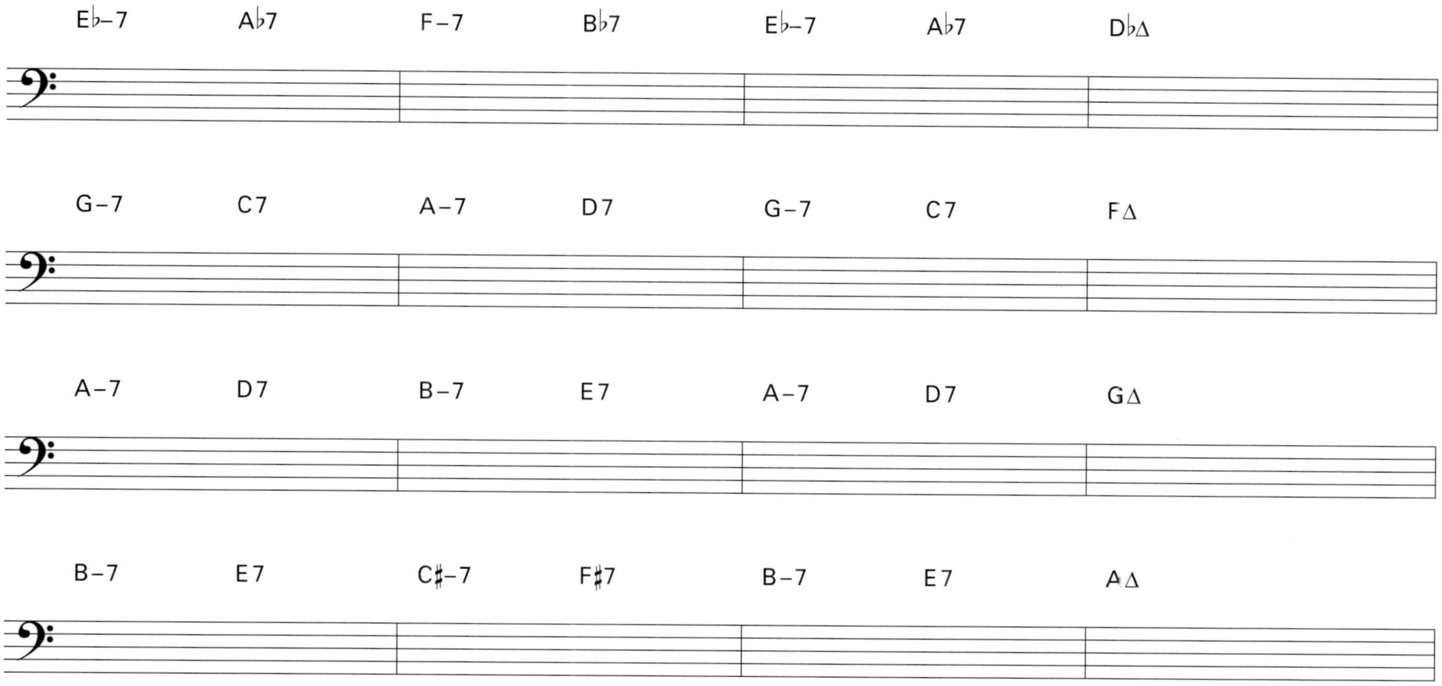

19. Breaking Away From Scales

An often asked question is "How can I use scales practically for a meaningful improvisation?". Although it does not fall in the realm of an instruction book for the bass I would like to answer anyway. "Use them to build melodies."

Another answer would be to include the elements of rhythm, sound, form, and harmony in your improvisation.

The consequence of the first answer is that one must spend the time to study melodic construction. Although melodic construction cannot be dealt with in depth in a "bass" book, here are some suggestions.

A) Practicing

- Practice scales in thirds, fourths, fifths, sixths, sevenths, octaves, ninths, and tenths. (The last is not so easy.) With just this alone you could fill a book. (For example look at such "classical" instruction books as those from Simandl, Montag, Hofmeister, etc.).
- Play single notes shifted by an octave.
- Play scales for a specific chord extremely slowly. Decide which of the individual notes sound good and which could be left out.
- Compose melodies based on scales and use them in your improvisations. Slow down the fast process of improvisation for the slow process of composing.
- Analyze the improvised solos of others observing all the elements that we have covered. What makes their solo interesting or uninteresting?

19. "Aufbrechen" von Skalen

Eine häufig gestellte Frage in der Improvisationslehre, die eigentlich den Rahmen einer Baßschule sprengt, die ich aber dennoch ansprechen möchte, lautet: "Wie kann ich mit Skalen musikalisch sinnvoll improvisieren?"

Erste Antwort: "Bilden Sie daraus Melodien".

Die zweite Antwort: "Beziehen Sie in Ihre Improvisation auch die Elemente Rhythmus, Klang, Form und Harmonik mit ein."

Als Konsequenz der ersten Antwort müßte man sich also mit einer Art von Melodielehre befassen. Das kann naturgemäß in einem Baßbuch nur ansatzweise geleistet werden.

Hier einige Vorschläge:

A) Beim Üben

- Üben Sie Skalen in Terzen, in Quarten, in Quinten, in Sexten, in Septimen, in Oktaven, in Nonen und Dezimen (letzteres ist nicht so einfach!) Damit allein läßt sich ein ganzes Heft füllen. (siehe z.B. die "klassischen" Baßschulen von Simandl, Montag, Hofmeister etc.)
- Spielen Sie einzelne Töne oktavversetzt.
- Spielen Sie Skalen extrem langsam zu einem bestimmten Akkord und entscheiden Sie, welche Töne gut, welche Töne nicht so gut klingen, welche man auch weglassen könnte.
- Komponieren Sie auf der Basis von Skalen eigene Melodien. Verlagern Sie den schnellen Prozeß des Improvisierens in den langsameren des Komponierens. Verwenden Sie diese Melodien dann in Ihren Improvisationen.
- Analysieren Sie Soli anderer Musiker bzgl. der genannten Kriterien. Was macht deren Spiel interessant oder langweilig?

B) Improvising

- Substitute rests for some of the notes.
- play active rhythmically whenever you improvise using scale devices.
- Use other elements such as dynamics and tone colors.
- Mix scales with chords.

B) Beim Improvisieren:

- Ersetzen Sie einzelne Töne durch Pausen.
- Spielen Sie bei einer skalenbezogenen Improvisation rhythmisch sehr aktiv.
- Setzen Sie weitere musikalische Gestaltungsmittel wie Dynamik oder Änderung der Klangfarbe ein.
- Mischen Sie Skalen mit Akkorden.

20. Scale Study: *Autumn Leaves*

20. Skalenstudie über *Autumn Leaves*

IX PRACTICE CONCEPT

By working through this book, you will undoubtedly gain a great deal of motivation and ideas for your own performances. However the question keeps coming to mind how one can use so much material in any kind of a practical way. A few thoughts about practicing in general, and a "tailored" practicing concept would be especially helpful.

The vast field of "practicing" is something which is not "fixed", but rather a dynamic system which is in continual flux. It is a system made up of different elements which have a continual influence on one another. For instance, the right-hand exercises not only have the effect of strengthening the hand and making it faster and more precise, but also effects the quality of the sound as well as the timing and coordination between both hands.

Within this system of interacting parts, the idea of "practice" takes on a whole new dimension. Looking at it as a "network" goes far beyond the conventional idea of just instrumental training. This way of thinking provides in a very natural way a clear, creative and individual method for learning jazz improvisation. It is not the usual step-by-step, anonymous, fixed method, but one that I would like to call "improvised practicing". Practicing becomes a voyage of discovery, experimentation, encourages selfawareness, inventiveness, and offers each a musical experience that is extremely personal.

Some people define creativity as the ability to put together things in a very uncommon and surprising way in order to produce new ideas. The above discussed idea of improvised practicing corresponds to this definition of creativity.

The field of jazz bass practicing can be divided into three parts.

1. Instrumental technique
2. Improvisation
3. Overall music training

Following is a list of subjects which can be individually expanded so that they themselves become a complete, individual field of study.

IX ÜBEKONZEPT

Sie werden bei der Beschäftigung mit diesem Buch sicherlich eine Menge Anregungen und Ideen für ihr eigenes Spielen und Üben erhalten.

Dabei taucht immer wieder die Frage auf, wie man mit der Fülle an Übematerial sinnvoll und effektiv umgeht. Es liegt also nahe, sich ein paar Gedanken über das Üben im allgemeinen und über ein individuelles "Übekonzept" im besonderen zu machen.

Das große Lernfeld Üben läßt sich als ein dynamisches System auffassen, als etwas, das nicht starr, sondern andauernd in Bewegung ist. Es ist aus vielen verschiedenen Einheiten zusammengesetzt. Diese sind ihrerseits Lernfelder, bei denen untereinander ganz offensichtlich Bezüge und Wechselwirkungen zu erkennen sind. Bestimmte einzelne Übungen stehen immer im Zusammenhang mit anderen. So haben z.B. Übungen für die rechte Hand nicht nur den Effekt, daß diese kräftiger, schneller, präziser, sicherer wird. Es wird auch die Qualität des Sounds, des Timings, der Koordination zwischen beiden Händen beeinflußt. Unter diesem Aspekt der Vernetzung bekommt der Begriff Üben eine neue Dimension, die weit über das konventionelle Verständnis von Üben im Sinne von Training am Instrument hinausgeht. Dabei ergibt sich ganz selbstverständlich eine kreative, dem Jazz adäquate Lernmethode, die sehr individuell ist, die sich nicht nach einer starren und anonymen Schritt für Schritt Methode richtet, und die ich als improvisierendes Üben bezeichnen möchte. Es ermöglicht Üben als Probehandeln, fördert das Selbstentdecken und Erfinden, und damit den Erwerb sehr persönlicher Erfahrungen. Überdies entspricht es der Auffassung von Kreativität als einer Fähigkeit, Elemente in ungewohnter und überraschender Weise so zu ordnen, daß eine neue Idee zum Ausdruck kommt.

Das gesamte Lernfeld Üben eines Jazzbassisten läßt sich zunächst in drei Bereiche gliedern:

1. Instrumentaltechnik
2. Improvisation
3. Allgemeine musikalische Übungen

Zu diesen drei Bereichen folgt hier eine Liste von Lernfeldern, die Sie natürlich je nach Ihren eigenen Bedürfnissen erweitern und vervollständigen können:

A Technique

1. Left Hand
1.1 Strengthening
1.2 Change positions
1.3 Intonation
1.4 Pizzicato
1.5 Trills
1.5 Thumb position
1.6 Changing strings

2. Right Hand
2.1 Exercises in plucking
2.1.1 Index finger
2.1.2 Middle finger
2.1.3 Ring finger
2.1.4 Combinations
2.1.5 Changing strings/drops

3. Coordination of both hands
3.1 On a single string
3.2 With string changes
3.3 Studies
3.4 Transcriptions
3.5 (Jazz) theme playing

4. Arco playing
4.1 Bowing techniques
4.2 Changing strings
4.3 Studies
4.4 Transcriptions
4.5 (Jazz) theme playing

5. ....(your own ideas)
5.1 ....
5.2 ....

B Improvisation

1. Comping
1.1 Walking bass
1.2 Binary bass lines
1.3 Miscellaneous grooves
1.4 Chord studies
1.5 Scales

2. Solo playing
2.1 Phrasing and articulation
2.2 Chord studies
2.3 Scales
2.4 Patterns
2.5 Soloing concepts
2.6 Metrically free playing
2.7 Harmonically free playing
2.8 Structural exercises

C General Music Practicing

1. Rhythm
1.1 Develop a feeling for time. Be able to match any tempo and keep it constant. Learn tempos by their metronome markings.

A Technik

1. Linke Hand
1.1 Kräftigung
1.2 Lagenwechsel
1.3 Intonation
1.4 Pizzicato
1.5 Triller
1.5 Daumenaufsatz
1.6 Saitenwechsel

2. Rechte Hand
2.1 Anschlagsübungen
2.1.1 Zeigefinger
2.1.2 Mittelfinger
2.1.3 Ringfinger
2.1.4 Kombinationen
2.1.5 Saitenwechsel/Drops

3. Koordination beider Hände
3.1 auf einer Saite
3.2 mit Saitenwechsel
3.3 Etüden
3.4 Transkriptionen
3.5 (Jazz)Themen spielen

4. Arco-Spiel
4.1 verschiedene Stricharten
4.2 Saitenwechsel
4.3 Etüden
4.4 Transkriptionen
4.5 (Jazz)Themen spielen

5. ....(eigene Vorschläge)
5.1 ....
5.2 ....

B Improvisation

1. Begleitung
1.1 Walking Bass
1.2 binäre Baßlinien
1.3 verschiedene Grooves
1.4 Akkordstudien
1.5 Skalen

2. Solo
2.1 Phrasierung/Artikulation
2.2 Akkordstudien
2.3 Skalen
2.4 Patterns
2.5 Solo-Konzeptionen
2.6 metrisch freies Spiel
2.7 harmonisch ungebundenes Spiel
2.8 formale Übungen

C Allgemeine musikalische Übungen

1. Rhythmik
1.1 *Time feeling* entwickeln, d.h. ein Tempo aufnehmen und konstant halten können, sowie verschiedene Tempi und deren Metronomzahl kennen.

1.2 Use of a metronome or drum machine
1.3 Different groupings (3 in 4, 4 in 3, 5 in 4, etc.)
1.3.1 Polymeters (3 over 4, 4 over 3, 5 over 4, etc.)
1.4 Micro timing (ahead, behind, on the beat.)
1.5 Odd meters

2. Analysis

2.1 Watch live musicians and listen to live music.
2.2 Recorded music (Tapes, Records, CDs, Videos, etc.)
2.3 Chord progressions
2.4 Listen to and analyze rhythm patterns from different rhythm groups.
2.5 Styles
2.6 Solo transcriptions

3. Communication

3.1 Practice along with other musician
3.2 Practice with play-along recordings

4. General

4.1 Sight reading
4.2 Piano playing
4.3 Memorize tunes
4.4 Ear training
4.5 Simple instrument repairs
4.6 Mental training for performance
4.7 Composing
4.8 Developing "work techniques"
4.9 Concentration practice
4.10 Singing
4.11 Music theory
4.12 ....
4.13 ....

From the already mentioned interaction between the different elements, comes the individual "learning-strategy". When it is made clear what material belongs to what element, how that element influences, and is influenced by the others, then it can then be decided what and how one is to practice.

For instance, the element of "Improvisation".

Improvisation combined with other fields of learning

1.2 Arbeit mit Metronom oder Drum Machine
1.3 Verschiebungen (3 in 4, 4 in 3, 5 in 4, usw.)
1.3.1 Polymetrik (3 über 4, 4 über 3, 5 über 4, usw.)
1.4 Mikro-Timing (vor, hinter, auf dem Beat)
1.5 ungerade Metren

2. Analyse

2.1 Live Musik hören und sehen
2.2 Konserven (Bänder, Kassetten, Platten, CDs, Videos, ...)
2.3 Akkordverbindungen
2.4 Rhythmus-Patterns von Rhythmusgruppen abhören und analysieren
2.5 Stilistik
2.6 Soli transkribieren

3. Kommunikation

3.1 mit anderen Musikern üben
3.2 zu Play-Alongs üben

4. Allgemeines

4.1 Blattlese-Übungen
4.2 Klavier spielen
4.3 Stücke und Kompositionen auswendig lernen
4.4 Gehörbildung
4.5 einfache Reparaturen am Instrument
4.6 mentales Training für Konzerte und Auftritte
4.7 eigene Stücke und Kompositionen schreiben
4.8 Beschäftigung mit dem Bereich "Arbeitstechnik"
4.9 Konzentrationsübungen
4.10 Singen
4.11 allgemeine Musiktheorie
4.12 ....
4.13 ....

Aus der angesprochenen Verknüpfung der Lernfelder ergibt sich die individuelle "Lernstrategie". Ist man sich darüber im klaren, welche Inhalte das jeweilige Lernfeld hat, welche Vorgänge wie ablaufen und welche Verbindungen bestehen, kann man entscheiden, was und wie geübt wird.

Als Beispiel das Lernfeld Improvisation:

Improvisation in Verbindung mit anderen Lernfeldern

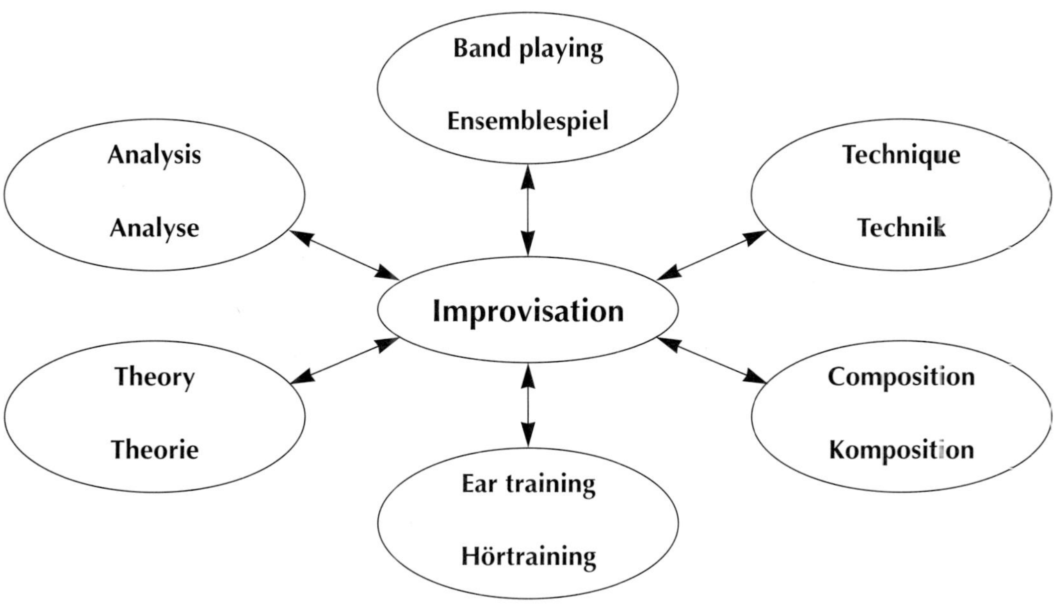

The typical practice plan might look like this:

Analysis

- While listening to a particular recording you have discovered a melodic phrase that is of special interest.
- You transcribe the phrase since it is too difficult to play immediately.
- Analyse the harmonic, structural and rhythmical environment of the phrase as well as the sound.

Technique

- You practice the phrase in a comfortable tempo.
- You notate the best fingerings for both the right and left hand.
- You control your practicing of the phrase by recording.
- You transpose the phrase to other positions and keys.

Theory

- You discover that the phrase sounds good in other harmonic situations.

Composition

- You develop different variations of the phrase.
- You notate the exercise and compose an etude.

Ensemble playing

- You play the phrase and its variations during your next group rehearsal or performance.

The element of composition is a good starting point. For example you discover a useful melodic phrase by trying different possibilities while you are improvising. Using this "composed" phrase you are able to create various connections to the other "fields of learning" thus developing your own very personal practice concepts.

If one looks at music, the instrument, and performer as separate parts of a dynamic "whole", it will become clear that there are influences and connections between all of the different elements. Of course within the framework of a bass instruction book, the subjects of the instrument and the performer cannot be dealt with at depth.

A list of the more important issues follows.

1. Concerning the instrument

- acceptable sound
- correct string placement (strings that are too high from the fingerboard demand too much strength, too low allows the strings to rattle)
- good fingerboard condition (correct shape, smooth surface)
- Acceptable string quality

2. Concerning the player

- Certain physical and mental prerequisites.

Ein typischer Lernvorgang könnte so aussehen:

Lernfeld Analyse

- Sie haben beim Hören einer Aufnahme eine besonders interessante melodische Phrase entdeckt.
- Sie transkribieren diese Phrase, da das unmittelbare Nachspielen zu schwierig ist.
- Sie analysieren, in welchem Zusammenhang die Phrase gespielt wird: harmonisch, formal, rhythmisch, klanglich.

Lernfeld Technik

- Sie üben diese Phrase in einem ausführbaren Tempo.
- Sie notieren dafür den besten Fingersatz, sowohl für die linke als auch die rechte Hand.
- Sie kontrollieren sich durch Aufnehmen Ihres Spiels.
- Sie übertragen die Phrase in andere Lagen (Register) und in andere Tonarten.

Lernfeld Theorie

- Sie entdecken, daß die Phrase auch in anderen harmonischen Zusammenhängen gut klingt.

Lernfeld Komposition

- Sie entwickeln Variationen der Phrase.
- Sie notieren die Übungen, schreiben eine Etüde.

Lernfeld Ensemblespiel

- Sie spielen die Phrase, bzw. Variationen davon bei der nächsten Ensembleprobe oder bei Ihrem nächsten Auftritt.

Denkbar wäre natürlich auch ein Einstieg über das "Lernfeld Komposition": Finden Sie z.B. durch wiederholtes Probieren eine melodische Phrase , die Sie sich gleichsam "erimprovisieren". Mit dieser selbst "komponierten" Phrase könnten Sie dann ähnlich wie beim obigen Beispiel verschiedene Verbindungen zu den einzelnen Lernfeldern herstellen und so Ihr persönliches Übekonzept entwickeln.

Betrachtet man Musik, Instrument und Spieler als Teile eines zusammengehörigen Ganzen, als Teile eines dynamischen Systems, wird klar, daß zwischen allen Elementen Wechselwirkungen und Bezüge bestehen. Im Rahmen einer Instrumentalschule kann naturgemäß auf Instrument und Spieler nur kurz eingegangen werden. Dabei spielen eine Rolle:

1. Beim Instrument

- akzeptabler Klang
- gute Saitenlage (zu hohe Saitenlage erfordert zuviel Kraft, zu niedrige läßt die Saiten klirren)
- guter Zustand des Griffbretts (richtige Kehlung, keine Unebenheiten)
- akzeptable Qualität der Saiten

2. Beim Spieler

- bestimmte physische und psychische Voraussetzungen

The complexity of both issues leaves me no choice but to give only a hint of the specialized literature.

Another example, a common ostinato figure, is provided here to illustrate the network among the fields of learning once more.

Beide Gebiete sind so komplex, daß mir hier nur der Hinweis auf die entsprechende Fachliteratur bleibt.

Die Vernetzung der Lernfelder möchte ich anhand eines anderen Beispiels, einer Ostinato-Figur, wie sie so oder ähnlich häufig gespielt wird, noch einmal aufzeigen.

Example: **Beispiel:**

Before you can play this ostinato on your instrument, you are faced with the problem of translating the written music into actual performance.

Here I would like to suggest a step-wise solution.

- Read and understand all available information, meter, tempo, clef, key, etc., that the graphic notation gives you: (4/4 time, tempo ♩ = 160 means 160 quarter-note beats per minute.)
- Learn the rhythm one measure at a time by singing an indefinite pitch.

Bevor Sie das Ostinato auf Ihrem Instrument spielen, steht hier der Prozeß des Notenlesens, die Umsetzung der Notenschrift in Klang.

Hier empfiehlt sich ein schrittweises Vorgehen:

- Lesen Sie zuerst die grundlegenden Informationen, die im Notenbild vorhanden sind, wie Taktart, Tempo, Notenschlüssel, Vorzeichen:
  4/4 Takt, Tempo ♩ = 160, (das bedeutet 160 Schläge pro Minute), Baßschlüssel, keine Vorzeichen.
- Lernen Sie dann den Rhythmus, indem Sie ihn taktweise und ohne eine definierte Tonhöhe laut singen:

Example: **Beispiel:**

- Put both measures together, beat time with your hand while singing the rhythm.
- Play the first tone of the ostinato (E♭) on the bass. Sing the rest of the phrase using the correct pitches and rhythm. In this way you learn the phrase with your "inner ear" before you play it on your bass.
- Find a practical fingering for the left hand.
- Play repeatedly without stopping the first example on your instrument.

Going through some mental training like this in advance will noticeably speed up the process of learning a particular phrase on your instrument. Use a metronome (clicks on two and four) and record the phrase to tape.

When listening observe the following:

- Do you keep a steady rhythmic flow? Are the notes placed exactly according to the rhythmical structure?
- Are the dynamics of the individual notes what you expect?
- Does your intonation suffer with repetition?

- Setzen Sie nun beide Takte zusammen, indem Sie den Rhythmus singen und ihn gleichzeitig mit der rechten Hand klopfen.
- Spielen Sie den ersten Ton des Ostinatos (E♭) auf dem Baß. Führen Sie die Phrase laut singend weiter, wobei Sie den bereits bekannten Rhythmus mit den richtigen Tönen "auffüllen". Auf diese Weise hören Sie die Phrase bereits mit Ihrem "inneren Ohr", bevor Sie sie auf dem Instrument spielen.
- Überlegen Sie sich einen günstigen Fingersatz für die linke Hand.
- Spielen Sie erst jetzt das erste Beispiel mehrmals hintereinander auf Ihrem Instrument.

Sie werden bemerken, daß durch den Vorgang des vorgeschalteten mentalen Übens die Figur zügig auf dem Instrument verwirklicht werden kann. Benutzen Sie ein Metronom (Klick auf zwei und vier). Nehmen Sie die Figur auf Band oder Kassette auf.

Achten Sie beim Anhören auf die folgenden Punkte:

- Bleibt der rhythmische Fluß konstant, ist die rhythmische Plazierung der Noten exakt?
- Entspricht die Dynamik der einzelnen Noten genau Ihren Vorstellungen?
- Werden alle Töne auch nach mehrmaligem Wiederholen noch gut intoniert?

- Are you satisfied with your sound? (Do not let the quality of the recording machine influence your critic of your playing.)

Generally, the following skills have a definite influence on your overall performance quality.

A) Technical abilities

- Left hand: strength, stamina, change of position, intonation
- Right hand: strength, stamina, precision of string crossing
- Coordination of both hands

B) Basic musical skills

- Rhythmic consistency (timing)
- Feeling for dynamics
- A preconceived idea of your sound

If you are not completely satisfied with the quality of your playing, ask yourself how you might be able to make an improvement. In the beginning it is not so simple to decide whether the problem is musical, technical, or perhaps lies somewhere else. Detailed practice and observation can be a great help in answering these questions.

In the area of "technique", here are a few suggestions how you might go about discovering the cause of a problem.

- Left hand (find the correct fingerings)

Example:

- Sind Sie mit der klanglichen Realisation zufrieden? Achten Sie dabei bitte mehr auf Ihr Spiel als auf die durch Ihren Recorder bedingte Aufnahmequalität.

Ganz allgemein läßt sich feststellen, daß auf die Qualität der Ausführung entscheidenden Einfluß haben:

A) Technische Fähigkeiten

- Linke Hand: Kraft, Ausdauer, Lagenwechsel, Intonation
- Rechte Hand: Kraft, Ausdauer, Präzision beim Saitenwechsel,
- Die Koordination zwischen beiden Händen

B) Grundlegende musikalische Fähigkeiten

- Rhythmische Konstanz (Timing)
- Ein Gefühl für Dynamik
- Eine vorhandene Klangvorstellung

Sind Sie mit der Qualität des Gespielten nicht ganz zufrieden, stellt sich natürlich die Frage, wie Sie diese verbessern können. Vor allem zu Beginn ist es nicht so einfach, genau festzustellen, ob die Ursachen eher im technischen oder im musikalischen Bereich (oder irgendwo anders) liegen. Detailliertes Probehandeln und eigene Beobachtung können dabei wertvolle Hilfe für die Verbesserung der Durchführung sein.

Für das Lernfeld Technik hier einige Vorschläge, wie Sie mit entsprechenden Übungen spielerisch "Ursachenforschung" betreiben können:

- Linke Hand (herausfinden des passenden Fingersatzes)

Beispiel:

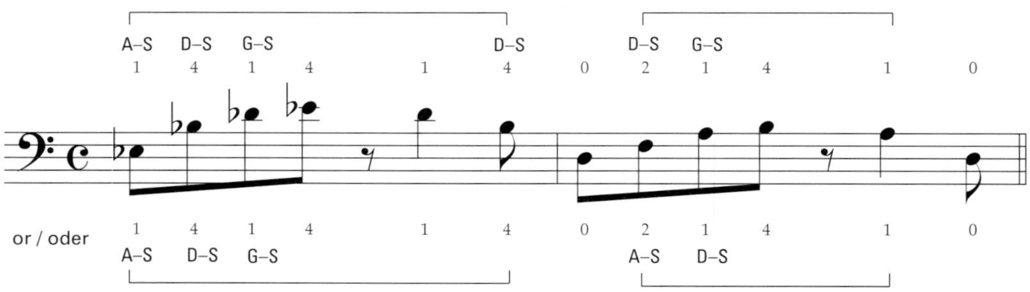

The fingerings given below the example have the obvious advantage that in the 2nd measure only an ascending half position shift needs to be made. This makes intonation much easier.

The right hand is more responsible for the detailed rhythmic practice, expecially here by numerous string crossings.

- Right hand (different fingerings, index finger, middle finger, and combinations.) See which of the four suggestions you like the best. Respectively, finding the fingerings that are best for you.

Der untere Fingersatz hat den offensichtlichen Vorteil, daß man zum Spielen des 2. Taktes nur eine halbe Lage nach oben wechseln muß. Das erhöht die Sicherheit bei der Intonation.

Für die rhythmische Feinarbeit ist hauptsächlich die rechte Hand zuständig, hier besonders bei mehrfachen Saitenwechseln:

- Rechte Hand (verschiedene Fingersätze: Zeigefinger, Mittelfinger, Kombinationen). Prüfen Sie, welcher der vier Vorschläge Ihnen am besten gefällt, bzw. finden Sie einen für Sie optimalen Fingersatz.

Example: **Beispiel:**

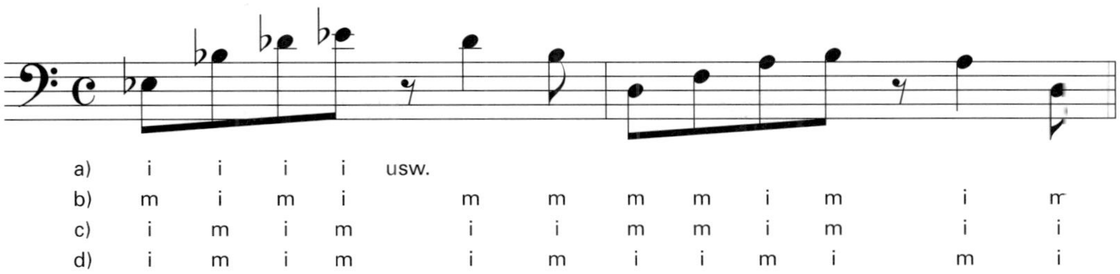

- Right hand only: the same string changes but only with open strings. (By not using the left hand, you can concentrate fully on the right.)

- Nur rechte Hand: die gleichen Saitenwechsel, jedoch allein mit Leersaiten (durch das Weglassen der linken Hand können Sie sich allein auf die rechte konzentrieren)

Example: **Beispiel:**

After numerous tries you will see (perhaps) that the lower fingerings are better. With most bassists, rhythmic precision (timing) is best when an ostinato like this one in a moderate tempo, is plucked with only one finger. Decide for yourself.

Also observe the effect that a change of tempo (faster or slower) has on the quality of the exercise. Which tempo sounds best? At which tempo does the rhythmic exactness or sound begin to suffer? At which tempo do you feel the best?

Discover different possibilities for playing the ostinato.

Nach einigem Ausprobieren erweist sich (vielleicht) der untere Fingersatz als besser. Bei den meisten Bassisten ist die rhythmische Präzision (Timing) dann am besten, wenn diese oder ähnliche Ostinati im mittleren Tempo nur mit einem Finger gezupft werden. Entscheiden Sie selbst.

Beobachten Sie ebenfalls, welchen Einfluß Veränderungen des Tempos (schneller/langsamer) auf die Qualität der Übung haben. Bei welchem Tempo klingt es gut, wann leidet die rhythmische Genauigkeit, wann der Klang? Bei welchem Tempo fühlen Sie sich wohl?

Entdecken Sie verschiedene Möglichkeiten, das Ostinato zu spielen:

Element Rhythm

- Rhythmic variation

Element Rhythmus

- Rhythmische Variation

Example: **Beispiel:**

- The ostinato in uneven meters.

- Ostinato über ungerade Taktarten.

Example:

Beispiel:

a up-tempo

b up-tempo

You can practice the examples above using your own variations of different fields of learning.

- Timing practice (the even note-placement on, before, or behind the beat.)
- Use different accents, especially on the off-beats.

Sie können die oben gezeigten bzw. Ihre eigenen Versionen auch innerhalb weiterer Lernfelder üben:

- Timing üben (gleichmäßige Plazierung der Noten, auch vor, hinter oder genau auf dem Beat)
- Verschiedene dynamische Akzente, besonders Betonungen auf den Off-beats

Example:

Beispiel:

- Rhythmic Variation (example with triplets).

- Rhythmische Variationen, z.B. mit Triolen.

Example:

Beispiel:

- Combining different rhythmic variations (example in four-measure groups).

- Kombinationen verschiedener rhythmischer Varianten z.B. zu viertaktigen Einheiten.

Example:

Beispiel:

Harmony

- Ostinati over different chord qualities.

Element Harmonie

- Ostinati über verschiedene Akkordqualitäten.

Example: / **Beispiel:**

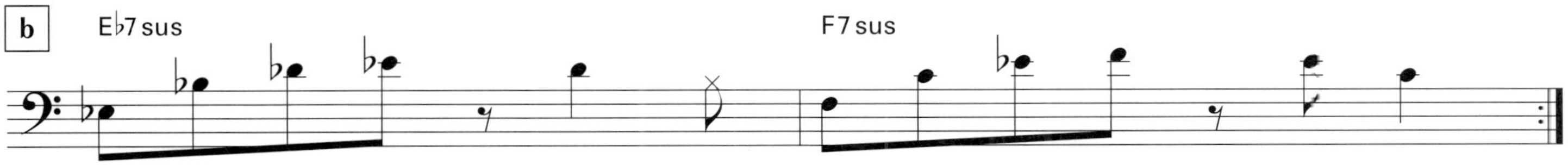

Combine different elements that result in different rhythmic variations of the ostinato is played with different chord progressions.

Verbinden Sie beide Elemente, indem Sie verschiedene rhythmische Versionen des Ostinatos über verschiedene Akkordverbindungen spielen.

Example: / **Beispiel:**

These examples are intended to show the countless possibilities of utilizing and combining the different elements and their influences that are available to you whenever you think in these terms, and to motivate you to develop your own individual practicing and study program.

For one to use this method of discovery, and gain confidence in this kind of improvisation method, one needs above all patience and practice. With increasing ability to focus on and use the different elements for a specific purpose, your improvement will greatly increase.

While certain areas are practiced only for a specific time to solve a specific problem, other areas like the training of motor-skills, belong to a daily-practice program. (warm-ups, strength and conditioning training.)

With this system of thinking in terms of interactive elements, you have the possibility tailoring your practicing to better fit your needs.

Here is an example of a time-structured personal practice plan.

Section A

Routine, plus

1	(Intonation)	
2	(Left hand)	
3	(*arco* playing)	50% practice time

Section B

Routine, plus

1.1	(Walking bass)	
5.1	(Articulation)	
6.3	(Free, unaccompanied soloing)	20% practice time

Section C

Routine, plus

4.1	(Sight-reading practice)	
7.1	(Ear training)	30% practice time

total 100%

In conclusion I would like to make one last point. Concentrated practice is only the first step towards the following.

Make music joyfully!

Diese Beispiele für vernetztes Denken und die sich daraus ergebenden zahlreichen Möglichkeiten zur Kombination der Lernfelder sind dazu gedacht, Ihnen methodische Anregungen für Ihr sehr persönliches Übeprogramm zu vermitteln. Um sich mit dieser Methode des Entdeckens und des improvisierenden Übens vertraut zu machen, braucht man vor allem zu Beginn etwas Geduld und Übung. Mit einiger Erfahrung entwickeln sich jedoch, durch die damit einhergehende Konzentration auf das Wesentliche, Effektivität und Erfolg des Übens enorm.

Während bestimmte Lernfelder nur über einen bestimmten Zeitraum und mit einem bestimmten Ziel geübt werden, gehören andere, vor allem motorisch-gymnastische Übungen (Aufwärmen, Kraft- und Konditionsübungen) zum täglichen Übeprogramm. Unter dem Aspekt der Vernetzung sind Sie jedoch in der Lage, auch hier variabel vorzugehen.

Hier ein Beispiel für einen persönlichen Übeplan in Verbindung mit einer zeitlichen Strukturierung:

Bereich A

Routine, sowie

1	(Intonation)	
2	(linke Hand)	
3	(*arco*-Spiel)	50% Übezeit

Bereich B

Routine, sowie

1.1	(Walking Bass)	
5.1	(Artikulation)	
6.3	(freies, unbegleitetes Solo)	20% Übezeit

Bereich C

Routine, sowie

4.1	(Blattlese-Übungen)	
7.1	(Gehörbildung)	30% Übezeit

insgesamt 100%

Zum Abschluß möchte ich noch darauf hinweisen, daß konzentriertes Üben nur die Vorstufe zu einem Ziel sein kann.

Mit Freude Musik machen!

Blues 4 U

for 2 basses / für zwei Bässe

More Bass Hit

for 2 basses / für zwei Bässe

25
29
33
37
D A G A D A G D
solo
41
45

Cephalocereus

for 2 basses / für zwei Bässe

Daddy B.

for 2 basses / für zwei Bässe

♩ = 104 (even eighths)

Georgia On My Mind

for solo bass

Hoagy Carmichael

Selected Recordings By Sigi Busch

Ausgewählte Diskographie von Sigi Busch

Association P.C.	Earwax	Munich 6802 634 M 1
	Sun Rotation	MPS Stereo 21 21329-3
	Erna Morena	MPS Stereo 21 21524-3
	Rock Around The Cock	MPS Stereo 21 21763-9
Association P.C. with Jeremy Steig	Mama Kuku	MPS Stereo 21 21840-6
Joe Viera – Ed Kröger Quartet	Essay In Jazz	Rote Reihe 52, UE 20052
Jazztrack	First Call	Happy Bird/Bellaphon 5015 Stereo
	Jazztrack	Happy Bird/Bellaphon 5023 Stereo
	Listen	Happy Bird/Bellaphon 5030 Stereo
Jazztrack with Norma Winstone	Flying Stork	Musicians Record Co/EMI 066-45 422
Uli Beckerhoff Quintet	Dedication	Spygel Fusion Stereo 8009 LC 7596
Sigi Busch/Charlie Mariano/Wolfgang Dauner	Age Of Miracles	MPS Stereo 20 22457-1
Sigi Busch/Alexander Sputh Duo	A New Way Of Living	Ego Records/Pläne 4020
Manfred Schoof Big Band	Manfred Schoof Big Band	Mood 28641
Quartet & Brass	Culloo	Line COCD 9 00919
Quartet & Brass	More Than Four	Line COCD 9 01068
BuschMusic	The Berlin Song Book	Klangräume LC 30240

Whom To Listen To — Wichtige Bassisten

Jimmy Blanton	Duke Ellington Orchestra
Charles Mingus	Charles Mingus Band
Oscar Pettiford	Duke Ellington Orchestra, Ben Webster, Thelonious Monk
Ray Brown	Oscar Peterson Trios
Paul Chambers	Miles Davis, John Coltrane
Sam Jones	Cannonball Adderley, Eastern Rebellion
Scott LaFaro	Bill Evans Trio, Ornette Coleman
Gary Peacock	Bill Evans, Miles Davis, Keith Jarrett
Richard Davis	Elvin Jones, Thad Jones/Mel Lewis Orchestra
Charlie Haden	Ornette Coleman, Liberation Orchestra
Rufus Reid	Dexter Gordon, Kenny Burrell, Kenny Barron, Lee Konitz, Jack DeJohnette
George Mraz	Tommy Flanagan, Slide Hampton, John Abercrombie
Nils Henning Œrsted–Pedersen	Oscar Peterson Trio, Kenny Drew, Dexter Gordon
Palle Danielsson	Jan Garbarek Group
Ron McClure	Keith Jarrett, David Liebman
Eberhard Weber	Colours, Jan Garbarek
Dave Holland	Miles Davis, Chick Corea, Jack DeJohnette
Eddie Gomez	Bill Evans Trio, Steps, Jeremy Steig
Ron Carter	Miles Davis, Herbie Hancock
Mirouslav Vitous	Weather Report, Chick Corea, Vitous Trio & Quartet
Mike Richmond	Stan Getz, Jack DeJohnette
David Friesen	David Friesen Duo, Trio, Quartet
Stanley Clarke	Chick Corea, Stanley Clarke Bands
Jaco Pastorious	Weather Report
Slam Stewart	Art Tatum, Don Byas, Lionel Hampton
Christian McBride	Jazz Futures, Joshua Redman
Steve Swallow	Carla Bley Band, Gary Burton
Marc Johnson	John Abercrombie, Bass Desires
Marcus Miller	Miles Davis
Dennis Irwin	John Scofield
John Patitucci	Chick Corea

About The Author

During his long career as jazz bassist, Sigi Busch has performed with Ben Webster, Philly Joe Jones, Sonny Stitt, Jeremy Steig, Gary Burton, David Liebman, Mose Allison and John Zorn, and gained much of his reputation as a member of "Association P.C." "Jazztrack", and the "Manfred Schoof Big Band".

At ten, Sigi began violin lessons, at 16 trombone, at 20 bass, and in the military learned the tuba. He gained experience with amateur bands before beginning his studies at the Bremen Conservatory.

During the years from 1968 to 1971 Busch performed with Joe Viera-Ed Kröger Quartet and from 1971 to 1975 with Association P.C. Late 1973 the first recording "Age of Miracles" was released under his own name. Charlie Mariano and Wolfgang Dauner were also featured.

After studying at Berklee College of Music in Boston, Busch worked from 1975 to 1979 with "Jazztrack". Afterwards he worked with drummer Pierre Courbois and founded the group "In 'n Out". In the fall of 1989 he performed with the Gil Evans Orchestra.

Sigi Busch taught at the Hochschule für Musik in Hannover, the Musikhochschule in Hamburg, Bremen University, Oldenburg University, and for many years taught a jazz course for Jeunesses Musicales, Germany.

In 1979 Sigi Busch was the first to be awarded the "Förderpreis Musik" from the city of Bremen. In addition to this book, Busch has also published a three-part ear training course and a basic jazz and pop theory book.

Since 1989 Sigi Busch has been professor for jazz pedagogy at the "Hochschule der Künste" in Berlin. He has also been appearing as a duo with pianist Walter Norris. In 1994 he reassembled and toured with his group "BuschMusic", and has lately produced the CD "The Berlin Songbook".

Über den Autor

Sigi Busch spielte im Laufe seiner Karriere mit Musikern wie Ben Webster, Philly Joe Jones, Sonny Stitt, Jeremy Steig, Gary Burton, David Liebman, Mose Allison oder John Zorn, ist aber vor allem als Mitglied der Gruppen "Association P.C.", "Jazztrack" und der Manfred Schoof Big Band bekannt geworden.

Er hatte als Zehnjähriger Geigenunterricht, lernte mit 16 Posaune, mit 20 Baß und beim Militär schließlich auch Tuba. Erste Erfahrungen hat er mit diversen Amateurbands gemacht, bevor er am Bremer Konservatorium studierte.

1968 bis 1971 gehörte Busch fest zum Joe Viera - Ed Kröger Quartett und 1971 bis 1975 zur "Association P.C.". Ende 1973 ist die erste Platte unter eigenem Namen, "Age of Miracles", mit Sidemen wie Charlie Mariano und Wolfgang Dauner erschienen.

Nach einem Studium am Berklee College of Music in Boston USA arbeitete er 1975 bis 1979 mit "Jazztrack" und gründetet danach mit dem Drummer Pierre Courbois die Gruppe "In 'n Out". Im Herbst 1989 spielte er im Gil Evans Orchestra.

Sigi Busch unterrichtete außerdem an der Hochschule für Musik in Hannover, an der Hamburger Musikhochschule, hatte Lehraufträge an den Universitäten in Bremen und Oldenburg und leitete viele Jahre lang die Jazzkurse der Jeunesses Musicales Deutschland.

1979 erhielt er den erstmals verliehenen Förderpreis Musik der Stadt Bremen. Der Bassist hat neben der vorliegenden Baßschule Bücher wie eine dreiteilige Gehörbildung (Hörtraining 1, 2 & 3) und eine Jazz & Pop Musiklehre verfaßt.

Seit 1989 ist Sigi Busch Professor für Jazzpädagogik an der Hochschule der Künste in Berlin. Seitdem spielt er auch mit dem Pianisten Walter Norris im Duo. 1994 stellte er auch wieder seine Gruppe "BuschMusic" zusammen, mit der er in den letzten Jahren Konzertreisen unternahm und eine CD unter dem Titel "The Berlin Songbook" produzierte.

Photo by Hiam Halawa

MIKE DOWNES
THE JAZZ BASS LINE BOOK
• ORDER NO. 15019 (CA. 140 PAGES)

This is a comprehensive approach to the construction of improvised bass lines. Intended for beginners and professionals alike, the book deals with playing in "2", creating walking bass lines, 3/4 time, using a "broken feel", modal and slash-chord harmony, ballads, and much more.
Each chapter is full of fundamental and advanced concepts and ideas, accompanied by transcribed examples from the masters of jazz bass playing.
Mike Downes is currently the head of the bass department at prestigious Humber College in Toronto. He is much in demand as a clinician, and he continues to be one of the most sought after bassists in Canada.

FERNANDO MARTINEZ
FUNK GROOVES FOR BASS (E-S)
• ORDER NO. 15025 (80-PAGE BOOK W/CD)

This book/CD set provides a bridge to the professional-level books by John Patitucci or Dave Weckl and includes:
a play-along CD, featuring 12 grooves in the styles of Marcus Miller, Me'Shell Ndegeocello, Anthony Jackson, a.o.; detailed practicing concepts; tune descriptions; groove transcription; practical exercises and hints

BILL MAYS
THREE SHORT STORIES
• ORDER NO. 06003

For double bass and piano.
Three Short Stories, written for bassist John Goldsby, is an extended, through-composed three-movement piece. It contains improvised sections for both instruments, challenging passages of bass harmonics and extensive use of both arco and pizzicato techniques.
Recorded by John Goldsby and Bill Mays on "Tale of the Fingers" (Concord CCD-4632).

*"[...] a major new work for improvising bassists who have formidable arco technique." **(International Society of Bassists)***

MICHAEL MOORE
MELODIC PLAYING IN THE THUMB POSITION
• ORDER NO. 15006 (100-PAGE BOOK W/CD)

This book/CD set offers a method to solve the problem of being ›ruled by roots‹ in a solo. It can be used as a thumb position method to explore the upper reaches of the instrument with a logical harmonic approach, and will aid in developing a more melodic approach to solo playing.

*"A gifted player and influential teacher, Moore puts much of his unique insight into this remarkable book, now available in an imposing illustrated edition. Starting with simple diatonic material, Moore leads you through the full spectrum of diminished, pentatonic, and altered scales, illustrating each stage with notated and recorded examples based on standard chord progressions." **(Simon Woolf, Bass Player)***

MICHAEL MOORE/CLEM DEROSA
THE MICHAEL MOORE BASS METHOD
• ORDER NO. 15013 (140-PAGE BOOK)

A first of its kind approach to the learning of double bass, incorporating traditional classical studies with practical jazz and popular music applications.
Michael Moore, who has been at the top of the jazz bass scene since his arrival in New York in the 1960s, and pioneer of jazz education Clem DeRosa, combine to produce an easy to follow method designed for individual or classroom application.

PETER O'MARA
A RHYTHMIC CONCEPT FOR FUNK/FUSION BASS (E/D)
• ORDER NO. 15026 (48-PAGE BOOK W/2 CDS)

This book/CD set features 16 challenging original tunes in Funk/Fusion style by renowned Australian guitarist Peter O'Mara. Patrick Scales adds his ideas on musical interpretation to give the aspiring bassist an insight into the creative process from a professional's point of view. The tunes cover a variety of tempos and grooves and are presented using a real rhythm section: Patrick Scales, Christian Lettner and Peter O'Mara (from Klaus Doldinger's "Passport")
The audio play-along tracks are presented in an order of increasing complexity. CD 1 contains complete recordings of all instruments so that you can hear each instrument working together. CD 2 omits all bass tracks so that you can playalong with the rhythm section and also create your own basslines.
Midifiles of all compositions are also included.
Also available are editions for guitar, by Peter, and drums, by Peter O'Mara and Christian Lettner. The books are fully compatible and can be used in a combo setting.

RON MILLER
HOW TO PLAY BASS IN A BIG BAND
• ORDER NO. 15022 (76-PAGE BOOK W/CD)

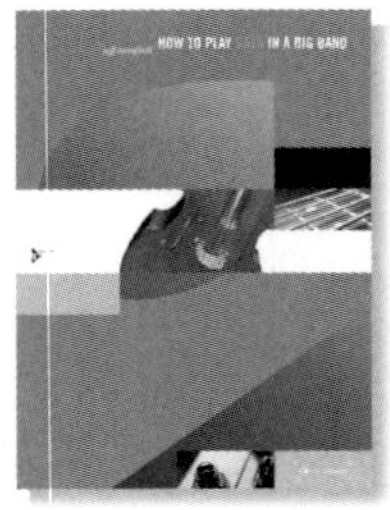

Improvisation is at the heart of jazz, but knowing how to play stylistically correct in a large jazz ensemble is also a necessity. *How to Play Bass in a Big Band* offers tips, suggestions, examples and a play along CD to help you put it all together. The repertoire covers many jazz styles from Basie to Latin and African-influenced music to ECM and contemporary jazz (the Vanguard Jazz Orchestra, Bob Brookmeyer, etc.).

CHUCK SHER/MARC JOHNSON
CONCEPTS POUR L' IMPROVISATION D'UN SOLO DE BASSE (F-D)
• COMMANDE 15001 (200 PAGES AVEC 2 CDS)

SOLOKONZEPTE FÜR BASS (F-D)
• BESTELLNR. 15001 (200 SEITEN MIT 2 CDS)

Auswahl der Töne, Phrasierungsübungen, Das Üben von Soli über die Akkordfolge von Standards, transkribierte Soli von Jimmy Haslip, Eddie Gomez, Dominique Di Piazza, John Patitucci, George Mraz, Gary Willis und Scott LaFaro. Mark Johnson demonstriert auf der CD alle Übungen und Techniken.

JIM SNIDERO/JOHN GILL
EASY JAZZ CONCEPTION BASS LINES
• ORDER NO. 14768 (40-PAGE BOOK W/CD)

Simplified bass lines, as played by John Gill

JIM SNIDERO
INTERMEDIATE JAZZ CONCEPTION BASS LINES (E-D)
• ORDER NO. 14788 (BOOK W/CD)

Paul Gill, bass

JIM SJIM SNIDERO/DENNIS IRWIN
JAZZ CONCEPTION BASS LINES (E-D)
• ORDER NO. 14736 (BOOK W/CD)

Exact transcriptions as played by Dennis Irwin plus 21 simple piano lead sheets. Turn off the bass track on the CD and comp with Mike LeDonne and Kenny Washington.

JIM SNIDERO/PETER WASHINGTON
JAZZ CONCEPTION FOR BASS (E-D)
• ORDER NO. 14728 (BOOK W/CD)

Soloist: Peter Washington, bass

DAVE WEIGERT
JAZZ WORKSHOP FOR BASS & DRUMS (E)
• ORDER NO. 14601 (134-PAGE BOOK W/CD)

The primary focus of this book/CD set is on jazz and the related styles of funk, Brazilian and Afro-Cuban jazz. The CD features 16 play-along tunes, including jazz classics by John Coltrane, Miles Davis, Herbie Hancock and Sonny Rollins, choice standards, as well as Latin and funk tunes by "Pee Wee" Ellis, Russell Ferrante, James Brown, a.o., plus 9 rhythmic etudes by three Berklee faculty members. In addition the book contains written parts and playing suggestions for bassists and drummers.
Soloists and rhythm sections include Berklee faculty members Hal Crook, Bruce Gertz, Rick Peckham, Billy Pierce, a.o.

*"Jazz Workshop is loaded with very important essential information for the aspiring drummer and bassist! It is clearly presented and covers vast intricacies of playing this music, Jazz! If you aspire to become a 'world class player', check this book out, NOW!" **(Rufus Reid)***

*"This text and accompanying CD should prove to be an invaluable tool for the developing rhythm section player. Dave has touched on all the significant points regarding rhythmic foundation and has emphasized 'listening'. We all know you can lead a horse to water but you can't make him drink. Hey drummers and bassists, if you're thirsty, the water is there!" **(Marc Johnson)***

JAZZ WORKSHOP FÜR BASS & SCHLAGZEUG (D)
• BESTELLNR. 14602 (134 SEITEN MIT CD)

Dieses Buch/CD Set konzentriert sich in erster Linie auf den Jazz und Funk, sowie brasilianischen und afrokubanischen Jazz. Es enthält ausgeschriebene Stimmen zu 16 Stücken von Miles, Hancock, Rollins, James Brown, Pastorius, Russel Ferrante u.a.
Aus dem Inhalt: Die Geschichte von Bass und Schlagzeug im Jazz; Notation; Das Verbessern des Blattspiels; Interpretation eines Leadsheets; Sinnvolles Üben; Üben mit Aufnahmen (CD und Video); Setups und Fills; Time; Jazz Feel; Form; Improvisation; Latin Feel; Begleitung und Time Spielen; Touch, Ton und Dynamik; Funk Feel, Hören und Gehörbildung; Vorbereitung auf eine Probe; 9 Rhythmik-Etüden; Basslinien nach Stilen; Zusammenfassung der Feels nach Stilen; Musikervokabular; Bibliographie.
Die Demo/Play-along CD wurde von 22 (!) Berklee-Dozenten, wie z.B. Hal Crook, Billy Pierce, Rick Peckham und Greg Badolato in den Berklee Studios eingespielt.

*"...enthält eine Fülle sehr wichtiger, essentieller Informationen für interessierte Schlagzeuger und Bassisten." **(Rufus Reid)***

*"...ein unschätzbares Werkzeug für die Rhythmusgruppe." **(Marc Johnson)***

SIGI BUSCH

Sigi Busch
JAZZ & POP: HARMONISCHE GRUNDLAGEN
• Bestellnr. 11202 (192 seiten)
Die bisherige Jazz & Pop Musiklehre ist nach der 8. Auflage grundlegend erneuert und erweitert und in *Jazz & Pop Harmonische Grundlagen* umbenannt worden. Der Aufbau dieses Buches ist nach dem Prinzip „Schritt für Schritt" gegliedert. Die übersichtliche Gliederung erlaubt jedoch auch, bei Bedarf an einer beliebigen, den Leser/die Leserin besonders interessierenden Stelle „einzusteigen". Zudem können Sie den überwiegenden Teil der Beispiele und Aufgaben als so genannte MIDI Files aus dem Internet herunterladen und anhören. Der theoretische Anteil des Bereiches Harmonielehre kann so individuell vertieft, je nach eigenem Bedürfnis genutzt und auf einfache Art und Weise mit der täglichen musikalischen Praxis verknüpft werden..

Sigi Busch
IMPROVISATION IM JAZZ – EIN DYNAMISCHES SYSTEM
• Bestellnr. 14405 (118 seiten)
Improvisation im Jazz – ein dynamisches System bietet, unabhängig von stilistischen Vorlieben, zahlreiche Beispiele und Anregungen. Sowohl im elementaren als auch im fortgeschrittenen Bereich werden verschiedenste Wege zum Erwerb vielfältiger, eigener Erfahrungen ermöglicht.

Sigi Busch
EAR TRAINING, VOL. 1
• Order No. 16002 (48-page workbook w/cd)
A basic ear training text for self-study. CD narrated by Jerry Granelli.
Each of the ten lessons is divided into three parts: Intervals/Chords, Rhythm, Melody. Examples and exercises are played by different instruments, including piano/keyboard, saxophone, trumpet, drums, percussion, and synthesizer. The answer section at the end of the book is ideal for self-study.

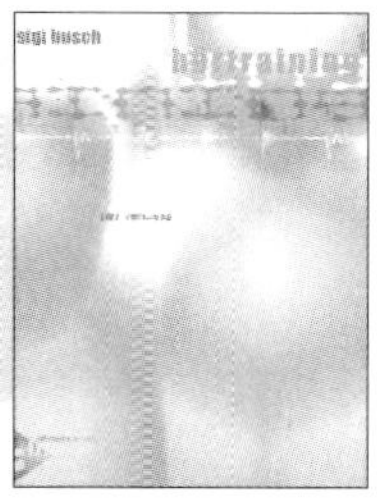

HÖRTRAINING KURS 1 (D)
• Bestellnr. 16001 (48 Seiten mit cd)
Intervalle, Melodiediktate, Rhythmusdiktate, Skalen, Modi, Dreiklänge, Akkorde, Akkordverbindungen etc.

HÖRTRAINING KURS 2 (D)
• Bestellnr. 16101 (64 seiten mit cd)
Melodiediktate, Antizipation, ternäre und binäre Rhythmusdiktate, Akkordlagen (Voicings), tonleitereigene Septakkorde und Umkehrungen,
4-stimmige Akkorde, mehrtaktige Akkordfolgen, harmonische Klischees, 12-taktige Akkordfolgen, 2-stimmige Melodiediktate, lineare Akkordverbindungen, Akkordfolgen mit erweiterten Akkorden etc.
*„Vieles von dem, was als Beweis für ein gutes Gehör angesehen wird, ist eigentlich nur das Wiedererkennen von vorher schon Bekanntem." **(David Baker)***

www.advancemusic.com